Potent Landscapes

Southeast Asia

POLITICS, MEANING, AND MEMORY

David Chandler and Rita Smith Kipp

SERIES EDITORS

Potent Landscapes

Place and Mobility in

Eastern Indonesia

CATHERINE ALLERTON

UNIVERSITY OF HAWAI'I PRESS   *Honolulu*

© 2013 University of Hawai'i Press

All rights reserved

Printed in the United States of America

18 17 16 15 14 13   6 5 4 3 2 1

Library of Congress Cataloging-in-Publication Data

Allerton, Catherine, author.

  Potent landscapes : place and mobility in eastern Indonesia / Catherine Allerton.

    pages   cm.—(Southeast Asia: politics, meaning, and memory)

  Includes bibliographical references and index.

  ISBN 978-0-8248-3632-0 (cloth : alk. paper) — ISBN 978-0-8248-3800-3 (pbk. : alk. paper)

    1. Manggarai (Indonesian people)—Social life and customs.   2. Cultural landscapes—Indonesia—Manggarai (Kabupaten)   I. Title.   II. Series: Southeast Asia—politics, meaning, and memory.

  DS632.M287A44 2013

  305.899'22—dc23

                                                                    2012042515

Series designed by Richard Hendel

Printed by Sheridan Books, Inc.

For Simon

CONTENTS

ACKNOWLEDGMENTS

As an ethnographic investigation of the power of the landscape, this book is shaped by my own experience of becoming entangled in and involved with Manggarai places and pathways. With respect to houses and field-huts, a good part of this process was focused on *food*. Indeed, when I think of my fieldwork in southern Manggarai, I remember constantly being given glasses of sweet coffee, invited to lunch, and presented with gifts of bananas, avocadoes, or peanuts. I would therefore like to thank all of the Manggarai villagers who have fed and nurtured me, who insisted that I eat even when I was full, who complained when I didn't eat enough, and who gave me bags of Manggarai coffee to bring home. I am sorry that I cannot mention them all by name. However, there are a number of villagers whose significance to my work demands individual acknowledgment.

Gabriel Ngantur (Amé Gaba) and Anastasia Anus (Iné Anas) took me into their Wae Rebo house, fed me, explained my purpose to others, and have become family. My heartfelt thanks to them and to my adoptive siblings and their spouses: Teres, Marsel, Yus, Frans, Maksi, Dete, Primus, Selus, and Fian. Thanks also to my "other house" in Kombo: Tote, Tina, and their sons Sil, Frid, and Rober, as well as their neighbor Dete. A good part of my time in Wae Rebo was spent next door, in the house of my "old father." There I enjoyed the company and stories of Amé Huber, Iné Sisi, Lome, Frans, Anna, Regi, and Geni, as well as the laughter and tantrums of Aben, Rinus, and Densi. Later they were joined by Kon and Edit. I am particularly grateful to Anna for her continual kindness and friendship. Thanks to my family in the "mountain house," particularly Amé and Iné de Yos, for their hospitality. Nina, my "walking friend" and Meren, her sister, took me under their wing and told me many stories. Sita, Teus, Odi, and Talis always welcomed me to their house and involved me with their family lives. The two Tanta Tinas, Fita, Les, Matil, Kris, and Kata provided stories and friendship, as did Niko. Thanks to the teachers at the school in Lenggos, particularly Guru Frans, Guru Alec, and Ibu Guru Medi, for their hospitality both in and out of school. Thanks also to Guru Stanis and Guru Sius at the school in Denge. Amé Dorus, the ritual leader of Wae Rebo, was always forthcoming with information about ritual events and let me record many of his songs and stories. Amé de Rikus, the political leader of the community, told me the history of Kombo and explained some of the community's future plans.

Sadly, some of the villagers with whom I have worked in Wae Rebo-Kombo have since passed away. Several of these have been women, who died in pregnancy or childbirth, including the lovely Edit. Of the older inhabitants who have died, I must mention five old men who contributed to my research. Amé Paulinus, born at the beginning of the twentieth century, told me stories of Japanese soldiers and Polish priests, and made me laugh by demanding to know the salaries of my entire family. Amé Michael was gentle and friendly. Amé Nabas welcomed me to his field-hut and fed my craving for *markis* fruit. It is hard to imagine this book without the words of Amé Bertolo, the charismatic ritual speaker during my first fieldwork. Finally, I must mention Amé Huber, my "old father," who died in July 2008. A shy man of few words, he nevertheless taught me much about what it means to be a good Manggarai person and introduced my eldest daughter to his land and ancestors.

Any Darung and Tony Rumondor in Ruteng have, over the years, provided friendship and support in many forms. Thanks in particular to Any for her delicious cooking and work on tape transcription, as well as her support when hosting my visits in 2001, 2005, and 2008. During fieldwork in 1997–1999, my visits to Ruteng were made comfortable by the kind hospitality of Moira Moeliono and Pam Minnigh. I must also thank Tin, Eti, Pater Marsel Nahas SVD, and Pater Gabriel Mite SVD for their help during my first months in Manggarai in 1997. Shuichi Matsuda, a Japanese photographer, visited Wae Rebo during the drum house rebuilding, and generously sent me some of his photographs. Thanks also to John Ryan for his photographs of Wae Rebo and to Jeanine Pfeiffer for delivering and sending letters in 2008. Maribeth Erb and Stanis Mucek have supported this research in many ways, and have provided friendly hospitality in Singapore. Thanks in particular to Maribeth for always answering my queries, and for providing the initial information that led me to Wae Rebo.

This book owes much to the critical support of Maurice Bloch and Fenella Cannell, for whose intellectual inspiration I remain grateful. Thanks in particular to Fenella, and to Simon Jarvis, for visiting me during fieldwork and enthusiastically engaging with my Wae Rebo friends. Webb Keane and Susanne Küchler provided me with a raft of generously critical questions and comments, from which I have drawn much inspiration over the years.

Among friends and colleagues who have helped steer this research towards publication, I must particularly thank Charles Stafford, who read the whole book, and Matthew Engelke, who has read all sorts of things. Huge thanks are also due to Rita Astuti, Peggy Froerer, and Richard Chenhall for their friendship and support. Deborah James, Chris Fuller, and the late Olivia Harris have all been helpful and encouraging as heads of the Anthropology Department at the London School of Economics. For comments on earlier or partial versions of the chapters, I also thank Nick Allen, Matthew Amster, Judith Bovensiepen, Janet Carsten, Nicolas Ellison, Maribeth Erb, Stephan Feuchtwang, Gregory Forth, Luke Freeman, Eric Hirsch, Brian Howell, Michael Lambek, James Leach, Nick Long, Michael O'Hanlon, Albert Schrauwers, Michael Scott, Edward Simpson, Mary Steedly, Kari Telle, and Lee Wilson. I thank the audiences in anthropology seminars at LSE, University College London, Aberdeen University, Queen's University Belfast, Edinburgh University, and Oxford University, as well as those who attended numerous conferences. Thanks also to Harold Herrewegh for his translation of Dutch materials and to Mina Moshkeri of the LSE's Design Unit, who drew the maps and diagrams. All of the photographs in this book are my own.

At the University of Hawai'i Press, I would like to thank Pam Kelley and Ann Ludeman for their enthusiasm and efficiency. I am grateful to Barbara Folsom for her careful copyediting. I would also like to express my thanks to the book's anonymous reviewer for frank and helpful editorial suggestions.

A number of institutions have funded and supported my research. Fieldwork in Manggarai between September 1997 and March 1999 was sponsored by the Indonesian Institute of Sciences (LIPI) and Universitas Nusa Cendana, Kupang. Financial support came from an ESRC Research Studentship (award no. R00429634133). Two subsequent trips to Manggarai, between March and August 2001, were conducted while I was a Junior Research Fellow at Wolfson College, Oxford, with funding from the British Academy's Fund for Southeast Asian Studies. Trips to Manggarai in 2005 and 2008 were partly funded by the London School of Economics.

The path I have travelled towards this book has been a long and winding one, interrupted—like the lives of the people I describe—by new work, houses, and children. For grandparental childcare services, and much more, I thank Angela and Michael Allerton and Joan Nicholson. For providing many delightful detours and for making my life truly "lively" I must thank Olive, Eliza, and Roxana Nicholson. My debt to Simon Nicholson is, as Manggarai people would say, most heavy, and I therefore dedicate this book to him, with love.

Introduction
The Shape of the Land

When you visit a village in southern Manggarai, one of the first things that people say to you after they have gently shaken your hand and offered a greeting is "This is the shape of our land here." They do so in a manner that combines humorous apology with modest pride. The statement implies both "this is the way we do things here" and "what you see is what you get." This is not a land of modern houses, busy highways, or electricity, but of steep slopes and stony fields, where hardworking people enjoy the products of their land and labor. If you visit a person's house for the first time, they will often adopt the same tone, looking around at dirt floors or bamboo walls, saying, "This is the shape of our house here." Similarly, if you scramble down steep paths to visit someone in their garden-hut, they are likely to declare, with a laugh, "Eh, Auntie, this is the shape of our field here." These statements seem to stress a connection between people and place: "our house here" may be a humble dwelling, but it is ours and we are part of it; "our field" may be perched on a stony mountainside, but it is our land and we eat its produce.

Taking its cue from the many everyday ways in which people in west Flores emphasize or humorously comment on their connection with fields, houses, and villages, this book draws a cumulative portrait of Manggarai places, revealing their shape, significance, and value. It describes the intimate connections between the land of Manggarai and its rural inhabitants, and shows how these connections are remembered, practiced, and debated in both ritual actions and everyday life. However, because Manggarai people stress the importance of paths as well as houses, rivers as well as fields, and movements as well as settlements, the book uses the notion of landscape as a way of drawing out the mobile entanglements of people with their historical and contemporary environment. This is a potent landscape, replete with personal and collective memories, but it is also a landscape formed by people, spirits, and goods *on the move.*

In 1997, shortly after arriving in the Manggarai region of eastern Indonesia to begin my fieldwork, I visited the mountain village of Wae Rebo for the first time. With a new friend from Ruteng, I hitched a lift with a priest travelling to the church at Denge, driving for many hours along a bumpy stone road through numerous villages. That night, we stayed in the house of the head of the local administrative unit (*kepala desa*). The next morning, the head, his daughters, and the local unit's security guard accompanied us on the steep walk, through dense rainforest, up to Wae Rebo. Reaching the summit of one section of the path, I looked to the south and saw the houses and fields of the lowlands beneath us, with the strangely shaped island of Pulau Mules just off the coast. Three hours later, emerging from another dense section of forest, I glimpsed the village of Wae Rebo for the first time. Resting snugly inside a bowl of mountain ridges was a grassy village yard encircled by a number of houses, including four round structures with tall, thatched, conical roofs sloping to the floor. My companions emphasized to me (in Indonesian) that this was a unique village: nowhere else in Manggarai were original specimens of such traditional housing to be found. This was why the district head (Bupati) of the Manggarai region was currently planning a visit to the village, to see for himself its unique housing forms.

My memory of that first, steep descent through coffee gardens into the center of Wae Rebo and my first entry into the dark interior space of a round house (*mbaru niang*) are now something of a blur, but the confusion provoked within me is not. The village was beautiful, its houses were clearly fascinating, its residents seemed friendly enough, but was it an appropriate site for my research? Wasn't Wae Rebo rather too remote? Did I really want to live somewhere unique, somewhere that was due to receive an official state visit? How should I know when I had found "my" fieldsite?

Our visit was a short one, and we returned to the lowlands that afternoon. I was keen to get back to Ruteng and to investigate other possible fieldsites. As we wearily climbed back down the mountain paths, my friend asked the *kepala desa* where Wae Rebo children went to school. He replied that they went to school in Lenggos, in the lowlands, but they didn't travel there from Wae Rebo every day. This was because Wae Rebo also had a site in the lowlands, called Kombo, where many of its villagers lived. Wae Rebo people were strong walkers, he told us, as they were always travelling up and down the mountain between their two villages. Sure enough, having met no one on the path when we climbed up earlier in the day, on our way back down we bumped into several men carrying large sacks on their shoulders, their machetes rattling in their holders as they briskly climbed. As he described Kombo to my friend, the *kepala desa* said the site had been founded by order of the local government and mentioned some kind of related dispute. Frustrated by my poor language skills, I struggled to understand the details of this conflict. However, my curiosity had been aroused, and Wae Rebo suddenly seemed a more possible fieldsite. Why, I wondered, had the government ordered the community to build a lowland site? How often did people walk up and down between the sites, and what motivated their journeys? What was it like for schoolchildren raised in the highlands to move to the lowlands to attend school?

A week later, with a photocopied Manggarai-Indonesian dictionary weighing down my bag, I moved to Wae Rebo to begin fieldwork. Though initially based solely in the highlands, over the months that followed I gradually began to accompany my informants on their journeys to the lowlands or other villages reached by mountain paths. I also began to gain a more complex understanding of the many similarities and differences between Wae Rebo and Kombo as sites and to hear different accounts of their history. Thus, from the start my ethnographic attention was drawn to the historical significance and emotional power of movements within a landscape of named, potent, yet profoundly different places. As my fieldwork progressed, I heard ever more complex stories of the entanglement of places and people, narratives that stressed the metaphysical connections between Wae Rebo-Kombo people and their land, but that also hinted at the dangerous consequences of the intermingling of spilt blood, potent places, and human fate. Thus, this book analyzes the power of a collective, shared landscape shaped by state development policies and responses to religious change, while also taking seriously the intense personal connections between Manggarai individuals and certain places and pathways.

Although this book is unique in exploring the multiple aspects of the power of a Southeast Asian landscape, approaches to power in the region have of course long stressed its distinctive materiality. In his classic paper ([1972] 1990) on "The idea of power in Javanese culture," Benedict Anderson argued that Javanese power was not, as in the modern European conception, an abstract aspect of a relationship, but was something concrete, an "existential reality" (1990, 22). In the Javanese context, power was amoral, unitary, of a constant quantity, and always embodied, whether accumulated by a person or concentrated in an object or place. Anderson describes how people on Java constantly read the *signs* of power's accumulation or diffusion in the person and environment of a ruler. Powerful persons could be recognized by the heirlooms they amassed about themselves but also by their "poise, restraint and equanimity in all situations" (Brenner 1998, 148). Though there has been a fair amount of comparative regional research on conceptions and consequences of such distinctively Southeast Asian "potency" (Errington 1990, 42) as materialized in both persons and objects, less attention has been paid to the pooling of such potency in the landscape. This is surprising, since Anderson's original paper emphasized how Javanese power, as an "intangible" and "mysterious" energy, was "manifested in every aspect of the natural world, in stones, trees, clouds, and fire" (1990, 22). Indeed, Anderson stresses that this conception of "the entire cosmos being suffused by a formless, constantly creative energy" is what provides the "basic link" between the "animism" of Javanese villages and "the high metaphysical pantheism of the urban centers" (ibid.).

As subsistence farmers who baptize their children as Catholics and marry in church, but who continue to hold sacrificial rituals in fields and houses and to take note of a range of nonhuman persons, people in rural Manggarai continue to approach their environment in a distinctively "animistic" manner. In Chapter 4, I draw on recent phenomenological approaches to animism that have emphasized its significance, not as a system of beliefs, but as a way of being-in-the-world. These approaches not only help make sense of why, despite Catholic conversion and state-sponsored village resettlement, Manggarai understandings of an animate landscape remain strong, but also help elucidate what is *specific* about animism in this context. More generally, phenomenological approaches not only to animism but also to landscape, influence this book's aim of evoking the sensual specificity of, for example, houses as places, or people's temporal movements along marriage or other paths.

In his work on dwelling and the perception of the environment, Ingold has emphasized how human environments are not neutral backdrops to activity, nor an external world of "nature" over which people gain a conceptual hold (2000, 42). Instead, against what he calls "the logic of construction," he draws attention to the fundamental historicity of our environments, "forged through the activities of living beings" and continually emerging "in the process of our lives" (ibid., 20). This broadly phenomenological perspective is in striking contrast to the Durkheimian tradition within social anthropology that saw relations among social groups as the natural basis for symbolic classifications mapped onto spatial arrangements (Durkheim and Mauss ([1903] 1963).[1] It is also an explicit reaction against theoretical approaches that understand a "landscape" as a distinct way of seeing: "a pictorial way of representing or symbolising surroundings" (Cosgrove and Daniels 1988, 1). For Ingold, those who *inhabit* landscapes do not confront them as a world "out there" (2000, 173). This means that no meaningful distinction can be drawn between a "natural" landscape of physical features and a "cultural" landscape of representations and projected symbols (2000, 189).

Ingold's approach to the social temporality of the landscape influences this book's argument in a number of ways. His emphasis on the ongoing incompleteness of a landscape under perpetual construction is, as we shall see, helpful for understanding the experience of Wae Rebo-Kombo villagers who inhabit a two-placed, partly resettled village and who continue to deal with outsiders' perceptions of their highland and lowland sites. In his refusal to distinguish between the "built" and "unbuilt" environment (2000, 19), Ingold's dwelling perspective also helps make sense of the many connections between Manggarai houses and "the land" more generally. Such connections tend not to be emphasized in the literature on Indonesian houses, which, as will become apparent, focuses on architectural form and cosmological order. Perhaps most significantly, at the heart of Ingold's approach to landscape, as well as his more recent attempt to connect lines and place making (2007), is an acknowledgment of the importance of *movement*. As mentioned, the Manggarai landscape is one defined by mobility, not only in Wae Rebo-Kombo villagers' journeys up and down mountain paths, but also in the daily movements between houses and to fields, or the more poignant journeys along marriage paths or to "outside" realms. The significance of this mobility, its role in creating places of value, and the particular challenges it presents, will be explored in detail in the chapters that follow. So too, however, will some of the problems in adopting an *exclusively* phenomenological approach to place and landscape, at the expense of overemphasizing *bodily* interaction or neglecting broader political and economic forces.

In adopting a nonrepresentational approach to place and landscape, inspired in part by phenomenological accounts, this book gives equal prominence both to the taken-for-granted, often unspoken aspects of everyday life and to the interpretations offered by Manggarai "experts." I consider such a stress on the everyday to be important for two reasons, though I acknowledge that it is by no means a simple or uncomplicated strategy. First, this dimension of life has long been neglected in anthropological work on eastern Indonesia, in part of because of the domination of scholarship on this region by the structuralist "Leiden School." This Dutch school sought to identify cultural areas

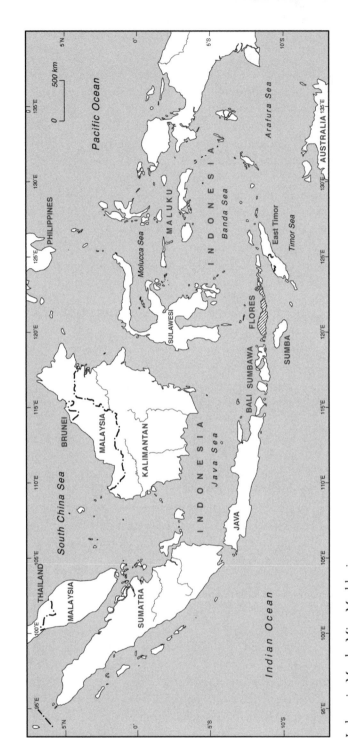

Indonesia. Map by Mina Moshkeri

that were sufficiently homogeneous and distinctive to form a separate "field" of investigation (Locher 1968, ix), and "eastern Indonesia" was most definitively identified as such a "field of study" by van Wouden's *Types of social structure in eastern Indonesia* ([1935] 1968). In this work, van Wouden argued for the importance to eastern Indonesian societies of "connubium" (forms of cross-cousin marriage), associated cosmological classifications based on "oppositions," and systems of dual sovereignty combining secular power and mystical authority. Research within the Leiden School has produced many detailed ethnographies, and its influence continues to be seen in some of the neostructuralist work of the "Comparative Austronesian Project" based at the Australian National University. However, in its search for cosmological order, the Leiden tradition has not only ignored or trivialized the messy and contradictory aspects of what eastern Indonesian people say and do in everyday life, it has also taken it as given "that a certain kind of coherence existed and could be discovered and given a name" (Keane 2004, 148). By contrast, an ethnographic interest in "the apparently trivial and humdrum" (Gullestad 1991, 480) can be linked to shifts in conceptions of culture—no longer seen as coherent or unified, but increasingly recognized as "negotiated, contested and (sometimes) resisted" (ibid., 480).

Ethnographies of eastern Indonesia that follow in the footsteps of the Leiden tradition have, as Keane notes, tended to approach the task of mapping cosmological coherence by seeking out experts, or "those persons apparently responsible for speaking on behalf of society" (2004, 148). Indeed, many female ethnographers of the region appear to have adopted the fieldwork strategy outlined with admirable honesty by Hoskins, who states that for most of her fieldwork on Sumba "men served as my 'teachers,' while women were my 'companions'" (1993, 9).[2] By contrast, from the beginning of my fieldwork in Wae Rebo-Kombo, I explicitly avoided concentrating only on those with ritual expertise, but aimed to uncover the taken-for-granted, implicit notions in which *all* Manggarai people might be considered to be "expert." I focused on somatic experiences of living and sleeping in different kinds of dwellings, and on the practical skills necessary to being and becoming a competent Manggarai person. I listened as much to the stories of women as to those of men, and to "backtalk" (Tsing 1993, 152) as well as the ritual speech that is the focus of so much eastern Indonesian ethnography (see Fox 1988).

However, I chose this strategy not only as a reaction *against* neostructuralist traditions of anthropological research and a feeling that there must be more to the character of eastern Indonesian life than the rather solemn practice of ancestral ritual, but also, in the second place, because of work critiquing the ways anthropologists conceptualize human thought and culture. In a series of writings, Bloch (see especially 1991, 1998) has argued that most anthropologists ground their representations in a false theory of cognition, which assumes that everyday thought is "language-like." This is why both informants and readers may often feel that anthropological accounts are missing something, that they do not convey what a culture "was really like." By contrast, Bloch himself emphasizes the importance of paying close attention to the nonlinguistic side of practical activities, a side that anthropologists, through their method of participant observation, are uniquely placed to understand. This means that, in order to avoid exoticizing our subjects, anthropologists should focus, not only on formal events, speech, or rituals, or on the verbal explanations given to us, but also on "so-called domestic life and everyday activities" (Carsten 1997, 20).

Nevertheless, explicitly turning one's attention to the taken-for-granted, unspoken aspects of daily life is by no means a straightforward or easy strategy. Marianne Gullestad, for one, has cautioned that, while appearing "transparent and simple," the actual meanings of the idea of everyday life are "both complex and variable" (1991, 480). Certainly, socioeconomic position, gender, age, and other differences within any society mean that what is considered "everyday" by one person may be experienced as "extraordinary" by another. More significantly, and as Gullestad notes, not all societies can be said to necessarily have an "everyday life" in the Western (in her case, Norwegian and home-based) sense of the word (ibid., 481). In Manggarai, there is no one, local, positive conception of something we might call everyday life. In particular, there is no sense that such a sphere could be mapped onto the "domestic." Instead, there could be said to be a number of axes of difference between different styles of activity, in which a more ordinary or humble way of life is contrasted with a more extraordinary, unknown, or ancestrally focused one. One such axis of difference is the contrast between village (kampung) and town (kota) life, where the former is associated with a more rough-and-ready, less "developed" (maju), yet highly valued existence. Indeed, this humble, village-based existence is the one alluded to in statements such as "This is the shape of our land." Another axis of difference relates to the widely held understanding that human life is mirrored by an immanent realm of spirits and ancestors, of those explicitly described as "people on the other side," whose concerns and habits are different from, but should never be forgotten by, living humans. A third axis contrasts today's time and people with that of "the old people in the past," who handed down those practices which people see as "just our character/custom" (*ruku muing*), even though the *purpose* of the "old people" may now be obscure, and even though present practices may only *imperfectly* correspond to the templates passed "from above in the past." A fourth axis of difference is that between periods when the tempo and activities of productive life—weaving textiles, clearing fields, collecting firewood, digging up cassava—are interrupted by both ritual activities and resulting taboos or prohibitions. Though ritual sacrifice in fields, or events to name babies or welcome brides, are considered part of the essential *work* that contributes to health, wealth, and fertility, this work nevertheless involves a different kind of collective focus and *effort* to that expended during, say, the "weeding season" or the "coffee season."

The Manggarai everyday life described in this book therefore emerges out of a series of contrasts with other realms of existence, modes of being, or collective tempos. As we shall see, paying serious attention to the everyday qualities of life inside household rooms, to ways of walking and arriving, or to personal recollections is not simply a way to paint a more three-dimensional portrait of eastern Indonesian life. It is also a strategy for uncovering the implicit, practical knowledge and values of Manggarai sociality. However, despite its explicit interest in the everyday, this book does not ignore the extraordinary, the ritual, or the ancestral. Indeed, at times it makes them the focus of sustained attention. Although works within the Leiden tradition may have gone too far in emphasizing unchanging cosmological coherence, or in neglecting the perspective and experiences of women or children, their focus on ritual did reflect something of both its ubiquity and its significance in eastern Indonesia. Life in southern Manggarai is continually punctuated by life-cycle, agricultural, or other rituals in which chickens are sacrificed and after which people eat together. Indeed, so frequent are such events that—with the exception of very large-scale endeavors involving the whole community—they even have something of a habitual flavor. What intrigues me about such events is both what they make *explicit,* and what they make *possible* in respect to place. Why are ritual speeches often addressed to village sites, rooms, or the land? How do rituals influence the power of place, or the connections between places and people? How might they bring about material and other changes to the landscape?

Steep ravines and deep river gorges, the waters of which are swollen during the intense rainy season, dominate the landscape of west Flores. Indeed, with its mountainous interior and potholed, winding roads the fragmented terrain of Flores reflects a wider cultural and linguistic fragmentation. The island

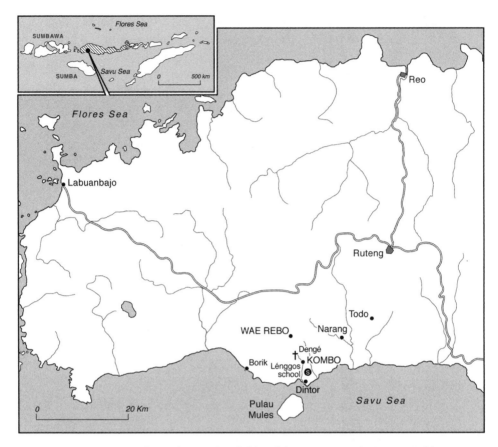

Manggarai, West Flores, showing key fieldwork locations. Map by Mina Moshkeri

never had a common language or, until Indonesian independence, any form of sociopolitical unity. For the Dutch colonial authorities, who achieved nominal sovereignty in 1859, Flores was an "unprofitable" island, suitable only for a policy of "non-interference" (Dietrich 1983). Prior to Dutch sovereignty, Manggarai (the area of which covers roughly one-third of Flores) had been the focus of a struggle between the Makassarese empire of South Sulawesi and the Sultanate of Bima on the island of Sumbawa. These powers fought for control over parts of Manggarai until well into the nineteenth century, in part to control the lucrative slave trade from the region.[3] With the establishment of their "Ethical Policy" in 1907, the Dutch took a more active interest in and control over Manggarai, sending out military patrols in the name of "pacification," and in 1929 elevating the leader of Todo, the most powerful area (*dalu*), to the newly created position of raja or king of Manggarai (Steenbrink 2007, 89). However, as with other regions of Flores, for much of the twentieth century, it was not the local government that took the central role in development in Manggarai, but rather the workshops, clinics, schools, and plantations of the Catholic mission.

Whereas Protestantism dominates many other islands in eastern Indonesia, Flores is well known throughout the country for its high percentage (over 90%) of Catholics. A Portuguese Dominican mission was established in the sixteenth century in Larantuka, east Flores, creating a legacy of names and sacred objects that continues to this day (Lewis 1988, 330). However, because Portuguese influence did not extend to the west of the island, Catholicism was not introduced to Manggarai until missionaries of the Societas Verbi Divini (SVD), or Divine Word Society, entered the region in the 1920s. Today, the majority of Manggarai inhabitants strongly identify as Catholic. Children are baptized as babies and receive first communion during their primary schooling; couples marry in church in addition to village-based marriage rituals; most people try to observe Sunday as a day of rest; and many people are interested in discussing the life of Jesus. However, beyond this fundamental, and strongly felt identity, there is considerable diversity of practice and discourse. Though town dwellers in Ruteng tend to attend church regularly, this is by no means the case in all rural areas. People hold a variety of attitudes towards Catholic worship and its relationship to older practices categorized as "custom/tradition" (*adat*) or, more colloquially, as "chicken speech" (*tura manuk*). Though these different attitudes will emerge in the chapters that follow, it is worth stating at the outset that the majority of my informants did not see Catholicism as relevant to all areas of their lives. For example, throughout my fieldwork, most villagers emphasized to me that "only believing in prayers" does not protect them from sickness or harm, and that "leaves and grasses" or "village medicine" involving magic are essential to good health.

Today, Flores is located in the modern Indonesian province of Nusa Tenggara Timur (NTT), one of the poorest and least urbanized provinces of eastern Indonesia, itself the poorest national region (Barlow and Hardjono 1996, 12).[4] After Indonesian independence, Manggarai became one of the five districts (*kabupaten*) of Flores, under the rule of the Bupati or district head based in the central town of Ruteng. In 2003, as a result of both population increase and political tensions, the region was split into two districts, West and Central Manggarai, each with its own Bupati. The new "capital" of

West Manggarai was the port of Labuanbajo, a town that sees a regular influx of tourists come to view the famous dragons of Komodo island. Though tourism, as we shall see, has reached Wae Rebo, it has had little significant economic impact beyond Labuanbajo and the Komodo National Park. The majority of Manggarai people, like most of the population of Flores, continue to be economically dependent on agriculture. In addition to subsistence cultivation of wet and dry rice, maize, tubers, and vegetables, people increasingly invest their time and resources in cultivating cash crops. These include candlenut, vanilla, cloves, and cacao, though in many areas the most notable cash crop is coffee. A good coffee crop can generate a significant income for farmers, yet most will also save a large quantity of beans for their own personal use. This is because glasses of sweet coffee (even when served in "mixed" form with roasted maize) are, in addition to betel quids, the basic requirement of Manggarai hospitality.

My first, coffee-fuelled fieldwork in southern Manggarai was for a period of twenty months between September 1997 and April 1999. During this time, I lived with a married couple in Wae Rebo whose children were either married and living in different villages or away for long periods at school elsewhere in the region. I also undertook various journeys to other villages, staying in Kombo at Easter, Christmas, and times of important events as well as on my way to and from administrative trips to Ruteng. I returned for a further period of four months from April to August 2001. This time, I deliberately based myself in the lowlands, visiting the school at Lenggos and gaining a better understanding of the tempo of life in Kombo. I also paid two week-long visits to Wae Rebo-Kombo in 2005 (with my family) and in 2008 (to attend a death ritual). The ethnography in this book is therefore based on a total period of about two years' fieldwork.

It will not escape the attention of readers interested in Indonesia that my first fieldwork dates almost exactly coincided with what is broadly known as the country's *krisis:* a period of environmental, economic, political, and social upheaval that saw extreme weather conditions, the devaluation of the Indonesian currency, the resignation of President Suharto from office, and violent incidents in some areas of the archipelago (see Vel 2001). Though subsequent research has tended, with good reason, to focus on the political repercussions and significance of this period, it is worth emphasizing the multiple elements of the crisis, as these were crucial to local responses in southern Manggarai. In 1997, my informants experienced rising prices of consumer goods simultaneously with an unusually prolonged dry season, while in 1998 people connected radio accounts of demonstrations in Jakarta with news of church burnings.

This led some Wae Rebo-Kombo residents to recall the past prophecies of a Dutch priest who had warned them of the potential for cataclysmic events at the dawn of the new millennium. When local news reached my informants of a Manggarai man killing his sister over a land dispute, some people asked one another whether these cumulative signs were evidence of the end of the world prophesied for the year 2000.

Responses to the political *krisis* in southern Manggarai were many and varied. Some older informants criticized the students demonstrating in Jakarta and linked them with young people in Manggarai who, on leaving their "big schools," return to the village with overeducated and overcritical voices. Other, male informants spoke of Indonesia's endemic corruption and seemed genuinely excited by the possibility of political change. A schoolteacher wrote a poem to be read on National Education Day extolling the virtues of teachers who "serve[d] every day," even while reformation was "shaking the corners of the fatherland." Some spoke of their fears that, with Suharto out of office, Indonesia would become an Islamic state and argued (in some cases quite vociferously) for a separate, Christian state in eastern Indonesia. Yet many more informants (particularly women), when asked their opinions regarding the political crisis, would claim ignorance or indifference, or would self-parody their lack of understanding (cf. Kuipers 2003, 181). One woman said it didn't matter to them, as "village people," whether the president had changed or not; another self-deprecatingly described herself as a "person who ate leaves" and asked how she was supposed to know what was happening in Jakarta? In this vein, throughout 1998, the language of "crisis" began to enter into local speech in various humorous ways. Female friends began to refer ironically to large piles of washing as a "clothes crisis," or to a lack of participants at particular events as a "people crisis." A boy losing a game with friends would be named "Suharto," while a bossy woman might be called "Mega," after the opposition politician Megawati Sukarnoputri. My friend Nina enjoyed remarking that, while people in Jakarta were rioting, the only thing she was planning to burn was her new field.

The impact of the crisis for some was thus a heightened sense that, as citizens of Indonesia, they were first and foremost *Christian* Indonesians, and that this identity was potentially under threat. However, for many of my informants, their identification as Indonesian was at best somewhat vague and patchy. None of them had access to television and to the awareness of national issues that watching television can bring (cf. Vel 2001, 154).

Even more important, though rural children begin to learn the national language, Bahasa Indonesia (BI), in primary school, very few of my informants spoke Indonesian with any kind of fluency or regularity. This makes southern Manggarai very different to other areas of western Flores, most notably the towns of Ruteng and Labuanbajo, where many children now grow up speaking Indonesian as their first language. In the villages I know well, competence varies widely from person to person, with schoolteachers and those educated beyond primary school the most fluent, but with many elderly people having no understanding of or interest in the national language. When local schoolchildren are prepared for their first communion by visiting nuns from other regions of Flores, the latter are often surprised to discover that what they say to the children is met with blank looks and must be translated into Manggarai by schoolteachers. The majority of adults say that they can understand a little Indonesian but that they find it too "heavy" to speak. Indeed, if the Manggarai notion of the "everyday" emerges through the series of contrasts outlined above, then one further, significant axis of difference is that between the Manggarai and Indonesian languages. The national language is not considered appropriate for use in many contexts, and I have often heard visiting state officials criticized for addressing villagers in Indonesian. During collective events and village meetings, young men's overuse of what is referred to locally as "high Malay" (*Melaju tinggi*) can also generate considerable conflict. My fieldwork has therefore been conducted entirely in the local language, and all foreign words in the text (with the exception of those explicitly labelled as BI or Bahasa Indonesia) are Manggarai.[5]

In what follows, I have made no attempt to disguise the identity of the two-placed village of Wae Rebo-Kombo. As I describe in Chapter 5, the village was visited in 1997 by a number of state officials, as a result of which my research featured in a number of articles in the provincial newspaper, *Pos Kupang*. This fact, together with the uniqueness of Wae Rebo's housing and the nature of social connections and knowledge in Manggarai more generally, makes designating the village with a pseudonym practically impossible. However, with regard to individual informants, I do frequently use pseudonyms in the text. When describing public or positive events, or quoting from life histories where the person has given me explicit consent, I use the shortened names by which people are addressed in daily life. For older informants, this involves following polite forms of address by attaching a prefix such as *Iné* (Mother), *Amé* (Father), or *Tanta* (Auntie). When reporting sensitive or very personal information, or when I rely on what other informants have told me in the absence of the person under discussion, I use pseudonyms and change identifying personal details. Certain individuals may therefore appear in the ethnography under two different names. This may make for possible confusion, but ethics in fieldwork and in anthropology is characterized by such contextual decisions rather than by blanket rules.

This introduction has outlined some of the book's main questions and overarching issues with a deliberately light touch. Manggarai people and places are too complex and multifaceted to speak to a single theoretical concern, and more substantive engagements with the literature on human–environment interactions, house societies, travel, agency, and custom (*adat*) revival in Indonesia will emerge from the ethnography in the chapters that follow. My portrait of a distinctive and complex landscape, as the reader will see, moves out from the most intimate places of daily life in a series of concentric circles. It begins with the smallest places of significance—household rooms and the everyday movements in and out of houses—and then gradually extends its focus to longer journeys and larger scales of place making. Each expansion or resizing reveals different aspects of the connection between people and place.

Chapter 1 examines sleeping rooms, showing how these are entangled with their occupants' bodies and souls during key phases in the human life cycle. It shows how rooms emerge as different kinds of entities at moments of their own social lives, and how particular rituals create the presence of the room as an agent. Chapter 2 considers ordinary houses and shows how everyday activities produce a house as a place of value through the creation of "liveliness." The chapter argues that the significance of Manggarai houses cannot be comprehended through an architectural or symbolic approach. Rather, a multisensory approach is needed, one that is sensitive to the permeability of the house to sounds, smells, livestock, and the movements of personnel. Chapter 3 considers the characterization of marriage as a "path." Based on women's evocative memories of their marriage journeys, it shows how such journeys form paths in the landscape, and how travel along physical paths is central to affinal relations. Together, these three chapters show how processes of kinship and marriage in Manggarai are inseparable from the landscape of places and pathways. To give analytical priority to either social relations or the material environment would be to fail to understand their mutual constitution in this context.

Chapters 4 through 6 investigate larger scales of entanglement between people and the landscape, and examine the influence of missionization, state development, resettlement, and migration. Chapter 4 considers the agricultural and forest landscape. It shows how the agricultural cycle structures people's recollections of the past, and how sacrificial rituals are inseparable from farming, as they are considered to be "what the land wants." It explains why

Catholicism has had so little influence on ritual procedures and argues that Manggarai conversations with the environment are a specific form of agricultural animism. Chapter 5 examines the ways in which place is made, not only through everyday activities, but also through more self-conscious discourses and engagements with wider powers. It considers the question of what makes a settlement a real village and shows both the ritual implications of resettlement programs and the cultural and political implications of a state-sponsored house-building project. Chapter 6 describes everyday, extraordinary, and mythical movements within the landscape. It argues that the Manggarai orientation system is one that implies movement towards others and shows how the notion of "rooting" in place is not opposed to mobility but is what makes safe travel possible.

As readers progress through this book, they will see how valued places emerge both through the explicit creation of presence in ritual performance and through everyday practices and movements that do not have the creation of place as their explicit goal. In the conclusion, I draw out the book's arguments about the necessity of taking "everyday life" seriously, even in this context of frequent sacrifice and powerful ritual speech. It is through the repetition of numerous everyday practices that the landscape gains potency as a source of memories and a record of mobility. However, it is through ritual performance that people explicitly create the presence, or utilize the power, of the landscape's agency. Anthropology may occasionally take for granted the links between place and culture, but for people in southern Manggarai, these are links that must be continually remade, rethought, and recontested.

1

Rooms

A Place for Souls

Not only our memories, but the things we have forgotten are "housed." Our soul is an abode. And by remembering "houses" and "rooms," we learn to "abide" within ourselves.
—*Gaston Bachelard, 1994 [1964]*, The Poetics of Space, *p. xxxvii*

Let me invite you, reader, inside a Manggarai house. Having entered through the front door, leaving your sandals by the house ladder, follow me through, past the main guest-mats, to a small door curtain. Lift up the curtain and step inside, ducking your head if necessary under the low ceiling. As your eyes adjust to the dim light inside, you will see either that the floor is covered in sleeping mats or that the room is almost completely filled by a wooden bed, over which is hung flowery fabric to keep out mosquitoes. In the room's wooden chest, you will discover best-quality sarongs as well as smart clothes for church, and perhaps a few old and faded photographs. On the wall, a small shelf may hold a mirror, soap box, oil lamp, and prayer books. If you look more carefully at the bamboo or wooden walls, you will see that combs, hair grips, small knives, and packets of half-used medicine have been pushed into its cracks and joins. Under the bed, or in a corner, the room offers a living archaeology of family history: broken flip-flops, empty bottles of talcum powder, rosaries, school textbooks, old batteries, odd bits of crockery, old weaving tools, and various plastic bags can all be discovered in nooks and crannies. Clothes are hung from hooks on the walls, and the room may house a sack of stored rice, candlenut, or coffee.

In this chapter I uncover the stories and significance of these small and modest rooms, the kinds of places that anthropologists have rarely written about and from which, quite justifiably, they may often be excluded. These dark, musty places—often containing little more than a bed—are arenas for everyday dramas of sleeping, sex, feeding, and childbirth. As small parts of houses, rooms are key places in a social landscape that includes various kinds of dwellings, graves, fields, satellite villages, and pathways. Investigating the use and significance of rooms reveals a good deal about the mutual entanglement of persons and place in Manggarai. Moreover, processes of kinship and the expansion of the domestic unit through marriage cannot be separated from these small sections of a house. Inside the room of their birth along with its closely connected hearth, most Manggarai children will learn a good deal about brothers and sisters, closeness and separation, in ways that will color many of their significant contacts with others.

Rooms are the focal points for individual households within houses shared between an average of three or four (but sometimes up to eight) households. Referred to mostly as *lo'ang,* though also called *kilo* in the context of household organization and *molang* in the context of ancestral origins, rooms are relatively private, intimate places. The household intimacy of rooms—in contrast with the more public areas of the house—is enhanced by their size and shape. In older houses, rooms are often extremely small, with low ceilings and barely enough room to stretch out to sleep at night. Bamboo or wooden walls mark off a room, or it may simply be screened off from communal areas by a flowery curtain. The equivalence of "room" and "bed" in these small house sections is quite marked, and rooms can be created or taken apart relatively easily. Rooms, as household places, are symbolically and emotionally connected to the hearth (*hapo*), particularly the set of three hearthstones used by each household. In round *niang* houses, which have a large, central hearth, women cook on the hearthstones nearest to their room, in front of or inside which they store utensils, plates, and glasses for coffee. In larger rectangular houses, hearths are located in a separate building at the back of the house and are referred to by the Indonesian word for kitchen, *dapur.* However, although these hearths are farther away from household rooms, women still tend to use hearthstones in a way that maps the arrangement of their rooms inside the main part of the house.

Rooms, the centrality of which I am stressing here, have not featured particularly prominently in the many writings on Southeast Asian houses. While scholars have explored the ritual significance of different house parts, such as hearths and posts (Sather 1993, 70–74) or altars (McKinnon 1991, 87–93), and the differentiation of symbolically gendered "front" and "back" sections (Forth 1991a, 8, 45), many accounts are unclear regarding the existence of sleeping rooms or similar areas inside houses. In many instances this is, of course, because there are no rooms, simply one main "living" area, possibly with sleeping platforms (Cunningham 1964, 40, 59). Moreover, societies where a number of people once lived together in "great houses" may have faced pressures from governments to build single-family houses, so that rather than being grouped in different rooms, households now live in small houses within compounds (Waterson 1990, 151). One exception to a lack of information on rooms is Freeman's (1970) work on the Iban of Borneo. Freeman described the Iban *bilek* as *both* the "living room" of a long-house family apartment *and* the term used to refer to the family group that is "the basic unit of Iban social and economic organisation" (ibid., 9).

As we shall see, Manggarai rooms and their occupants are entangled in complex ways. Such mutual entanglements of objects and human persons are common in the "exchange" societies of Indonesia. Hoskins (1998), for example, has argued that for the Kodi people of Sumba, certain things such as textiles, betel bags, and spindles should be considered "biographical objects" that tell the stories of individual lives and are central to projects of selfhood. Here, I am less concerned with individual biographies than with how the "cultural biography" (Kopytoff 1986) of a Manggarai sleeping room develops in tandem with the developmental cycle of domestic groups. Just as Freeman described the ruptures in membership of an Iban "apartment-family," so we shall see that at key moments in their "social life" (Appadurai 1986) rooms reach a crisis point after which new dwelling units may be established. A biographical approach to a room as a place that is made and changed by different kinds of activity helps to avoid an overly static analysis whereby particular parts of a house are said to be female or male. Though at certain times rooms are intensely associated with women, at other times they are linked with a married couple, or with groups of patrilineally related men. However, while biographical approaches to "things" have helped to break down the boundary between subjects and objects, what must be kept in mind is that a room, as a shelter for intimate activities, a symbolic womb, a link with ancestral origins, and a harbor for souls, is a very particular kind of *place*—both material and immaterial, relatively passive and active. Rooms do not simply symbolize or tell the story of human lives; rather, they can directly influence those lives.

Identifying the starting point of the "life cycle" of a room is impossible, since even rooms in newly built houses may be defined as continuous with another, previously inhabited room. This continuity may be made explicit in the rehanging of ancestral platforms and in ritual speeches that, despite material changes, declare the two rooms to be, in essence, the *same* place. My imposed point of departure is therefore the event that most fundamentally shakes up the composition of a room—marriage, and the arrival of a new bride. Though connections between families are described and experienced in terms of old or new paths, the lived experience of marriage involves the gradual entanglement of a husband and wife (and any eventual children) with their small, dark room.

"ROOM FRIENDS"

Sharing a room and a hearth is a source of much pleasure in Manggarai life. The relative privacy of a room means it is a place for massages or confidential conversations, where people can relax and let down their guard. One night, I slept in the mountain house of a renowned healer and coffee farmer. In the early hours of the morning before dawn, I heard a different side to this rather formidable man as, inside his household room with his family, he asked his two-year-old son Marcuse to scratch his back for him, praising the boy's efforts by calling him "my little brother." However, sharing a hearth and room can also be the source of many everyday tensions. This is seen most explicitly when a man marries and introduces his bride to the room and hearth of his parents, often provoking a crisis in the developmental cycle of that room. In Manggarai, where there is a patrilineal emphasis to kinship, residence after marriage tends to be patrilocal. After the various stages and rituals of the marriage process, the bride moves from her natal home to that of her husband in an emotionally significant marriage journey called the *padong*. The final stage of this journey is a relatively private evening ritual called "blood on feet" (*dara wa'i*), which introduces the bride to her new room.

While most house rituals are conducted in the front part of the house, with men sitting in formal lines around the edge of the main guest space, "blood on feet" rituals are notable for taking place in a more intimate setting, outside the groom's family room. The bride and groom sit together, leaning against the wall of the room, while other guests and family members crowd around. The ritual speaker sits near the couple holding a white chicken, and his speech announces the bride's arrival, stressing the alliance relationship that has been established or renewed and making general requests for fertility and growth. The ritual speech often includes one particularly well-loved couplet that requests "diarrhea striking calves, shit hitting feet." This is a typical "riddle" of such speech, and according to one woman, means "You seek children, you want to always have babies, always have their diarrhea falling on your legs." After the speech, the throat of the chicken is cut very carefully with a machete, so that blood flows into a plate. The ritual speaker then puts his thumb in the chicken blood and uses it to mark a big toe of both bride and groom. This action of putting "blood on feet" signifies that the couple is a new social unit and, in particular, is thought to introduce them as such to the household room.

Two aspects of this ritual are worth stressing at the outset. The first is the spilling of blood. Now this in itself is not so unusual in Manggarai, where life-cycle and agricultural events are marked by a seemingly endless stream of rituals at which chickens and sometimes pigs or other livestock are sacrificed. However, this ritual is unique in that its name actually refers to blood. Marking room membership by marking feet with blood is noteworthy since, as we shall see, blood is connected with rooms and their inhabitants in other, more mysterious ways. The second important aspect of this ritual is the fact that it is addressed, not only to ancestral spirits and to human onlookers, but also *to the room itself.* This is why the ritual must be held outside the actual room and is the first indication that, in certain contexts, rooms are approached and imagined as persons. During one "blood on feet" ritual that I attended, the ritual speaker intoned, "Listen well, you by the name of the room in which we sit, floor on which we live." This kind of direct addressing of place through the use of a descriptive, paired couplet is common in Manggarai ritual speeches. I was told that these place couplets refer both to the place itself and to all the human and nonhuman persons associated with it. To speak these couplets in a ritual, and to ask such places to "listen well," seems to awaken and demand the attention of both ancestral spirits and the places with which such spirits are fused.

The personification of the room as a place also emerges in comments people make about unsatisfactory ritual procedures. I once talked with a widow, Iné Kata, about the marriage of her third son, Stanis. Stanis had what is referred to as a *tungku* or "joining" marriage (see Chapter 3), as his bride was following the marriage "path" of her paternal aunt, the wife of Stanis' paternal uncle, Rober. Because of this, the "blood on feet" ritual was held in Rober's house. However, the couple were in fact planning to live in the room in another house of Stanis' mother, Kata. In view of this, Kata asked Rober if a second "blood on feet" ritual could be held in *her* room, but was told by him that this was not necessary. This upset Kata a great deal because, as she later told me, she was "scared that the room would accuse." People often say that they hold rituals in order to avoid the accusations (*babang*) and questions—Who is this? What do they want? Why have you forgotten me?—of ancestral spirits. When not properly informed of new events, or the identity of new people, ancestors may respond by causing sickness in the living. However, Kata feared the accusation, not of the ancestors, but of the room itself, and the possible repercussions for her son's and daughter-in-law's health. Stanis' wife's mother was also said to have been upset that, as she put it, her daughter would not be introduced to "the room where she will cook." Iné Kata stressed to me that marking the feet with blood was not just an acknowledgment of a renewed marriage "path" but a sign of "the beam above, the floor below." That is, the ritual makes the new couple one with the room in which, bounded by its beams and floor, they will live and reproduce.

The "blood on feet" ritual demonstrates the ways in which a new husband and wife are connected with a room—a connection that becomes more profound as their marriage progresses and they have children together. A polite way of referring to one's spouse is as one's "room friend" (*haé kilo*), perhaps also drawing on the equivalence of room and bed. A couple who have had sex together before marriage are described as having already "entered the room" (*masuk lo'ang*), and I was told that marriage rituals of the pre-Christian past involved a much more explicit accompanying of a new couple into the room in the hope that they would have sex.

In many respects, the growth of families can be mapped in terms of crowded rooms out of which new rooms and houses are established. Although a new couple should be introduced to the room of the man's parents, there are

FIGURE 1.1   A bride and groom posing with their new bed linen

often many practical issues that prevent a couple from sharing this room. Initial incorporation is thus frequently and necessarily followed by separation. The new couple may set up a new room in the same house while continuing to share a hearthstone with the man's parents. Another frequent pattern is for two newly married men to build a house together. If no young siblings remain in the parental room, or if a man's parents are old and frail, the new couple may take over the man's actual natal room. However, even in such a case a smooth transmission of the room from one generation to the next is by no means automatic. What is significant is that any conflicts, which generally center on the relationship between a woman and her new daughter-in-law (*woté*), tend to be expressed in terms of cooking and eating separately.[1]

As already mentioned, rooms and hearthstones are closely connected. One woman told me that brides cry after they have married, because "They remember this hearthstone. The hearthstone for cooking rice. When you move, you have a different hearthstone."

The ideal domestic arrangement following a marriage is for a new bride to cook together with her mother-in-law (*inang*), so that the groom remains "one saucepan" with his parents, eating food cooked over one set of hearthstones. In some cases this does happen, and women will talk proudly of having "just one saucepan of vegetables" with their mother-in-law. More often than not, though, either or both of the women will find cause for complaint. One frequent area of conflict concerns the inadequate reception of guests by young brides. However, the most common disagreements occur in the tense realm of shared household resources.

One older couple shared many vexed discussions with me about their daughter, Eti, who lived in a village to the west and had just started to "eat separately" from her husband's mother. This situation was precipitated by a row that took place one morning as the older woman cooked cassava on the hearth. Eti's husband, Stefan, was planning to spend the whole day in his garden, so Eti asked his mother to increase the amount of cassava she was cooking so that he could take some with him to the fields. Her mother-in-law responded to this request by snapping that Eti obviously had a "big belly," and perhaps she should cook separately. This upset Eti a great deal, as Manggarai people are expected, and indeed encouraged, to have large appetites, and accusing someone of greediness is extremely rude. When Eti's parents discussed this situation, they stressed that Eti's mother-in-law had obviously wanted to eat separately from Eti from the beginning, as she had chosen the occasion of a relatively minor disagreement to plant the idea of a household split. As relations between the two women deteriorated, a childless brother of

Stefan's deceased father spoke harshly with Stefan's mother about gossiping to other people regarding her daughter-in-law's behavior. This led the older woman, who had been cooking for this widower for many years, to suggest that, since he supported Eti, he should eat his meals with her.

These kinds of conflicts between new brides and mothers-in-law have no doubt always existed. However, they are probably more common today, with the decline of parentally arranged marriages and the increase in young couples eloping. A number of older women complained to me that today's brides prefer to spend the money given to them before their wedding on gold jewelry and clothes rather than investing in new saucepans for use on shared hearthstones. Such conflicts also show the very gradual process involved in the development and growth of a room as a household unit. Although the "blood on feet" ritual that welcomes a new bride seeks to create the presence of a room united with its inhabitants, the practical difficulties of sharing intergenerational spaces mean that a new couple may soon seek a room of their own.

BIRTH: ROOMS AS WOMBS

If marriage often provokes a crisis in the biography of a room, childbirth—literally described as being "in the room" (*oné lo'ang*)—consolidates the physical and metaphysical connections between a married couple, their children, and their room. To illustrate the links established between a baby and the room of its birth, I will describe the events surrounding the birth in 1998 of baby Gita, the fifth child of Odi and Talis.

Early one February morning in Wae Rebo, Odi arrived in my neighbors' back kitchen. She headed straight to where Sisi, an old woman with thick curly hair, was sitting by the fire watching the simmering cassava. Heavily pregnant, Odi was nearly in early labor and wished Sisi to come with her to her house, to "look at the signs" and gently massage her stomach "to make the labor quick." That morning, other older women gradually arrived in the small house up on the hill, which Odi shared with Sita and her family. When I arrived with Sisi's granddaughters, Odi was already "in the room," from which quiet moans could be heard.[2] As the old women arrived, they went behind the bamboo partition into Odi's room to assess her progress and give advice in hushed tones before coming back into the main area of the house to drink coffee, accept betel quids from friends, and chat in loud voices. Young, unmarried women from nearby houses were helping Sita with vegetable preparation or going to fetch water from the stream. Fabianus, a renowned healer, arrived in the house and, after seeing Odi in her room, gave her medicinal ginger, turmeric, and *jéngok* roots[3] to eat. As he returned to the main room, Odi called out, "Don't go anywhere, *nana,*" and he assured her that he would be staying, settling back comfortably onto a cushion and rolling himself a large cigarette.[4] Odi's own husband was away, buying rice in the lowlands. "Maybe it's better this way," said Anna, "what could he do to help?" As Odi's labor drew on, more women entered the darkened room and stayed to help, offering encouragement for her "lonely war," or holding her arms in a tight grip from behind. By the time the baby was born, the small house was full of people helping with cooking or waiting to hear the news.

As the newborn baby girl lay on a folded sarong on the floor of the room, preparations were made for the cutting of the umbilical cord and ritual declaration of the new arrival. Hubertus, a young father from a house down the hill, arrived with a length of thin bamboo. In this, he cut two notches to remove a small, sharp piece of bamboo for a blade, the *lampék*. This blade was used to cut the cord and was then wrapped in a scrap of cloth and pushed into the bamboo wall of Odi's room. The storage of this bamboo blade, which is closely associated with the baby's health,[5] is one of the first connections made between a baby and its room. The blade is not stored indefinitely in the room but only for as long as the child is considered a baby. Indeed, Odi later told me that during her labor the blade from the birth of her previous child, Yulin, had fallen out of the wall, as though making way for her younger sibling.

However, it is the remaining part of the bamboo stick, known as the *lambo,* that most obviously links a baby with its room. After Gita's birth, Hubertus took the meter-long *lambo* and went out the door and round to the side of the house. There, he banged with the stick on the wall of Odi's room, shouting, "Is it an outside person or an inside person?" This question is asked and answered three times, and in this case the new baby was emphatically declared to be an "outside person" (*ata pé'ang*). Girls are "outside people," as they move away from their home at marriage, while boys are "inside people" (*ata boné*) because they remain in their natal home and "receive fields." Following this ritual declaration of gender, the *lambo* is pushed up through the floor of the room and attached to a stick buried in the ground below. This stick, which can be seen from outside the house, is described as "the sign of a new birth." In a wooden or concrete house that is built directly on the ground, the *lambo* will simply be attached to the household's bed, although people say that this serves the same purpose as a stick underneath a house raised up off the ground. Like the *lampék* blade, the *lambo* is rather vaguely connected with the child's health and identity, and I once heard a woman describe the marriages of her adult daughters in terms of "collecting up their *lambo.*"

However, the full significance of the *lambo* is shown a little while after the birth, when the child's father buries the placenta in the ground near to the room. The baby may then not be taken out of the room until the occasion of its naming ritual, called "breaking the stick." We can therefore see the bamboo *lambo,* which links the baby to the placenta in the ground below the room, as continuing the function of the umbilical cord during the baby's postnatal limbo.[6] The *lambo* keeps the baby safe by anchoring it to its placenta and the ground, and by making the room a protective place. The need for such protection is explained by Manggarai views regarding the spiritual vulnerability of a newborn baby and its mother. Postpartum medicines, such as the roots given to Odi, help a mother to regain her strength but also, and more important, to ward off dangerous spirits who come from the undersides of houses to "sniff" the blood of childbirth and prevent it from drying up naturally (cf. Laderman 1983, 125; Carsten 1997, 119). One woman, Iné Kris, described the stillbirth of her first child. As she was in labor, she recalled, she looked down through the gaps in the floor and saw a pair of strangely glowing eyes. For her, this was an unequivocally evil spirit, probably sent by another person, and had caused the death of her baby. Indeed, fear of spirits or sorcerers who lurk beneath a house means that on occasion the *lambo* stick may be moved. Shortly after my friend Sita gave birth to her fourth baby, I spent a night with her and her children in their room. She told me then that she was pulling her *lambo* into the room every night because she had heard that this bamboo stick had become a recent target for sorcery.

The rather transitory state of a baby in its room-womb is also revealed in death rituals. After death, all Manggarai people of whatever age should have a ritual called a *kélas* held in their name, an important event thought to signal the end of a deceased person's involvement in worldly affairs. However, should a newborn baby die before its umbilical stick has been "broken," the ritual held is not a *kélas* but a *sikop,* the same kind of death ritual held after a miscarriage or stillbirth. Although they are considered fully human, unnamed babies who die while still confined to their room-womb are not thought to have created the same social relationships (with both living and ancestral kin) as those who are remembered with a *kélas.*

In the hours and days after the birth of Gita, neither Odi nor the baby left the room. However, the house received a stream of visitors, come in the Manggarai fashion to greet the village's "new guest." Women crowded into the room to hold the baby and see Odi, while men sat on guest-mats in the main part of the house, talking loudly to Odi through the wall of her room and asking after the baby's health by, for example, remarking, "I don't hear your new guest" if the baby wasn't crying. Odi's husband, Talis, had been down in the lowlands at the time of Gita's birth. On his return, his first task was to bury the placenta in a deep hole near to the room.[7] Once this hole was refilled with earth, ashes from the hearth were scattered on top and the site marked with a large, flat rock. The location of these flat stones marking the placentas of children acts as a kind of spatial mnemonic when recounting family histories. Sisi, the old woman who had massaged Odi, once described her extended family's movements between houses by pointing to and listing the places where the placentas of her grandchildren had been buried.

After burying the placenta, Talis' second major task was to make a miniature hearth inside a metal bucket. Like a normal hearth, this "baby hearth" consists of three hearthstones between which the embers of a fire glow. This special hearth is more likely to be made in the chilly highlands than the lowlands, and is used to warm the new baby's room-womb until the child's naming ritual. It is further evidence of the close association between Manggarai rooms and hearths, but is used only for warming the room or heating up medicinal liquids. The baby's mother, if healthy, will usually have begun to cook on the main hearth some time before the child is allowed to leave the room.

The naming ritual itself begins with the cracking of an egg beneath the supporting posts of the house, after which the *lambo* stick is pulled out of the ground and detached from the room or bed. The baby is then brought out of its room-womb, cradled by its mother, while gathered kin and affines search for its "real name" or "name of the chicken." Once this name, which is different from the Christian name given to a baby at baptism, has been decided, a little blood from the sacrificed chicken may be used to mark a toe of the child, who is no longer considered a "new guest" but a full village member. This marking echoes that of the bride and groom during a "blood on feet" ritual, and yet these events involve different aspects of a room. A "blood on feet" ritual involves huddling around a room, calling up that room as an ancestral entity, and introducing to it a new couple. In contrast, a baby's naming ritual comes at the end of a period of time in which the household room has been the baby's only world, a protective and nurturing container. When the "breaking the stick" ritual occurs, the baby is taken out of the room into the public part of the house and introduced, not to the room, but to the community in general. Thus, while birth procedures involve physical changes to a room, such as the placing of the *lambo* stick, they are part of a series of

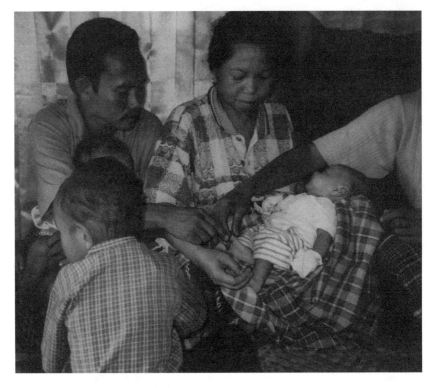

FIGURE 1.2   Naming a new baby

ordinary practices linking rooms and their inhabitants and do not involve the personification of the room, or its awakening as a powerful ancestral place.

SLEEPING, EATING, AND SIBLINGS

As more children are born in a room, it gradually changes from a place associated with a married couple as "room friends," to a place connected with young children, and eventually, to a place occupied by unmarried young women and their mother. A room such as that of Odi is directly linked with its children, who fall asleep on its woven mats or bed, hide things in its walls, and emerge from it bleary-eyed in the mornings to demand rice. While much important ethnographic work on the significance of houses in Southeast Asia concentrates on cooking and eating (Carsten 1997; Janowski and Kerlogue

2007), the practice and place of sleeping is also crucial. When children are young, they always sleep in the household room with their mother and father. This is the case even when they spend much of their time with other children living in their shared house. One evening in Kombo, I ate dinner in a large house that was home to four households. As the adults sat talking, various young boys from the house's various rooms lay down together on mats in the wide house corridor, singing songs and telling stories and riddles. After a while, the boys all dropped off to sleep, some covered with sarongs but others still in their school uniforms. Significantly, later that evening when the adults of the house were retiring to bed, they picked their children up from this small huddle of bodies and carried them into their individual rooms.

Just as Manggarai people will always invite casual visitors to stay and eat with them, so they will also, emphatically and routinely, invite people to sleep in their house. Especially when visiting a house at twilight, a person rising to return home will often be told, "Sleep here tonight." Certainly, people do enjoy sleeping in the rooms of friends or extended family members, particularly after someone has been ill or when other house members are away. However, despite being valued as an expression of intimacy, sleeping in rooms other than one's own is a rarity. In everyday circumstances one should always return to one's house and room to sleep. One of the strongest criticisms leveled at one young man in the village was that he always slept in the houses of his gambling friends and rarely returned to sleep in the house of his parents.

As children grow older, this intimate routine of the whole family sleeping together in one room begins to change, a reflection of transformations in the room's developmental cycle. Older children (particularly, but not exclusively, boys) may be encouraged to sleep in other rooms in the house, such as those of a grandmother or of unmarried aunts. One woman told me that her six-year-old son had begun to sleep in the room of his grandmother in their shared house rather than with her and her husband, because—in a euphemistic reference to sex—he "understands." In general, though, the pattern is that while girls continue to sleep in the household room of their parents, boys as they grow older will gradually move to sleep on the house's guest mats (*lutur*). Eventually, once a family's last child has been born, a father will join his sons on these outer mats. This gradual development, whereby boys and men sleep away from their room, while a mother and her daughters remain in it, provides a strong contrast to Bahloul's evocative descriptions of the "peregrinations of female bedding" in colonial Algeria. Bahloul argues that, in the context of a "strongly patriarchal family," a stationary bed "corresponds to power within the family," while the temporary and movable nature of young women's beds demonstrates their "weakness and submission" (1996, 34). By contrast, in Manggarai, ideas about propriety mean that whereas young men can sleep in the more public areas of the house, young women should not; moreover, young women can continue to sleep with their mother in her room, while at a certain age this becomes inappropriate for boys.

Sleeping is perhaps the predominant activity that takes place in rooms. This is not to say, though, that feeding and eating are not also important in strengthening ties to the room and its associated hearth. Within a multifamily house, people cook rice (the main foodstuff) for those they share a room with, though dishes of vegetables may be shared between households. Great importance is also attached to the whole household eating together at the same time. Small children are encouraged to eat together in order to learn to share with their siblings. I once saw a woman solve the problem of her two small nephews not eating their lunch by unceremoniously plonking their food onto one, shared plate, whereupon they both happily started to eat. "Ah," she said, "they don't want to eat alone." Poignant memories of household commensality mean that when a person is working or studying away from home, fellow household members will "call their soul" (*bénta déwa*) at mealtimes with a cry of "Come and eat!" One woman, Berta, described how after her mother died her maternal kin were keen for her to go and live with them. However, though still a child, she declined their requests and chose instead to take her mother's place as the provider of cooked food for her natal room. Tellingly for the concerns of this chapter, she chose to express her desire to remain with her father and cook for him and her younger siblings by informing her mother's kin that she didn't know "how to cook in a stranger's room."

However, just as sleeping arrangements reveal a gradual process whereby boys and men must move away from their family room, so too do eating arrangements stress gendered aspects of closeness to or separation from one's room and siblings. As boys grow, they also move away from their mother's plate and begin to eat sitting with their father. Although household members should eat together at the same time, men are served their individual plates of rice and vegetables by women and tend to eat them either sitting on woven mats in the kitchen or on the guest mats in the main room of the house. In contrast, women—particularly mothers and daughters, or groups of sisters— tend to eat together, huddled near the hearth, spooning rice and vegetables from shared plates.

SIBLINGSHIP AND ORIGINS

These gradual processes whereby, as children grow, a room and hearth become more associated with a mother and her daughters are intriguing, as Manggarai kinship, though not organized entirely by descent, involves a marked emphasis on patrilineality and ties between male siblings. Moreover, I have explained how at birth male children are described as "inside people" and female children as "outside people." To explore these apparently paradoxical issues of closeness to and separation from the natal room, I now turn to an examination of siblingship. The Manggarai term *ahé-ka'é* when literally translated means "younger same-sex sibling—older same-sex sibling," though people sometimes translate it using the Indonesian word *keluarga* (family). The key aspect of this term—as Forth has argued for the similar term *ka'é-azi* among the Nagé of Flores—is that it denotes "a variety of relationships that contrast with affinity" (1998, 311). Hence, I translate it here as "siblings." The female grandchildren of two brothers or the male grandchildren of a group of sisters are all "siblings." In addition, various families in Wae Rebo-Kombo who do not share (or have forgotten the nature of) a genealogical link also consider themselves "siblings" because they are "people who speak together" at alliance events. However, a brother and sister, or the children or grandchildren of a brother or sister, can never be "siblings," for theirs is a relationship framed by potential affinity. Yet, although the terminology of siblingship differentiates between brothers and sisters, it does not differentiate between a group of same-sex siblings and their spouses. In Boon's terms, we can say that the "parallel" tie between brothers and brothers (which includes their in-married spouses) indicates the "absence" of gender (1990, 219). Under these conditions, a man and a woman *can* be considered siblings. For example, Lome, who is married to Frans, refers to Frans's older "brothers" and their wives as "older sibling," and his younger "brothers" and their wives as "younger sibling."

Since, in general, land and other forms of wealth such as buffalo are inherited by sons from their fathers, relations among male "siblings" are extremely important. Groups of such men (for example, the male grandchildren of a male ancestor) should work together to conduct rituals for common ancestors and are expected to contribute jointly to funds and food supplies for one another's alliance and other ritual events. There is much to be said about the day-to-day significance of these relationships, but what I am particularly interested in here is the role played by rooms in the remembering and reactivation of connections between male "siblings." This is particularly evident in a group of rituals known as *mora* that are held to praise specific ancestors, and thereby to ensure the ongoing health and wealth of current and future descendants. Although varying slightly according to whether they concern an individual family, clan branch, or village, all such "praising" rituals center on acknowledging and remembering origins through a return to an ancestral room. Moreover, the crucial fact about "praising" rituals is that, like "blood on feet" rituals, they are held, not in the main part of the house, but directly outside the relevant room. At a relatively simple "praising" ritual held by a group of brothers to praise their deceased father, a chicken and a white goat will be sacrificed. After the ritual speech, some of the meat from these animals is taken, mixed with cooked rice, and placed on a platform made from woven sugar-palm fronds. Wing feathers of chickens or ears of sacrificed livestock are also attached to this platform, and married sisters (*woé*) who have been called to attend the ritual are asked to place money on it. In a syncretic adaptation, the platform may be decorated with small candles and described as an "altar" before being hung outside the room of the ancestor being praised.

These platforms, which remain hanging outside a room long after the "praising" ritual has taken place, are described as the "plates" of the ancestors, which are "rinsed" by the ritual. Failure to refresh the plates in this manner is thought to invoke the wrath of the ancestors, who would feel forgotten, and would thus withhold the blessings that are necessary for growth. This concern with remembering origins has been stressed in studies of many Austronesian societies (Parmentier 1987, 132; Fox 1996, 5–6; Sakai 1997, 42). What is significant in Manggarai is that this remembrance occurs through reestablishing the unity of male "siblings" in their origin room. Moreover, since the unity of a room is closely connected with the hearth, the ritual is followed by a meal in which the family eats in the company of both living members and ancestors, who are presented with a meat and rice offering known as *hélang*. Although this re-created unity is only temporary, it is part of an ongoing process through which "siblings" become detached from, and are then reintegrated with, a room as the central place of family intimacy. Indeed, as a group of brothers grow up and have children and grandchildren, there is some sense in which their ideal sibling unity can *only* be re-created in ritual form.

"Praising" rituals are the third example I have considered of rituals connected with a household room. Like "blood on feet" rituals, but unlike the ritual events connected with birth, these rituals create the presence of a room as an ancestral entity. With "blood on feet" rituals, a new couple is introduced to their room and a request is made for children, growth, and health. "Praising" rituals, in contrast, offer thanks for such growth and stress its origins in a particular room. Moreover, through "rinsing" the plates of the ancestors and leaving physical signs of remembrance, these rituals are a way of continuing to ensure the beneficent presence and interest of ancestral spirits in a room of origin.

However, although the ideal form of male siblingship may be one of mutual respect and cooperative closeness, in reality such connections are often a source of tension and difficulty. In part, this is because a particular kind of hierarchy is implicated in relationships among "siblings." In Manggarai, as in many eastern Indonesian societies, an older male "sibling" (and his descendants) has certain rights—mostly of a ceremonial and ritual nature—which reflect what ethnographers have called his "precedence" in time and space (Reuter 1992; Fox 1996). Throughout Manggarai, clan origin stories frequently concern violent struggles between an older and a younger brother. When in daily life sibling relationships become strained, the results are often traumatic. One notorious case in Kombo concerned two young men whose argument over the control of water flowing into a wet-rice field escalated to involve their respective fathers, the sons of two original brothers. Eventually, the political leader of the community (*tu'a golo*) intervened in the dispute. Keen to prevent a confrontation between male siblings, he simply imposed the fine of a chicken on each man, instructing them to bring these chickens to a joint occasion where they would be cooked and eaten by the two families. Significantly, this fine attempted to reconcile differences by symbolically re-creating the original hearth-room out of which the "siblings" came and through which their descendants were connected. However, despite this formal attempt to reestablish the unity of the origin room, most people subsequently regarded this relationship as "broken" (*biké*).

Despite the ideology of close ties between male "siblings," many men, given the choice, opt to avoid the obligations of siblingship. For example, one man, Tomas, told me that his marriage with his wife, Meri, *could* have been classified as a socially preferable *tungku* or "joining" marriage, along the "path" of his father's brother's wife (Meri's paternal aunt). However, this older woman's son, Ben, was a somewhat arrogant and argumentative man whom Tomas tried to avoid, despite their connection as "siblings" (the male children of brothers). In order to avoid involving himself with Ben any more than was necessary, Tomas chose *not* to recognize this connection, and instead (despite the extra expense that this involved) preferred to have his marriage with Meri classified as a new connection (*sangkang*). What this example shows is that, even in the context of apparently "given" relationships, there are still areas of *choice* regarding which aspects of such relationships to play up or emphasize.[8]

By contrast with male siblingship, which is structurally significant but marked by hierarchy and tension, relationships among female *ahé-ka'é* are characterized by a certain amount of freedom and equality, perhaps because they carry less organizational weight. Within a house occupied by the extended family of a group of brothers, young female "siblings" move between one another's rooms with ease, borrowing combs and hair-clips, practicing hymns, and comparing weaving designs. Their relationships are intense, and as they prepare vegetables or cook rice together, they will often jokingly refer to one another as *weta* (the term by which a man refers to his sister) or *ipar* (meaning "sister-in-law"). During 1998, two younger sisters continually referred to their older sister as Mega, after the Indonesian politician Megawati Sukarnoputri. Such joking is common among certain close kin, as when fathers praise their young sons by calling them *kéha* (brother-in-law), a relationship with rather "matey" connotations. In the case of unmarried female "siblings," calling one another "sister-in-law" seems to be an ironic reference to future affinal relationships that, as we have seen, may not always be so easygoing.

After marriage, which involves a woman's moving away from her natal home, female "siblings" see one another less frequently, although a woman's unmarried sisters will often visit her for the birth of her children or to help with harvesting. Once all the sisters are married, contact between them becomes more irregular, largely being dictated by events in their natal family they are required to attend as "married daughters and sisters" (*woé*). However, there are also some obligations that matrilineally related kin are expected to fulfill for one another. When a woman's son marries, the sons of her other married sisters are expected to make a contribution ("be in on things") towards the bride-price, as well as contributing "dirty money" for the purchase of cigarettes and palm wine from the bride's family. When married female "siblings" meet, they will try to impress on their children the importance of these maternal connections. For example, at one event, I saw a woman telling her son to be gentle with the son of her younger sister. "Play well with him," she said, "he's your sibling, and he'll be in on things when you look for a wife." Although exempt from such monetary contributions, female children of sisters are also encouraged to be close when they meet. As with sisterly relationships in one house, this is often expressed in rather demonstrative joking. For example, Nina said it was obvious that her and her mother's sister's daughters were "siblings," since they "joked together."

The connections I am delineating here between siblingship and household places and activities resonate with work on houses and siblingship among the cognatic societies of Southeast Asia (Headley 1987; Errington 1989; Boon 1990; Carsten 1995). Such everyday connections tend not to have been analyzed in work on eastern Indonesian societies where, as mentioned, there has been a preoccupation with the ritually elaborated difference between older and younger brothers in terms of "precedence." However, as Carsten has noted, paying attention to the significance of everyday activities in houses tends to bring women and children to the forefront of our analytic attention (2004, 49). As I have shown, rooms as ancestrally significant places are central to processes that stress patrilineal kinship. Thus, a "blood on feet" ritual usually welcomes a new bride to the room of her groom's father, while a "praising" ritual presents a room as indisputably patrilineal, the origin point for a group of male siblings. However, everyday activities of sleeping and eating obscure this view of an ancestral, patrilineal room and suggest a more complex gendering of connection to, and separation from, place. From an early position of shared childhood intimacy, brothers and sisters grow to have rather different connections to the room of their birth. Although infant boys may be declared "inside people," as they grow older they become nocturnal "outsiders," and their household room becomes dominated by the possessions and activities of their sisters. Moreover, relationships structured by female siblingship are by no means structurally insignificant, as we have seen with regard to the practicalities of marriage.

Carsten (1997) has stressed how, although Malays on the island of Langkawi consider blood and bodily substance to be partly derived from procreation and birth, they see them as equally affected by the processes of sharing involved in house life. At first sight, Manggarai understandings of relatedness could not appear to be more different. This is a context where people are members of groups ideally related through patrilineal descent and where, by contrast with even some eastern Indonesian societies (McWilliam 2002, 177), there is little adoption or fostering, even by childless couples. Moreover, my Manggarai informants told me many stories that emphasized the importance of speaking the truth about a child's biological parentage, as "not knowing your father," in particular, could have physical and spiritual effects. For example, I was told the story of a high-status woman, a teacher, who experienced continual ill-health. Her mother eventually confided that the teacher's "real" father was not her (the mother's) husband but a poor villager. When the teacher visited this man, she gave him a gift of a sarong and some money in order to declare herself his child. After this, because she "knew her father," the

teacher's health problems disappeared. It is hard to imagine Carsten's Langkawi villagers, for whom adopting and feeding children gradually involves
sharing substance with them, telling this kind of story.

Nevertheless, even in Manggarai, residence and locality, and in particular
shared food, are acknowledged as influences on ties of relatedness. This is
revealed, not by statements about how those who eat together become kin,
but by rules about who may *not* eat together. When the *separation* and not
the similarity or closeness of siblings is required, eating together takes on connotations of incest and is "forbidden." For example, two sisters (including
classificatory sisters) who are pregnant at the same time may not eat from the
same plate. One informant told me that if they did so, their unborn babies
would be sure to ask of one another "Where is yours? Where is mine?" and,
because of a lack of difference between them, the babies might not both sur-
vive.[9] This bears similarities to the treatment of babies born at the same time,
who are known, in reference to their respective *lambo,* as "sticks which overlap together." Such babies may not be breast-fed by one another's mothers,
although breast-feeding the babies of other women is a common, positively
valued practice in Manggarai. In the case of "overlapping sticks," there is a
fear that breast-feeding by the other's mother might insufficiently mark out
the baby as an independent being. Although Manggarai people value the
intimacy and closeness established by feeding at the same hearth or breast,
in cases where persons are already extraordinarily linked by time, place, and
relationship, such feeding threatens to destroy the separation that must occur
in order for normal growth to take place.[10]

BLOOD, FATE, AND SOULS

The description of two babies born at the same time as "sticks that overlap together" reminds us of the significance of the stick that connects a room
with an infant's buried placenta. This, and the practice of keeping the bamboo blade used to cut the umbilical cord in the wall of the room, is one of a
number of practices that promote the entanglement of rooms and human
persons. For example, I was often scolded by female friends for "throwing
away" the hair from my comb and noticed that most women would wind up
comb hair into a little ball and push this into a crack in the wall of their room.
No specific reason for this practice was given to me other than a general fear
of other people getting hold of such hair and using it against a woman in
magical practices.[11] Hiding hair in the wall of a room keeps it safe, as rooms

are protective places for bodies. However, ideas about blood, to which I now turn, reveal more profound understandings about the connections between rooms and bodies.

We have seen how both the ritual to welcome a new bride to a room and the naming ritual for a newborn infant involve marking feet with blood. Although all sacrificial rituals involve the spilling of blood, these are the only two that physically mark human bodies with that blood. Thus, in the context of room rituals, blood from sacrificed chickens not only communicates with ancestral spirits but also marks a place identity on people. However, in Manggarai, blood has not only physical but also important metaphysical aspects. In particular, blood is connected to ideas about fate and destiny, especially through the ways in which traumatic events are thought to infect the blood of later generations. The term "body-blood" (*dara-weki*) is sometimes used to refer to "luck," as when a person who walks through the forest without encountering rain is said to have had "good body-blood." However, "body-blood" also refers to "fate" or "destiny," as the blood that links the generations may sometimes carry a kind of bad karma. What is crucial for my argument here is that the bad blood of a room's previous inhabitants, or ancestors, can become so closely associated with a room that the room itself may threaten to "infect" later occupants. This is particularly the case with the "green/unripe blood" (*dara ta'a*) caused by a "green/unripe death" (*mata ta'a*).

Kari Telle has persuasively examined how the concept of "compatibility" or of a good "fit" (*rasi*) informs person–house relationships among the Sasak (2007, 199). In Manggarai, it is the fate (and blood) attached to a room that threatens to render it "incompatible" (*toé cocok*) with later inhabitants. Two examples will show how "green blood" can be transmitted to others both through bodily inheritance and through association with a room. The first example concerns a woman, Lusi, who in the late 1970s became the third wife of a man I shall call Tinus. Both of Tinus' previous wives had died after only a very short time in Wae Rebo. The deaths of these women were rumored to be because of the "bad magic" that Tinus had been practicing. Therefore, when Lusi was due to give birth to her first child, certain efforts were made to protect her from the "unripe blood" of Tinus' two deceased wives. In particular, the male healer who was overseeing Lusi's care made sure that she did not labor and give birth in Tinus' room. Instead, she was moved to another room in their shared house. This room belonged to the natal kin of Tinus' own mother, known in southern Manggarai as Tinus' "mother-father" (*iné-amé*). Since women who marry into a village are often (in a process called "finding a mother-father") encouraged to call their husband's wife-giving affines "mother" and "father," moving the woman to this room was rather like allowing her back into the safety of her natal room. Through this temporary move, an alternative, intimate place was sought in order to protect the woman from the "unripe blood" and uncertain fate connected with her household's *actual* room. While "unripe blood" might appear to have an agency of its own, it is significant that this only becomes potent or dangerous when attached to a specific room.

The second example occurred during my fieldwork in 1998 before the "blood on feet" ritual for Mus and his new bride, Imel. Before the room ritual commenced, a number of older men moved to the doorway of the house, where they crouched somewhat secretively. Here, they sacrificed a gray chicken before firmly shutting the door and gathering near Mus' room for the "blood on feet" ritual. When I asked about this later, I was told that it related to Mus' grandfather, who many years before had killed another man and been deported to a prison on Sumba. The "unripe blood" spilt in that murder was thought to have infected the fate of his family afterwards, and in particular was deemed responsible for the family's subsequent "lack," since Mus was the only male child of his generation. Some people said that the ritual with the gray chicken was performed to stop or impede the "unripe blood" of this ancestral event and prevent it from infecting Mus and Imel's room.[12] Others said, more specifically, that it was to prevent the continuation of a "lack" of male descendants and to ensure that Mus and Imel would be able to produce male children. Crucially, the ritual was held in the doorway of the house: the murderous ancestor could be invited there, but not into the room, and once the sacrifice was made, the door was tightly shut.

Carsten, in her work on Malay kinship, has demonstrated how "blood" as a substance has a fluid quality, is produced by food, and in particular is changed by the consumption of maternal milk and rice meals (1997, 127). In Manggarai, blood as a substance linked with fate can be shaped, not by everyday house activities such as eating, but by the room with which the malevolent potency of bad blood is entangled. The examples I have considered both demonstrate how the "unripe blood" of an early or sudden death can infect the fate of humans, partly through descent, but more precisely—since Lusi did not inherit blood from Tinus' previous wives, nor Imel from Mus' grandfather—through association with rooms as places. It is as though certain kinds of blood literally seep into the fabric of a room. And while ritual precautions can be taken to dissociate a person from the fate embodied in a room, these are risky and uncertain. When I visited Wae Rebo briefly in 2008, Imel had given birth to her second child, a boy, an event on which everyone familiar with the family history commented. However, Lusi, who bore Tinus five children, died while these children were still young; she was finally unable, people said, to escape her fate.

These connections between individuals, rooms, and fate are also demonstrated in what people say about a category of guardian spirits commonly referred to as "body siblings" (*ahé-ka'é weki*), though they are also known by other names. Ideas about such "body siblings" draw on the association between siblings and the family room, revealing an idealized image of close kin who protect and comfort us, sharing intimate places. I was told that it is "body siblings" who make young babies laugh,[13] and who can be called on to remove grit from your eye if no one else is around. They are associated with the nape of the neck and explain why people will sometimes say that you should not sleep with anything hanging near your head, as this obstructs the "spirit of the nape of your neck." Many people now talk of these spirits as beings like Christian angels (BI, *malaikat*), but the essential idea of a comforting companion remains. Indeed, a revealing dimension of these spirits is that they are often spoken of as a kind of spiritual spouse. Many people told me that your "body sibling" is the opposite sex from you, and moreover looks exactly like your human spouse.

However, ideas about body siblings are also merged with notions of a person's soul or spirit and reveal intriguing connections between souls, sickness, and household rooms. People generally refer to human souls using either the Manggarai term *wakar* or the Indonesian term *déwa,* though I have also heard "souls" talked about in terms of "breath" (*nai*).Though talk of souls is ambiguous and unsystematic, three things are clear from what Manggarai people say: the first is that it is easy for souls to become detached from bodies; the second is that souls or spirits continue to exist after death; and the third is that souls are either the same thing as "body siblings," or else are closely connected to them. One woman, Meren, told me that your soul is the same as your "guardian angel," or "spirit of the nape of the neck," and is connected with a person's ancestral name—the very "name of the chicken" that is given to a baby at the ritual to "break the stick." As this ritual is the one at which a room ceases to act as a second womb to a child, it would appear that body siblings or souls are further linked in complex ways with rooms as protective, intimate places.

As mentioned, souls are thought to occasionally wander away from their bodies. Indeed, people say that this is why we sometimes see other people—both the living and the dead—in dreams. However, too much "soul wandering" causes sickness in the living. This is why, if a person suffers a long or inexplicable illness, a ritual will often be held to "collect up their soul" (*hilir wakar*). As the ethnography I have considered in this chapter might lead us to expect, such rituals are always held in front of a person's room. Similarly, the night before any major communal ritual, smaller rituals to "collect together souls and spirits" will be held in front of all the occupied rooms of a house. Although these rituals are conducted at night, it is considered extremely important that every member of the household should be awake for the ritual speech. Children will be woken up and the whole household will sit next to their room for the duration of the speech.

In southern Manggarai, the boundaries between people and place are blurred in such a way that a room can transfer blood from person to person, can be the abode of a person's spirit, and can be the place to call back wandering souls.[14] Human problems can be addressed by speaking to, remembering, and calling upon the protective agency of a room. When Edy, a ten-year-old boy, kept playing truant from school, a respected elder told his father that the boy's wanderings were caused by a failure to "work together" with his "body sibling." To correct the problem, the elder told Edy's father to sacrifice a chicken for this guardian spirit near to the boy's room. Indeed, since forgetting such a body sibling can cause confusion and illness (often expressed as senseless wandering), some people say that one should hold an annual ritual to "feed" or "praise" these spirits. However, talk about soul wandering and forgetting body siblings can also be a way to express criticism of people who do not act correctly towards their kin. When one old man became mentally ill and could not stop wandering around, one person asked "Ai, has he forgotten something in his room?" The implication of such a question is that a man may have neglected certain key relationships and connections, whether with his wife, with siblings, or even with a deceased parent. These are the very relationships connected with his room, and maintaining them is central to maintaining good health. The death of one young child was linked to her parents' neglect of the ritual and other obligations involved in "sibling" relationships. Significantly, this neglect was voiced in terms of the child "not knowing her own room." In several important respects, then, to "know" and "remember" one's room is to know one's self, properly placed and fully knowledgeable of kinship connections.

ROOMS AS AGENTS

In focusing on the developmental cycle of Manggarai house rooms, we have seen how these small places shift through time, from a center for a newly married couple, to a nurturing place for babies and children, to a dressing and sleeping place for female kin, to an origin point for male "siblings." Narrating the social life of a Manggarai room reveals how rooms have at their core a tension between the separation and incorporation of family members, as well as a tension between relationships of siblingship and those of marriage. As seen from the perspective of a "praising" ritual, the family room is the focus for a group of (male) siblings. However, as seen from the perspective of a "blood on feet" ritual, a room is the focus for a married couple and their future children. The tensions between these aspects of relatedness are not resolved or "objectified" (Lévi-Strauss 1987, 155) in the room, but are an ongoing dynamic in a room–household's developmental cycle. A room emerges as a different kind of place in the context of both different practices and different temporal cycles. Moreover, rooms are materially changed by these cycles, as sticks are thrust into them as a sign of new birth, ancestral platforms are "rinsed" and rehung, and new brides bring into them new bed linen blessed with holy water during their church wedding.

Lévi-Strauss, in his writings on house-based societies (or societies-with-houses), has stressed how "houses" in such places as Southeast Asia combine material and immaterial aspects (1983, 174). If we take a room as a place central to personhood and marriage, as a kind of "house" in Lévi-Strauss' sense, then the combination of material and immaterial aspects is striking. Rooms in their concrete materiality make possible the intimacy of spouses, the safe birth of babies, and the co-sleeping of siblings. Yet rooms also have a significant *immateriality:* they are addressed as unseen persons in rituals; they are places to "collect up souls"; and they may transmit the dangerous fates associated with unripe, or violently spilt, blood. This is why, in addition to focusing on the quotidian activities that take place in and around rooms, this chapter has also dwelt on the rituals held outside room walls. I have stated that both rituals, and comments made by ritual participants, appear to *personify* rooms. However, what kinds of persons might rooms be, and under what kinds of conditions? Lévi-Strauss states that a "house" can be considered to be a *personne morale,* usually translated as "a corporate body" (1983, 174). In using this phrase, Lévi-Strauss employs an idea with a long pedigree in kinship theory. This is the idea that, in certain societies, it is not individuals who act as jural entities or "corporate bodies" but particular kinship groupings, whether lineages (Fortes and Evans-Pritchard 1940) or houses. For Lévi-Strauss, then, the personhood of houses is of a purely corporate nature, and agency remains firmly invested in human subjects. Indeed, this is shown elsewhere by his use of the terminology of "fetishism" to describe Indonesian houses (1987, 155), a terminology usually employed with regard to "a kind of misunderstanding" (Keane 2006, 199), whereby the agency of human subjects is falsely (according to a critically distanced observer) imputed to things (cf. Pietz 1985, 14).[15]

In her comparative work on Southeast Asian architecture, Roxana Waterson describes how many societies of the region see the house as "living," an "animate entity" with a "vitality" of its own (1990, 115–137). She notes that this vitality may be connected with that of trees, may be formed during construction or ceremonies, or may be connected with the notion of the house as a body. Like Waterson's concern with the implications of a "living house," I want to take seriously local understandings of what kind of entity a room might be and to argue that room rituals do not simply treat rooms *as if* they were persons but call forth, and speak to, rooms *as* powerful agents. However, to describe these aspects of a room as "life" or "vitality" makes them sound only positive, and does not do justice to the ways in which rooms may punish or infect their inhabitants.

Edward Schieffelin has argued that performance is concerned with the "creation of presence," and that through these "presences" performances can "alter moods, social relations, bodily dispositions and states of mind" (1998, 194). As *performances,* certain Manggarai rituals seem to create the presence of rooms as powerful beings—that is, as agents—whose emotions and favors may influence the fates of human persons. This kind of process has been explored by Jon Mitchell (2006), who analyzes the emergence of objects-as-agents in ritual performance. For Mitchell, it is the "performance deployment" of bodies, things, and what he calls "space" that transforms them into subjects (ibid., 398). Thus, he argues that the masks of the Mande of western Sudan have a powerful agency, but that this agency or potency can only be "operationalized" through performance (ibid., 392). Unlike Mitchell's analysis of Mande masks, it does not seem that the agency or potency of Manggarai rooms can *only* be "operationalized" through performance. A recently married bride may be vulnerable to the fates embodied in a room at any time, and not merely during a ritual. Nevertheless, ritual performances held outside rooms do call forth the presence, or deliberately "operationalize," the agency of rooms. During such rituals, a room becomes a different kind of place to that which it may be in the course of ordinary life. This is perhaps demonstrated most significantly by the fact that, in the context of "blood on feet" or *mora* rituals, rooms tend to be called *molang,* while in the context of everyday life and of birth practices, they tend to be called *lo'ang.* As a *lo'ang,* a room is a material place. As a *molang,* a room may also be such a place, and indeed people do sometimes use the term in normal conversations to refer to a person's room. However, on most occasions when a room is referred to as a *molang,* it is more than simply a material place: it is an agent, connected with the ancestors, able to "listen" and to transmit fertility. There are limits to the actions of rooms as agents, and they do not involve themselves in all the details of everyday life. When a tired woman goes to sleep on the mats in her room, she is not thinking about the room's agency. Nevertheless, that rooms *can* act can be seen, for Manggarai people, in the post-ritual health of children whose souls no longer wander, or in the way that a room allows bad blood to infect the living.

An ethnography of rooms begins as an ethnography of everyday domesticity. However, as we probe more deeply into these dark and musty places, it becomes an ethnography of hierarchy among brothers, and of souls and illness. On the one hand, rooms are a focus for everyday actions of sleeping, sex, dressing, hair combing, breast-feeding, and (in their connection with the hearth) eating and feeding. In connection with these actions, rooms accumulate a distinctive materiality that might be unearthed by a casual visitor. However, on the other hand, rooms are places closely connected with mysterious "body siblings," places where ancestors are fed and souls gathered up together. This gives rooms a significant immateriality that cannot be casually observed. If rooms are dwellings for humans, they are also dwellings for various kinds of spirits. If rooms are connected with the messy business of family life, they also carry more mysterious traces of blood spilt in harmful actions. If rooms are able to act to protect their inhabitants it is because rooms too have agency.

2

The Permeable House

...porousness of boundaries is essential to place. A place could not gather bodies in the diverse spatiotemporal ways it does without the permeability of its own limits.
—Casey 1996, 42

One of the earliest accounts of architecture in Manggarai can be found in a published description of roof finials and changes in house form by C. Nooteboom (1939), a Dutch administrator who stayed there for eleven months in 1934. Nooteboom outlines two types of large houses that were once found in Manggarai, "often inhabited by several dozens of families" (1939, 221): an elongated, oval house and a round house.[1] He noted that in many villages the entire population was housed in one of these large structures, which were "pitch-dark in broad daylight and always stuffy by the smoke of the fires and the presence of so many people." According to Nooteboom, the house-posts of these large structures were relatively short, creating a "hotbed of germs" in the space occupied by "dogs, pigs and children" underneath. The occupants of these houses were consequently "very prone to all kinds of diseases," and the continued existence of these structures was, "from a hygienic point of view," untenable. Therefore, despite the "obviously very important objections" that these houses were a "general sanctuary" central to religious ritual and performances, the colonial administration in Manggarai decided to have them all pulled down, so that by the time of Nooteboom's stay in 1934 they were "lost as a cultural element." In their place, the Department of Public Health ordered the construction of "model houses of strictly controlled maximum measurements and a maximum number of occupants," with taller house-posts and a nearby "model lavatory" (ibid., 222–223). Nooteboom describes the preference of local people for building round houses, seven meters in diameter, since they "fitted much better with the adat" (ibid.,

224) but notes that in 1934 the loss of the larger houses was still "regretted" (ibid., 226).[2]

Since Indonesian independence, Manggarai housing structures have continued to be the subject of various state policies. At the height of the New Order regime (1966–1998), local governments in eastern Indonesia waged a strong campaign against traditional, and particularly communal, housing. This campaign, fought in the name of "sanitation," has been interpreted as an attack on social and religious systems (Fox 1987, 176; Fox 1993, 168–169). Graham, for example, describes drives for "modernization" by state officials in eastern Flores in the 1970s whereby new brick houses with windows were relocated close to thoroughfares, while so-called emergency housing made from forest materials was "placed well back out of sight of any visiting government officials" (1994, 125). In Manggarai, changes in house form have been inevitably linked to the relocation of mountain villages in the lowlands. My adoptive mother, Iné Anas, told me how as a child she moved from Modo, a mountainside village, to Kakor, laid out along a rough road in the lowlands, because the local government had instructed people to build rectangular "meter houses" with only one family per house.[3]

Campaigns against traditional housing were particularly effective in Manggarai. When Dorothy Pelzer, an American architect, travelled through the region in the 1960s, she was only able to photograph traditional circular houses (*mbaru niang*) in the villages of Pongkor and Todo (Waterson 1990, 39). These houses had been allowed to remain because of the prominent position of these villages in the region (Erb 1998, 184), but were in an advanced state of decay and collapsed soon after Pelzer's visit. However, having once destroyed "traditional housing," from the 1980s onward eastern Indonesian governments began to acknowledge the significance of such structures for marking ethnicity and promoting "cultural tourism," and therefore began a slow process of rebuilding. In Ruteng, the main town of Manggarai, a small, walled *niang* house with windows, originally built for a local ruler, began eliciting donations from tourists and other visitors (Erb 1998, 187). Then, from 1991 to 1993, the *niang* house of Todo was rebuilt in a project funded by a Swiss development agency and overseen by Polish missionaries (Erb 1999, 17–19).

This background is crucial to understanding the significance of the local government's "discovery," in the 1990s, of Wae Rebo's old *niang* houses, dwellings that villagers claimed were built between 1947 and 1949. At a time when Todo had to rebuild its *niang* house from scratch, Wae Rebo's isolation appeared to have enabled the unique survival of this architectural form. After his official visit to Wae Rebo in 1997, the Bupati of Manggarai drew up plans to remodel the highland village's center by dismantling its rectangular clan center or "drum house" and rebuilding it as a large *niang* structure. As Chapter 5 discusses, this "discovery" also had a more subtle impact on the village by promoting interest in and talk about Wae Rebo's apparently "authentic" status. However, in this chapter I am concerned with ordinary rather than drum houses, and therefore want to stress at the outset the diversity of housing in Wae Rebo-Kombo. Despite outside interest that focuses on "traditional" architecture, this two-placed village offers a material micro-history of wider processes of architectural change in the region, with house styles ranging from circular *niang* houses, to small huts, to large, rectangular dwellings and new cement buildings. Houses may be constructed from a range of different materials, including woven bamboo, wooden boards, cement blocks, *tuak* thatch, and metal roof sheets. They may have windows that let in light, or a roof that slopes to the floor and encloses the house in darkness. They may be home to eight different households, each with its own "room" off the main house center or corridor, or they may consist of a single room housing a single household. Yet, as I show in the next section, this material diversity masks commonalities of everyday use and significance.

As Nooteboom commented, the most striking feature of circular structures is their high, grass-thatched, "cone-shaped" roof (1939, 221). In Wae Rebo's round houses, small holes have been made in these roofs, allowing a limited amount of light to enter the house and enabling those inside to peer out at the rain or at passersby. These holes are covered with pieces of plastic and, together with sporadic re-thatching, give the roof a rather patchy appearance. Despite these "windows," entering a round house nevertheless requires adjusting one's eyes to the gloom as one dips under the roof and climbs a short, steep ladder to the door. Inside, the most notable feature is the central house-post (*hiri bongkok*), attached to which is often a bamboo ladder leading up into the main loft area.[4] While the larger circular structures of the past had multiple hearths (Nooteboom 1939, 222), Wae Rebo's round houses have one large, central hearth (*hapo*), with individual sets of hearthstones for each household/room. Around the edge of these round houses are between six and eight small household rooms, with a fabric curtain at the entrance offering some privacy (see Figure 2.1).

However, even at the time when I began fieldwork in 1997, Wae Rebo contained many more rectangular than round houses. Some of these rectangular houses were small and modest, with "planted" house-posts, walls of flattened-out bamboo, and thatched roofs. They tended to have only one

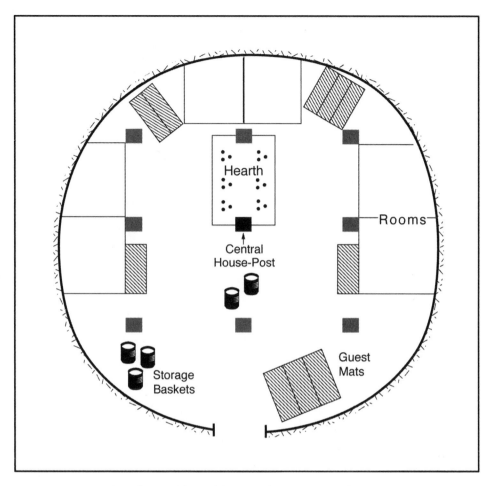

FIGURE 2.1   Plan of a round (*niang*) house with a central hearth. Drawing by Mina Moshkeri

or two household rooms, and because they had a central hearth rather than a separate "kitchen" (*dapur*), were rather similar to the kind of garden- or "monkey-huts" (*hékang kodé*) dotted in fields around the village. Other rectangular houses were more substantial and built on a larger scale, frequently using wooden boards for floors and walls, and sheets of corrugated metal for the roof. These larger houses were mostly "houses raised up on stones" constructed by a paid carpenter. Such houses have a front room (with guest mats) spanning the width of the house, leading through to a wide corridor between

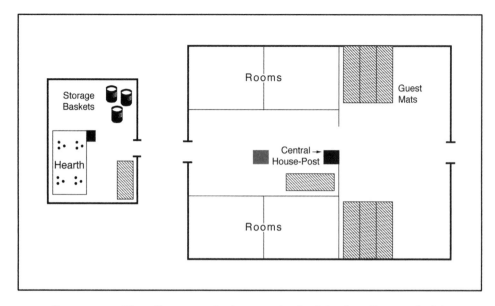

FIGURE 2.2   Plan of a rectangular house with a back kitchen. Drawing by Mina Moshkeri

household rooms (see Figure 2.2). The positioning of the hearth in a separate back kitchen is one of the major differences between such large rectangular houses and dwellings (including round houses) in which the hearth is located at the center of the house. The building of such separate kitchens was actively encouraged by government officials (Erb 1987, 198–200) and mirrors the enforced separation of "living" and "cooking" spaces elsewhere in Indonesia. Waterson has argued that in Tana Toraja, policies that encouraged the building of a kitchen in a lean-to or separate shed displaced the hearth as the focus of the household and were disadvantageous for women (1990, 42; cf. Feeley-Harnik 1980, 572). However, while women cooking on a central hearth are undoubtedly more physically central to the house, I do not find it easy to make such a clear-cut argument regarding the creation of back kitchens in southern Manggarai. Women themselves stress the considerable practical advantages of a back door, which means that they do not have to walk through or past crowded guests mats when, for example, they need to fetch more water. Moreover, as we shall see, the existence of walls does not necessarily imply the division of social space.

Kombo, like most lowland villages, consists mostly of these larger, boarded houses, though it also has a few smaller rectangular dwellings. Although the lowlands lack circular architecture, easier access to different building materials means that they demonstrate an even wider variety of housing styles than is found in the highlands. Some poorer villagers live in "houses on the ground" with dirt floors while, at the other extreme, Kombo has a few "cement houses" built by its wealthier inhabitants. Nevertheless, these cement houses still have something of an unfinished air to them, as glass is rarely installed in the "windows," and the kitchen is invariably a more humble lean-to. By contrast, the cement houses of schoolteachers, and of the Sino-Indonesian store- and truck-owner (known as *baba*) and Muslim fishermen on the coast at Dintor, do have glass in their windows and also tend to be decorated, both with colored paint and with posters of Komodo dragons, religious pictures, calendars, and vases with plastic flowers. These finished and decorated houses make very clear to ordinary villagers the use of architecture as a marker of social status and a form of "conspicuous consumption" (Thomas 1998).

THE EVERYDAY HOUSE: NOISE, SMOKE, AND SMELLS

Although I have begun my account with a brief architectural history, I now want to leave this history behind and turn to a more sensory exploration of Manggarai houses. For, while architectural descriptions and exterior photographs may reveal something of the basic form and layout of these dwellings, they say little about their everyday significance. Far from being orderly, static structures, these dwellings are in fact rather permeable and chaotic. Concentrating on the permeability of houses shows how, despite varying architectural styles, houses are animated by shared experiences.

In focusing on mobility and sensory experience, my account differs from other analyses of eastern Indonesian houses. For example, in one of the first anthropological investigations of house space in the region, Clark Cunningham described the house of the Atoni of Timor as a profoundly "ordered" structure, a veritable "model of the cosmos" (1964, 66). Cunningham noted that from the outside the Atoni house, by sharp contrast with the houses of the Batak or Toraja peoples elsewhere in Indonesia, did not appear to have particularly spectacular architecture. He focused instead on the ordering of house-posts and platforms, and on particular rules regarding the use of space by men and women, outsiders and insiders, arguing that Atoni house space revealed a series of ranked oppositions. Cunningham's analysis subsequently became a key example used by Lévi-Strauss to demonstrate the apparent "fetishization" found in Indonesian houses (1987, 155). Following Cunningham's initial work, symbolic duality has been described for other houses in Sumba and Flores, with gendered space being thought to express fundamental cultural divisions (Kana 1980; Forth 1991a; Fox 1993; Smedal 1994). Such studies can be compared with Bourdieu's (1973) famous analysis of the Berber house which, despite its apparent concern with daily practices, also constructs a distinctly structuralist picture of divisions of house space.[5]

Beyond architectural analyses, floor plans, or the shifting contexts of symbolism, we actually know very little about the perhaps more mundane significance of eastern Indonesian houses as *dwellings*. Here, I want to sketch an ethnographic portrait of the everyday use of Manggarai houses, in order to understand how houses (as places of value) emerge as a by-product of everyday activity that "does not have the 'production of place' as such as its avowed goal" (Weiner 2001, 15). This necessitates taking seriously, not only the ways in which houses, whatever their size or architectural style, operate as centers for the movements and activities of people, but also the multisensory aspects of houses as busy and productive places.

The permeability of the Manggarai house can be initially conveyed by attending to its significance as a soundscape. Domestic dwellings are the focus for noisy, productive activities and are defined and animated by the rhythmic thud of women pounding coffee and foodstuffs, the seesawing scrape of men sharpening their machetes, and what people call the *tok tok* sound that is made as women bang their weaving swords onto textiles on back-strap looms. Young children spend a good deal of their time in and around the house reproducing these sounds, pounding bits of mud and leaves with flat stones, or practicing machete sharpening with a spoon. When encouraging a young child to fall asleep at night, people often firmly pat the child's lower back at exactly the same tempo as a woman pounding rice or coffee in a large wooden container.

Because most houses are built out of wood or bamboo, with gaps between floorboards and slats in wall panelings, noise travels easily both inside and between houses. People fully exploit this fact and will happily conduct conversations with persons whose faces they cannot see, whether because they are in the back kitchen, the yard, or one of the inner rooms. Coming from a house culture where rooms are more bounded and private spaces, I frequently found this aspect of fieldwork unnerving. Sitting in my "room" writing, I would find myself having to conduct a conversation with someone in the main part of the house, who was quite unperturbed by not being face-to-face with me.

FIGURE 2.3
Rethatching a
round house

Other people would talk to me as they walked on the path round the outside of my house or, when I stayed in multifamily houses, after I had gone to bed in a household room at night. The longer I stayed in Manggarai, the more I learned to enjoy this aural permeability, calling out a joke or a greeting to a friend spotted through the house-plank gaps that served as my window.

The permeability of all parts of the house to sound, and the fact that people happily conduct conversations through walls, means that the kind of separation of space that might be implied by lines drawn to represent walls on a floor plan (such as in Figures 2.1 and 2.2), is actually far less clear-cut. Christine Helliwell (1993) makes this point in her eloquent critique of the separation between "public" and "private" space that informs most analyses of Bornean longhouses. Helliwell argues that the visual representation of apartment partitions on drawings of such longhouses belies the permeability of such apparent boundaries and obscures the significance of the longhouse as a "community of voices" (1993, 51). Similarly, in Manggarai, walls or partitions may signal the division of space into areas for different activities—for example, cooking, sleeping, or smoking—but they do not necessarily signal a division of *social* space. One rather authoritarian father, usually to be found sitting smoking on his guest-mats, would almost continually call out "You'll fall over soon!" to his eight-year-old son whenever he heard him running outside the house. In smaller rectangular houses with an internal hearth, guest-mats are often placed slightly behind the front wall of private house rooms, so that when sitting on them it is hard to see women cooking on the hearth fires. However, this does not mean that such women are not addressed by guests or do not take part in conversations. Similarly, during rituals or negotiations, women will periodically listen, sometimes intently, to the sounds of speech coming through bamboo walls. Although not in the same part of the house as the men who are speaking, they are nevertheless part of the audience. This is one of the reasons why I find it hard to argue that the moving of the hearth necessarily results in the social displacement of women.

This internal permeability of noise is also matched by the ways in which sounds travel *between* houses. Both in Wae Rebo and Kombo, my adoptive family would often comment on the sounds coming from neighboring houses. These ranged from the crying of children ("Ai, that boy doesn't stop crying"; "Never mind, that's called the sound of the village"), to laughter ("Weee, that house is really lively"), to the yelping of dogs who had probably been hit ("That. Is. It!"). People will always ask the inhabitants of a noisy or "lively" (*ramé*) house what they had been laughing about the night before, or quiz a mother on the reasons for her children's poor night's sleep. Certain kinds of low shouts also serve to notify nearby houses of a bird of prey flying over the village on the lookout for chickens or, at night, a suspected civet cat or wild pig near to a house. These warning calls create a sense of community that extends beyond the boundaries of houses as places.

Occasionally, neighbors will also call out to one another from inside their respective houses. As noise is in many ways the animating sign of a healthy house, people shout out, "Don't go to sleep too early," to a house that appears silent in the early evening. One Saturday afternoon in Wae Rebo, four-year-old Densi called out to Amé Gaba from the house next door, "Ooh, what are you doing?" followed shortly afterwards by a question regarding his wife (her great-aunt), "Hasn't Empo Anas gone to dig up some cassava?" Finally, after a pause, she shouted, "I thought she brought some fish!" Densi's calls were clearly prompted by her adult relatives in the house, and drew on the significance of hospitality and sharing between neighboring houses. These kinds of verbal exchanges are also connected with the ways in which even very young children move unselfconsciously between houses during the day, performing small tasks for their parents such as delivering maize cobs or borrowing a coconut grater. Because children can gather with little comment in the doors of houses and do not require the kind of hospitality that needs to be extended to adults, parents will often send their children to find out who a visitor to a neighboring dwelling might be, or what someone is buying from a travelling merchant. Houses, then, are particularly permeable to small children, whose considerable autonomy makes their presence in different houses neither remarkable nor disruptive.

However, it is not only the noise of cheerful conviviality that carries between houses. When a death occurs in a house, or when people bring news of a death in another village, the women of that house will set up a kind of wailing lament known as *lorang*. This sound reverberates through the village, and people in other houses listen closely, trying to interpret the sound and its direction for clues as to which house or woman might be affected. As my description of children's mobility might lead us to expect, children are frequently sent to a house to find out any bad news. The ways in which sound travels between houses also makes it hard to hide arguments. One night in Kombo, the sound of a man's and woman's impassioned shouting came from across the road, provoking much silent head shaking in my house and whispers of "Don't say anything." Perhaps because house walls provide such weak sound insulation, shouted arguments are actually extremely rare. When angry, the people I knew were much more likely to maintain a tight-lipped, frosty silence.

The permeability that I have described in terms of the soundscape of a house and its neighbors also applies to other senses and activities. Although, having few or no windows, Manggarai houses are hard to peer into, they are rather easier to peer *out* of. Occasionally, I would be chatting with a woman inside her house when she would spy one of her co-house residents returning home from the fields, baskets laden with produce. When boys returned from expeditions to collect firewood with piles of sticks balanced on their heads, people inside houses would call out to them "Ooh, leave some of that wood here, brother." More frequently, people sitting in houses in Wae Rebo or Kombo will see others walking past, heading off to the highlands or lowlands, and will call out, "Are you going to the north?" or, more jokingly,

"Hey, where's your chicken?" (a marriage alliance gift). Such calls are part of the everyday travelling practices crucial to flows of information between the two village sites. Houses, then, have a certain amount of *visual* permeability. They are also highly permeable to animals—particularly dogs—and to chickens, which slide noisily down metal roofs at dawn and continually saunter through houses looking for food. Children are often instructed to "go and look out for the chickens in the kitchen," and to chase them away with a cry of "*sikka!*"

Perhaps more noteworthy is the permeability of the house to smells: roasting coffee, perfumed talcum powder, hot medicinal roots, and, in particular, smoke. Both colonial and postcolonial officials were troubled by the health implications of large hearths at the centers of traditional Manggarai housing. However, for the people I know, a fire in the hearth and its resulting smoke are part of what makes a house lively and lived-in. The smoke from fires seeps gradually out of the roofs of houses and kitchens, giving the impression early in the morning that the house is quietly smouldering. Although people often complained about the smoke in round houses in particular, they also stressed its beneficial qualities: keeping a house warm, discouraging mosquitoes and other insects, and preserving both the roof thatch and foodstuffs stored in the loft (cf. McWilliam 2002, 228). One elderly woman, Ende Lina, had fallen out with her three unmarried daughters and therefore lived alone in a small, dilapidated house, while they spent most of their time in a remote garden hut. Such living arrangements were troubling to her co-villagers, but most troubling of all was when she fell ill and, as people said, there was "no fire in her house."

At this point I need to introduce the notion of "liveliness," or being *ramé*, which is central to the everyday significance of the house. Though liveliness is said to make life "feel delicious," it also has important protective qualities. The sounds of talk, the crying of children, the noise of machete sharpening or a weaving sword banging on a loom—these are all part of what makes a house alive, "lively," and therefore protective. People mentioned this notion of "liveliness" so much to me during fieldwork that I came to take it for granted (see also Allerton 2012). For example, a good wedding or other ritual is one that is "lively," with lots of participants, and perhaps some music and dancing. To join someone for a meal in their house is to "make things lively," while parents might encourage their son to marry because they need young children in their house again to make it "lively." This is why young women were often to be found setting up their weaving looms in the house of Ende Lina, having been sent there by their parents to keep her house "lively." It also explains why one elderly man was so fond of his radio, tuning in most evenings even though he was unable to understand any of the spoken Indonesian. "It's to make things lively," he said, "a little noise in my house." At times, the necessity people saw to make a house lively in this way surprised me. For instance, in the evenings following a death, young men would gather in the "house of sadness" to play cards and gamble. To my English sensibility, this seemed insensitive, somehow inappropriate. However, my Manggarai friends approved of and encouraged such behavior; the noise of the young men kept a house "lively," they said; it prevented "too much sadness" from permeating the thoughts of the inhabitants and their surroundings. Similarly, when someone is ill it is important that their house is kept *ramé* by frequent visitors. This liveliness is seen as a means of preventing the spiritual weakness—and its physical manifestations, such as a "lack of blood"—that too much sadness might cause, and means that there is nothing insensitive about such visitors cracking jokes or noisily passing round betel quids while the sick person rests.

The protective capacities of human noise are important because the house can also be permeable to unwanted and dangerous figures. Strange noises outside a house at night are greeted with alarm, and people fear shape-changing sorcerers who hide underneath the floor of raised houses in order to "steal the souls" of those inside. Such undesirable spirit visitors are also kept away by the barking of dogs and the smell of protective roots, such as *sumang*, a kind of turmeric.[6] When entering a house where someone has been ill, or where there has been a recent birth, one immediately smells this *sumang*, the juice of which is usually rubbed over the patient's back. Indeed, the permeability of the house to such a powerful smell means that the boundaries of protection are extended from a person's body outwards to their house. Just as the exposed parts of the permeable house—the floor, with its gaps and cracks, or open doors or windows at night—occasionally expose the bodies of its inhabitants to danger, so can the house at times become a protective body for all of its inhabitants.

RESIDENCE, MOBILITY, AND MULTIPLE CONNECTIONS

The notion of the "permeabilty" of the house to sounds, smells, animals, and children can be usefully extended to describe the historical movements of people between houses. People make decisions to move to other dwellings, or to build new houses, according to changing circumstances: for example, the collapse in a storm of a building, an expanding extended family, or tensions between different households. In addition, the contemporary situation of life in a "two-placed village" has further increased the permeability of houses in Wae Rebo-Kombo to changing inhabitants.[7] A key phrase people use when describing past and future moves, or connections with other dwellings, is "my own house" (*mbaru deru*). While this phrase might appear to refer to one's "home," I gradually came to appreciate that people actually call a number of different dwellings "my own house." Unravelling the different ways in which this phrase is used reveals much about historical movements of persons, and about connections between different houses.

In the previous chapter, I described how the origin room of a group of male siblings is the focus for "praising" rituals celebrating growth and fertility. People will often refer to the house of their father's or grandfather's origin room as their "main house" (*mbaru pokok*). Even if they do not live in this house, the descendants of a man who originated there will describe it as "my own house" and may spend a fair amount of time there. For example, during periods when her husband, Hubertus, is down in Kombo working in the wet-rice fields, Fin and her three young children spend most of their time in the original *niang* house of Hubertus' deceased father. Here, Fin enjoys the company of her husband's mother, sisters, and aunt, cooking, chatting, or helping set up a weaving loom. Although Fin and her children always return to their newer house to sleep, her daily movements to the "origin house" show that she has more than one house that is her "own."

During fieldwork, when visiting different houses, I would often encounter other visitors, who frequently explained their presence by stressing that "really" this was also their "own house."[8] Married women's movements to new villages after marriage also contribute to this landscape of mobility and multiple connections, since their sisters and sisters' children will be able to claim this new house as one of their "own." People thus claim houses as their own by tracing connections of male or female siblingship, links that are impressed on children from a very early age. When a baby or young child visits the house of one of its relatives for the first time, a glass of water will be fetched and a woman will dab some onto the forehead of the child, declaring "this is your house." This claiming of place influences daily movements and activities, and women happily take over cooking or serving coffee when visiting such a house. Unmarried women, in particular, lead multisited lives, frequently moving to different houses to look after the children of their brothers (see Allerton 2007c).

A house may thus have many more potential members than those who eat and sleep in it on a daily basis. Indeed, absent people still have a place

FIGURE 2.4
Winding cotton
outside a rectangular
house

in the house: kin will "call the soul" at mealtimes of children studying in
Ruteng or farther afield. The many ways in which people move among different houses that they claim as their "own" demonstrate the unbounded-
ness of houses as interconnected places in a landscape of mobility. For the
people of Wae Rebo-Kombo, the split of the community between two sites
brings out even more clearly the permeability of houses to shifting inhabitants, as well as the rather ad hoc nature of house building and composition.
Although a number of Wae Rebo-Kombo residents permanently inhabit
only *one* of these sites, most members of the community travel more or less
regularly between mountains and lowlands, in ways that I describe in more
detail in Chapter 6. This is why one unmarried woman, who moved continually between the two sites, referred to the community as "people who
swing" (*ata jéjong*). Such "swinging" necessitates, for all households, a base

in both Wae Rebo *and* Kombo. Following the logic of the claiming of houses as one's own, this base—particularly for those who travel relatively infrequently—may be the house of parents or siblings. For less frequent travellers, sleeping for a couple of nights in the house of a relative is enough. However, owners of households who maintain gardens in both mountain and lowland sites, or who have young children attending the lowland school but also substantial coffee fields in Wae Rebo, have, as circumstances arose, made more permanent arrangements. Some have a house—shared with different households—in each site, demonstrating both the greater significance of rooms in connection with households, and the ad hoc and shifting nature of house composition. Such households split their members between the two sites: for example, the mother and school-age children will live in Kombo, while the father and older children live in Wae Rebo.

In addition to their movements between houses, people also move, either daily or over longer time periods, between houses and garden-huts (cf. Dix Grimes 2006, 138). These are small, one-room thatched dwellings located in fields and used as a base from which to guard maturing crops from various scavengers, including monkeys, hence the term "monkey-huts." There is an interesting parallel between those who inhabit individual rooms within shared houses and those who work gardens (and inhabit garden-huts) within shared fields (*lingko*). Both groups form a community of equals not necessarily connected through kinship. However, despite these parallels, there are many differences between life in village houses and life in garden-huts. In particular, huts are places to which couples can escape with their children when the pressure of communal living becomes too great. After some minor disagreements with her husband's parents, one woman told me she was living in her garden-hut for a while because it was *aman* (safe and secure), and you didn't have to "listen to other people's talk." Garden-huts are also places of refuge and isolation after more serious disputes. One Kombo man with a notoriously short temper was once discovered threatening his wife with a machete. Attempts to punish the man were inconclusive, as his wife refused to speak about what had happened. Shortly afterwards, the couple moved to a garden-hut in a remote field, where they remained for two months, until the incident had blown over.

The movements of persons between different houses and to garden-huts are a clear illustration of Ingold's definition of places as "nodes in a matrix of movement" (2000, 219). Moreover, there is a specific temporality to these movements. During the months in which crops in newly opened highland fields began to flower or bear fruit, many people slept in their garden-huts continually, only occasionally returning to the village for Sunday morning prayers (cf. Dix Grimes 2006, 139), and then always with an anxious comment that "the monkeys will be all over my field." Similarly, people's movements between houses in Kombo and Wae Rebo reflect the agricultural cycle, the Catholic and school calendar, and the timing of ritual events or cooperative work tasks.

However, new forms of gendered travel, as well as a growing focus on houses as individual property, are changing some aspects of these easy movements between a nested series of houses. From 1999 onward, a number of young men (both married and unmarried) from Wae Rebo-Kombo and other villages migrated to find work on plantations and building sites in Malaysia. What was striking was that many of these men rationalized their temporary migration in terms of wanting to save enough money to build their own house. This reflects the growing expense of carpenter-built houses with metal roofs as opposed to smaller houses built using bamboo walls and thatched roofs. Increasingly, men aim to construct a new, individual house for their wife and children rather than sharing the house of a parent, sibling, or friend. In Wae Rebo, one man, Teo, had saved money through working felling timber in the forest and subsequently had a large new house built by a carpenter. When his younger brother married and had a child, many people assumed that the new family would move into Teo's house. However, it emerged that Teo wanted to "use a contract" and to charge his brother rent for occupying his expensive new house. His brother refused and instead chose to live with the large extended family of his paternal uncle. This was a completely new development in the village, and though Teo's attempt to charge rent may be a one-off, it does suggest that, as more expensive houses are built, mobility between houses may well be reduced.

HOUSES AS CENTERS: HOSPITALITY AND RITUAL

Domestic memory focuses not only on images of *places* but also on images of *concrete acts*. Its key dimensions are action, concreteness and immediacy. People remember *doing* things.
—Joëlle Bahloul, *The Architecture of Memory* (1996), p. 136

There are many activities that take place in or around Manggarai houses. Some of these, such as machete sharpening and weaving, have already been mentioned. Others are more seasonal, such as the post-harvest process of tying up cobs of maize to hang for preservation over the hearth, or the spreading of harvested coffee onto large mats in the yard to dry. I want to concentrate here on everyday practices of sharing and hospitality, as these reveal more about the flow of goods and people within and between houses. These are also the activities that many Manggarai people themselves stress as most central to their custom (*adat*) and identity. However, despite the permeability of the boundaries of a house, I also want to consider what makes a house a center, and to do this I must consider the significance of house rituals.

As we have seen, houses as dwellings may be occupied by a number of different households/rooms, whose inhabitants shift and change through time. Households are responsible for their own staple foodstuffs: rice, maize, and (to a lesser extent) coffee. However, the sharing of vegetables, fruit, and other seasonal treats is common practice in multifamily houses. Households will try to eat together at the same time, particularly when one has an unusual vegetable dish or has been lucky enough to get some meat from a wild pig or monkey killed during occasional hunting. By contrast, those who lived in smaller houses often joked with me about how impossible it was to enjoy a treat in large houses, as one immediately had to share it with the whining children of other families (cf. Kipp 1993, 62). While those living in houses with multiple rooms/households stressed that these were "lively," those in single or two-room houses said they preferred things to be "quiet." Nevertheless, those who live in single-household dwellings will often share with those who trace connections to their house. When Amé Gaba had particularly good sweet potatoes, oranges, or a piece of meat, he would frequently share them with Sita's family, who had once briefly shared his house. Paths of sharing, then, tend to follow historical connections between different houses.

Manggarai people are somewhat obsessed with their reputation as hosts, attach great importance to treating guests well, and always enjoy (while claiming to be horrified by) stories about visitors to other villages whose hunger was not recognized and who were not fed. The house activities of talking, chewing betel, drinking coffee, and eating are all surrounded by numerous ritualized procedures, which people continually emphasized as being Manggarai custom. One of the most basic forms of hospitality is to invite someone into one's house to talk. Indeed, although I earlier described the permeability of the house to noise, and the ways in which neighbors shout out to one another, there is a strong sense that any serious talk must take place face-to-face inside a house. On one occasion, Amé Gaba was spreading out coffee to dry in his yard, when another man emerged from the path through the coffee bushes. Seeing Amé Gaba was outside, this man then said, "I'm going inside," a clear sign that he wished to talk about something important.

In Wae Rebo and Kombo, people also frequently visit one another's houses more informally, seeking out betel quids or tobacco. In return for these stimulants, they offer a little bit of liveliness, jokes (*ganda ganda*), and gossip, and always (without being asked) join in to help with any work tasks, whether shelling beans or helping put the decoration on a woven basket. Less informally, when a guest enters a person's house for the first time, it is common for the host to say "Don't be angry, this is the shape of our house here." Once a guest is seated, members of the house will offer one of many different "greetings" (*ris*), which largely consist of a question, such as "You've arrived then?" If glasses of coffee are being served but there are no bananas or cooked roots to go with them, the host will say, "Don't be angry, you don't have an accompaniment." Conversation then continues, with the coffee completely ignored, until the host says "Let's drink" (*inungs gé*) or "How about it?" (*ajol gé*). I frequently saw coffee go completely cold during a conversation because no one was prepared to drink until requested to do so by the host. When cooked food is ready, the host will again often say, "Don't be angry, our vegetables are no good," even if the side dishes actually include both interesting vegetables and meat or fish. The ritualized uttering of these phrases of humility, particularly "Don't be angry" (*néka rabo*), occurs at all times of the day and in all Manggarai houses. Indeed, these phrases are one of the very everyday ways in which a house is marked as a humble but hospitable place.

Despite the importance of keeping home fires burning, an occasional meal or sleep taken in a co-villager's house is seen as good form, a way to be "lively" with others, acknowledging connections and friendships, proving that one is not too "proud" (*sombong*). Of course, some houses are more lively than others, just as there are some people who do a little too much visiting, particularly when another household is serving meat or fish. Children, as "little guests," will be given cooked rice when their mother is visiting another house, though mothers say that too much whining for food is a sign that a child has not yet learnt to feel properly "shy" or "embarrassed" (*séngger*) in other houses. One mother repeatedly told the story of how her toddler son, when visiting an old woman who had once fed him wild pork, shouted "Where's the meat, Sisi?" Though these stories are found extremely humorous, they also clearly serve to show young children's lack of awareness of ritualized humility.

These acts of hospitality are on a continuum with the use of communal meals as a kind of payment, the more formalized reception of guests at alliance and other events, and the feeding of ancestors and other spirits at house rituals. Occasionally, a household will pay other villagers to help them with agricultural tasks such as weeding or transplanting rice seedlings.[9] Despite the cash payment such workers receive, they still expect the household they are working for to provide them with morning coffee and snacks, and a large and hearty midday meal. More formal meals are also held both before and after a group of young men go to fell timber for a particular household, or before a carpenter starts work on construction of a bed or a house. The meal held after such work has been completed is particularly important and is called "massaging tiredness" (*kedur kamar*). A dog will usually be killed to provide extra meat, and the meal will be followed by speeches and the presentation of money (see Allerton 2012). When the workers for such an event are from within Wae Rebo-Kombo, there is usually some self-consciousness about turning a co-villager into a "guest" (*meka*). This is similar to the alliance events I describe in the next chapter, in which women are "made guests" at houses they normally visit as friends and neighbors.

Everyday processes of cooking, sharing food, and talking are therefore,

FIGURE 2.5   Eating together in a back kitchen

in the form of house hospitality, utilized to "make guests," to temporarily transform informal relationships into more formal ones in the context of which payments can be made. This process of activating different kinds of relationships through providing or receiving cooked food can also be seen in sacrificial rituals. Such rituals temporarily "make guests" of both human and nonhuman persons by providing them with speech and food. Manggarai people talk, for example, not of "going to attend Rensi's marriage ritual," but of "going to eat Rensi's chicken meat." Such a description may be humorous, but it also describes a transformed relationship to Rensi. Moreover, for most women in a house where a ritual is being held, the event *is* largely experienced in terms of the processing of uncooked and cooked food. At the beginning of the ritual speech, a chicken will be passed through to the ritual speaker. A short while later, the chicken will be passed back to the hearth, having had its throat cut over a plate in which its blood is collected. A woman or young man will then hold the chicken in the flames of the hearth in order to burn off the feathers. After this, the chicken is passed back to the ritual speaker for the inspection of its intestines (*toto urat*). It then returns again to the hearth, where a small amount of meat, including a piece of the liver, will be roasted. This roasted meat is then mixed with some boiled rice in a plate (one for each chicken or animal killed) and passed back to the ritual speaker as the "food for the ancestors" (*hang empo*). The witnesses to the ritual now settle back and enjoy glasses of coffee, while the women and young men begin to prepare and cook the meat. The end of any ritual, even one held in a field, is always marked by a communal meal, and no one who has witnessed such an event should leave before eating some of the meat.

This description of house rituals in terms of the processing and movement of chickens and meat is intended to show how hearth-based activities carried out by women and by young men are as central to house rituals as the speech of older men. The literature on eastern Indonesian rituals has tended to concentrate either on the symbolic meaning of ritual languages (Fox 1988; Kuipers 1998) or on the exchanges involved in large-scale events (Hoskins 1993; Keane 1997), and has had relatively little to say about the more ordinary practices that rituals employ. However, in Manggarai, a good ritual is not simply an event where the correct speech is spoken, or the correct goods received. It is also an event that is "lively," where food is cooked quickly and deliciously, and where guests are served politely and are able to eat their fill of meat. Indeed, the word *ramé* is often used as a noun to refer to lively events— such as bridewealth negotiations or a wedding party—whether or not these involve a sacrificial or ancestral element. During fieldwork at the Lenggos primary school, I asked children from Class 6 to draw and/or write a description of a *ramé* event in their village. What was noteworthy about their descriptions was that they gave as much emphasis to cooking, eating, and dancing as they did to ritual speech.[10] Indeed, there is no local word that could be translated as "ritual." Such events are referred to either by their rather pragmatic titles (such as "blood on feet") or as a *ramé*.

In considering household rooms, I argued that their full significance could only be understood if *both* everyday processes such as looking after children or sleeping *and* ritual activity were considered together. Here, I want to stress four points with regard to house rituals that are not specifically concerned with rooms. First, rituals are at the more formalized end of a continuum of practices of sharing and hospitality that animate houses. Second, rituals are one of a range of events that make a house "lively" and do so specifically by inviting nonhuman persons into the house. Third, this "liveliness" is part of what makes a ritual efficacious. Fourth, the ability to hold rituals is a crucial aspect of the distinction between different kinds of Manggarai dwellings, since although "monkey-huts" are valued as peaceful places to raise a family, they are not centers for hospitality or ritual in the way that a house is. Any major "talk" or life-cycle ritual must always be held in a house, and before such an event, people living temporarily in field-huts stress that they are going to "return to the house" (*wé'é mbaru*).

Significantly, the ritual to inaugurate a newly built house is also called "returning to/moving in to the house" (*wé'é mbaru*). A number of people stressed the importance of this ritual to me, from a teacher who had recently built a cement house to a middle-aged woman who reflected on how she didn't really feel comfortable in her Kombo house until after the ritual to "move in" to it. During this ritual, the speaker requests that the residents of the house will not be "itchy when lying down, disturbed when sleeping," a phrase that refers both to ill-health and to spiritual disturbance. In addition to chickens, a pig should be sacrificed at the ritual, to ensure the well-being of the house's residents and to provide food for the guests, but also, as one informant stressed to me, so that there will always be "the smell of pig's blood" in the house. People said that it was because a pig had been killed for "moving in" to a house that it could later host other, alliance rituals involving pig sacrifice. This "moving in" ritual is also said to "tame" and "persuade" the land to accept the new house and to protect its residents from harm. While rooms may have a specific agency of their own, in part connected with their role in patrilineal kinship, an ordinary house is a center to which other agents, including ancestral spirits and the land itself, are invited and offered hospitality. In making a house "lively" with such nonhuman agents, rituals make a house a protective place. By linking the house with the land, the "moving in" ritual is therefore part of the ongoing unfolding of relations between humans and the various agencies of the landscape.

Earlier, I argued that, because the potential community of people connected with a house is always much larger than those who live in it on a day-to-day basis, absent people always have a place in the house and may be called and remembered at mealtimes. Similarly, nonhuman persons, who are unseen in everyday life, also always have a place in the house. House rituals are largely about noting the presence of these unseen house occupants and treating them to the hospitality offered there on a day-to-day basis to living humans. Such rituals also attempt to re-create a house as in some respects the same place, despite the vagaries of time and the ongoing flow of occupants. This explains why, when people rebuild their houses, they always attempt to retrieve and reinstitute the offering platforms from the old structure. There is a permeability but also a potentiality to the ordinary Manggarai house, for it is a potential community of the living who are present, the living who are absent, and various spirits, and this is what makes a house different from a garden-hut. In addition, a house continues to be a home to the deceased, and it is to this connection between houses and the placing of the dead that I now turn.

DEATH AND DWELLINGS

By contrast with architectural or symbolic descriptions, which are prone to describing houses in somewhat static terms, an everyday, multisensory account of the house reveals its permeability to noise, smoke, smells and, most important, the movements of people. Manggarai houses have porous boundaries, but through rituals and other practices of hospitality, they have emerged as centered entities.[11] Despite my concern to draw out the everyday aspects of houses, I cannot ignore rituals altogether, both because they are part of what makes a house "lively," and because the ability to hold rituals is what distinguishes houses from those other everyday dwellings, garden-huts. Some of the most significant house rituals are the ordered sequence of sacrifices and ritual procedures that occur after a death. These demonstrate both the importance of the house as a protective shelter and the eventual necessity of directing the dead *away* from the house in order that their descendants may safely continue with the business of living.

Immediately after a death, the corpse is washed, dressed in its best clothes, and then "laid out on the floor" of the house. For this laying out, the head of the corpse should be near to the central house-post (*hiri bongkok*), with the feet pointing towards the front door. The corpse is covered in a shroud of woven *songké* cloths, and when people enter the house to cry over the corpse, they stroke the body through these cloths, which on this and other occasions can be said to function as "super-skins" (Allerton 2007b). The positioning of the corpse is particularly significant: the central house-post is associated with the (male) authority of household heads and is leant against by ritual speakers during key events. Laying the corpse (of whatever age or sex) out in this manner connects it with the power of the central house-post, which, as is the case with other such posts in southeast Asia is rather loosely thought to be the place where ancestral blessings are transmitted (Waterson 1990, 115–118; Forth 1991a, 35). However, the pointing of the corpse's feet towards the door indicates something equally significant about the "placing" of the dead.

A noticeable linguistic feature regarding the use of Manggarai houses are the direction terms that apply universally to all houses, whatever cardinal direction they may face. The two most important of these terms are *lé*, denoting the direction of the (front) door, and *hili*, denoting the direction of the hearth or kitchen. These terms are also used, somewhat differently, outside the house, although the system of external orientation (described in Chapter 6) does not affect the internal orientation of dwellings. Outside the house, *hili* is used to denote a place that is downhill or "behind," and this makes it apt for denoting the slightly sunken hearth or attached kitchen. *Lé*, when used outside the house, has a range of interconnected meanings but most generally means "towards the mountains." However, *lé* also refers to the vaguely defined "land of the dead," since the dead are *ata belé* (people on the *lé* side) and graves (on a steep mountainside in Waé Rebo) are always described as *lé*. Thus, pointing the feet of a corpse towards the door—the part of the house that is *lé*—directs it towards its future location in the grave, as a member of the "land of the dead."[12] As we shall see, the association of the recently deceased with the door of the house is particularly clear during the final death ritual or *kélas*.

The emotional significance of laying out the corpse in the house is shown by the horror associated with the category of deaths known as "green/unripe death" (*mata ta'a*). An "unripe death" is when the person is killed swiftly and suddenly outdoors, usually in their field, or in an act of cold-blooded murder, but also increasingly in road accidents (cf. Hoskins 1998, 162). In such cases, the body of the deceased must not be allowed inside the house (cf. McWilliam 1997, 112), in part (as we saw in the previous chapter) to prevent the infection of rooms with "unripe blood." One story I was often told was that of Domi, a young man who had died in his prime in the early 1980s, leaving behind a pregnant wife and one-year-old child. Domi had been crushed when felling timber, when the falling direction of a large tree had been fatally miscalculated. I was told that Domi's father carried his son's body into the village, where a raised platform was built near his eventual grave. It was on this platform that the corpse was laid out, and where, lit only by a gas lamp, people came to cry throughout the night. The number of times I was told about this death appeared to attest not only to the horror felt at a sudden death but also to the power of the image of a corpse laid out *outside* the protection of the house. Those crying for Domi in the open air were doubly exposed, to the elements of course, but also in the sense that extreme emotions are believed to make a person vulnerable to physical and spiritual harm. By contrast, those mourning inside a house are to some extent protected by the rituals that, over the years, have made the house into a protective shelter. As I showed earlier, the sheer number of people inside a house following a death also has a beneficial effect in keeping a house "lively." Prayer meetings held in a house after a death are similarly valued for both their lively and their protective qualities.

Deaths, of whatever kind, are described as "afternoon guests" (*meka mané*), as people will almost immediately begin to arrive in the house to cry over the corpse and comfort the bereaved. An "afternoon guest" is one who arrives unexpectedly, giving the house residents little time to prepare. Because a death involves "afternoon guests" in this way, Wae Rebo-Kombo villagers must all contribute equal sums of rice, coffee, and money to a bereaved household.[13] People also make important practical contributions, building temporary shelters outside very small houses, fetching water, or helping to move produce sacks or beds inside houses to make space for mourners. The description of death in terms of unexpected "guests" strengthens my argument that practices of hospitality are far from trivial but are central to the significance of the house. When guests arrive from farther afield, and particularly when *woé* (groups associated with out-married sisters and daughters) arrive, they will give small sums of money known as "tears," an expression of loss but also a means to help the family to buy sugar and other goods. These "tears" are also a way of paying respect to the deceased, who will then keep at a safe distance.[14] However, there may still be certain uneasy moments in houses when boundaries are broken down. For example, Maria, a woman in her forties, described to me a time when she briefly visited a house in another village. As she sat down, she became aware of a terrible smell of rotting. She called out to the women of the house, "Quick, pass me a betel quid," and then

FIGURE 2.6   Pouring glasses of coffee for guests at a final death ritual

"offered betel" to the ghost of a woman of that house. Maria told me that she had known this woman fairly well, but hadn't been able to visit the house to present her "tears" after the death. The terrible smell was that of the corpse of the deceased woman, whom Maria had not yet officially "remembered." Remembering the woman by offering betel caused the smell to disappear, as the ghost returned to the *lé* side.

Following the night of crying over a corpse, burial takes place fairly quickly, with prayers led by the *guru agama* (religious teacher). However, the removal of the corpse from the house does not signal the end of ritual procedures affecting the house and its inhabitants. Immediately after a death, all house residents and their families are forbidden to work in the fields, and all village women are forbidden to weave. The *tok tok* sound of a woman banging her sword on her loom is so closely associated with the everyday activity of houses that, people say, if it was heard by the deceased, he or she would ask why the weaver "didn't remember" or "didn't value" them. Again, this shows the importance of aural permeability to the value of houses as places. Fields may be visited only after performance of the small ritual known as "green/unripe leaves" (*haung ta'a*), held roughly three days after a death, after which the chief mourners may bathe for the first time. This real and symbolic cleansing continues a few days later with "shaking out the mats" (*wéntar losé*), when woven guest-mats are aired outside in the sunshine, simulating the spring cleaning of the house and its inhabitants. After this event, women in the village may weave again, and in Wae Rebo the drums (off-limits in the immediate aftermath of a death) may once again be played. People told me that after the "shaking out the mats" guests no longer come to sit and mourn on the mats of the "house of sadness," but rather mourn "each in their own house."

Death rituals mark the gradual transition of the deceased from inside the house to the grave "on the *lé* side." In the weeks immediately after a death, the often restless spirit of the deceased remains near to the house, and residents may feel signs of "spooking" (*katéng*), such as a sudden chill or goose bumps, or an awareness of a particular smell associated with the deceased. Such feelings are considered inevitable but unsettling, and one of the primary purposes of death rituals is to gradually signal the end of day-to-day contact between the living and the dead, to limit the future contexts in which the dead can share the liveliness of the house. The Catholic forty nights' prayers are usually held either inside the house or next to the grave and are considered an important way to demonstrate love for the deceased. However, it is the *kélas* or final death ritual that is crucial in placing a permanent barrier between the living and the dead. This is a large event held sometime in the year after the death, normally after harvesting rice. Paths of out-married women (*woé*) are sent formal requests for money (*sida*), part of which is used to recompense the natal families of in-married women, who are also invited and bring with them rice, pigs, *tuak,* and cigarettes. These guests arrive the night before the ritual sacrifice, an arrival described as the "return" (*wé'é*). Final death rituals are held for all age-groups, from small children to the very old, and are described as "the end of mourning," "the end of loving," or just "the end," a sign that affairs with the deceased are "finished." The climax is the sacrifice of a pig in the door of the house, after a ritual speech directly addressed to the deceased, in which they are exhorted to take with them "what is bad" (*ata da'at*), and leave behind "what is good" (*ata di'a*). The speech ends with the throwing of uncooked rice for the deceased in order that, in one man's words, they "don't keep coming to ask for food."

A *kélas* ritual marks "the end" of everyday involvement between the individual dead and the living. By sacrificing the pig in the doorway, the ritual continues the process of pointing the deceased away from the house and towards the land "on the *lé* side." After providing the deceased with a sumptuous meal, and with rice for cooking in the future, the ritual firmly draws a line under the everyday sharing of foodstuffs, coffee, and betel. The ritual is always held in the "main house" (*mbaru pokok*) of the deceased, which is often not the house in which they lived but that of a father or grandfather. Although in part a formal alliance event at which exchanges of money and livestock are made, the *kélas* is also the last chance for a family to show love for the deceased in the most poignant way, by eating together in their origin house. The arrival of paths of out-married women returning to their "main house" ritually emphasizes the movement of persons away from and back to a series of dwellings. Yet, in marking "the end" of the deceased's movements into the houses of kin, the ritual also marks the limits to safe and productive mobility.

BEYOND "THE HOUSE"

Despite the architectural changes outlined at the beginning of this chapter, many Wae Rebo-Kombo people do not see the difference between a round or rectangular, planted or raised house as one of great substance. Instead, they distinguish between the ritually significant "drum house," ordinary houses, and "monkey-huts" in fields. In this chapter—in part by evoking a *sense* of houses as places (Feld and Basso 1996)—I have shown how, despite architectural and other differences, ordinary houses show many similarities as highly permeable structures defined by the temporal flows of persons as well as the sounds, smells, children, and animals that move between neighboring dwellings. While in the previous chapter, we saw how household rooms, as both material and immaterial entities, play a shifting role in the organization of connections between spouses and siblings, in this chapter we have seen how ordinary houses are rather ad hoc collections of households. Though people utilize connections of siblingship to claim a number of different dwellings as "my own house," these have no particular implications for kinship organization.

Much of the literature on eastern Indonesian houses has followed one of two approaches. On the one hand, such houses have been approached from a standpoint of architectural or symbolic interest. These approaches have yielded many significant insights, for example into the meaning of house-posts (Waterson 1990, 118) or the interrelationship of houses and granaries (Barnes 1974, 55). However, such approaches do not necessarily reveal the local, everyday ways in which a house is made and understood as a place of value. Architectural diagrams or floor-plans, employed to help the reader visualize the particular buildings under discussion, obscure as much as they reveal. In particular, floor-plans emphasize walls and boundaries, whereas we have seen how the Manggarai house (probably like many other dwellings built of tropical materials) is highly permeable, whether to sounds, animals, sorcerers, smells, or ancestors. Chickens run about underneath it, substances drip through its cracks onto the ground below, smoke rises through its thatch, and chill winds blow through its walls. The boundaries between what is inside and what is outside the house are not always clearly defined. In addition, a Manggarai house is less a container than a stopping-off place for myriad journeys on many temporal scales.

That a house becomes a valued place in part through the movements of people can be seen by considering the negative evaluations of houses with few such movements, or with no visitors. One family, who were said to follow "charismatic" Christian practices behind closed doors, were criticized because it was said they "didn't answer the calls of other people," refusing aural permeability. Another house in Kombo, the home of an elderly couple, was criticized as a place where the door was always shut, where its inhabitants hid from their fellow villagers. When the wife died, very few villagers went to grieve or cry in this house, remembering when this woman had failed to cry for their own deceased relatives. One young woman told me that the husband, Lus, had been heard wailing, "Will this be what it is like when I die? Will I be all alone with no friends?"

What architectural and symbolic approaches share is that they focus on the house as a particular kind of *object*. Indeed, this is why, in his book on *Art and Agency,* Alfred Gell can include houses in a discussion of "art works" (1998, 251–258). Certainly, I do not intend to deny either the rather extraordinary architecture of *niang* houses or the materiality of the house (indeed, in my previous account of rooms, I was at pains to describe it). However, as a valued *place,* there is much more to a Manggarai house than its status as an object. If we focus on the taken-for-granted aspects of everyday life, we are drawn to both permeability and what I have called "liveliness." Though both of these aspects are influenced by the material qualities of houses, neither of them can be reduced to "materiality." A house is a place for numerous "lively" events—events that leave the smell of blood in the house, and that, partly through permeability, create a sort of protective, effervescent buzz. Similarly, ritual "liveliness" also helps ensure that a house is permeable to the right kinds of nonhuman persons. There is no better example of this than the way that a house door is left open and faced by the ritual speaker during marriage and death rituals. However, at times this kind of permeability is threatening, as when spirits attack through the undersides of the house, or when the wrong kind of ancestors enter a household room. Thus, ritual is also capable of creating barriers and boundaries, of turning the soul of the dead away from the house, or persuading a particular ancestor to keep away.

The second major approach to eastern Indonesian houses follows the concerns of Lévi-Strauss and seeks to outline the particular ways in which a society can be said to be "house-based" (see especially Errington 1989). This approach has also yielded many significant insights, but is hampered in two key respects. First, it follows predominant ways of theorizing in social anthropology by assuming that, ultimately, social relations have ontological priority over place. This is why, as we saw in the previous chapter, Lévi-Strauss can characterize certain houses as "fetishes" and can thereby fail to appreciate the specific ways in which such buildings (or parts of buildings) may be thought to exercise agency. For Lévi-Strauss, the point of the house as an institution is that it *fixes* (however temporarily) unstable and apparently contradictory social processes. However, the fact that, in Manggarai (as in many other places) people change residence and move, relatively easily, *between* houses makes it hard to see ordinary houses as *fixing* or fetishizing anything. The second problem with the literature on "house-based societies" is that it has led to analyses that stop, so to speak, at the door, and that fail to connect houses with the wider landscape of pathways and fields. My account of the permeability and mobility that lie at the heart of ordinary Manggarai dwellings is part of this book's overall strategy to connect different kinds of places and pathways rather than confining the house to something called the "built environment." As we have seen, even ritual, one of the most "centered" of house activities, seeks to reach *outside* of the house to the "land" it "persuades" and, through the door and beyond, to the ancestors on the "mountainside." Having focused on dwellings, let us now move out, beyond the house, to examine "paths" of marriage and family history.

3

Paths of Marriage

Iné Teres is a small, wiry grandmother with soft white hair tied up in a bun and strong hands for pounding maize with flat stones. She and her husband, the ritual speaker Amé Bertolo, preside over a large Wae Rebo house, home to several unmarried women and to Niko, a young boy with learning difficulties whose antics are the delight of the village. Iné Teres is often to be found watching the young women weaving in the shade underneath the house or feeding the two large pigs she has tethered to posts some distance away. The latter task fills her with exasperation; pigs, like chickens, are not polite diners.

Late one night, as dinner is cooked and rain falls on the thatched roof of the house, I interview Iné Teres about her marriage and children. Others in the house listen, occasionally adding their own comments. We speak of her final marriage ritual in her home village of Nandong and her accompanied journey (*padong*) to Wae Rebo. Remembering the *padong*s I have seen, I ask her if she cried. "Ai, I cried!" she replies, "I cried as I left Nandong." I ask her why, and she says she cried for her mother, who then told her, "Don't cry, *enu*." Tanta Tina, who is sitting in a corner of the large kitchen, adds that this probably made Iné Teres cry even more, and there is laughter of recognition. "Did your mother come on your *padong*, Iné?" I ask. No, she replies, she didn't come. We discuss her siblings, some of whom did accompany her, and then the conversation turns back to her arrival in Wae Rebo. Did she feel sad then? Yes, she says, but a month afterwards she went back to visit Nandong. She had gone west to Sarong for the *padong* of another woman, and as that woman cried, "I cried again myself. And because of that crying, that was when I went again, I went south west to Nandong." Later in the conversation, we discuss her children's marriages, and she tells me how her eldest son followed her "path" to Nandong and married her brother's daughter. Her husband, Amé Bertolo, tells me, "In the past, child, before the arrival of priests, we were all products of joining (*tungku*). Joining the path (*tungku halang*)."Marriage and alliance have been central topics in eastern Indonesian ethnography since the publication in 1935 of van Wouden's comparative study of social structure in the region. As a member of the Dutch Leiden School, van Wouden sought to uncover the basic patterns of social organization and classification that defined eastern Indonesia as a "field of study." In particular, he aimed to demonstrate the importance to these societies of "connubium" (forms of cross-cousin marriage), arguing that marriage customs were the "pivot" to a comprehensive organization of society and cosmos (1968 [1935], 2). Since this pioneering study, ethnographers have continued to reveal a variety of types of marriage alliance in the region while retaining a distinctive Leiden School stress on cosmology and classification (Barnes 1974; Fox 1980; Traube 1986; Lewis 1988; McKinnon 1991; Forth 2001). However, while these and other works have considered important and complex issues in relation to eastern Indonesian marriage, they have tended to be most concerned with the "rules" governing social action and with demonstrating the links between cosmological beliefs, ritual activities, and structural order.

This chapter challenges the hegemony of the Leiden-derived tradition of analysis by considering the topic of marriage from a new angle. In particular, I describe people's personal experiences of the marriage process, in order to show how relations of marriage can be understood not simply as a set of rules and classifications but as a sequence of place-based, practical actions. Throughout southern Manggarai, people speak of a particular marriage connection as a "path" (*halang*). For example, a proposed marriage with a previously unconnected family is described as a "new path," while those wishing a girl to marry her father's sister's son will hope she "follows the path of her aunt." Are such descriptions merely metaphorical, creating an image similar to the lines of anthropology's kinship diagrams? Or might there be a more literal connection between marriage paths and the "real," muddy trails through mountain forests and along lowland rice fields?

Fox's influential introduction to *The Flow of Life* (1980) notes the description of affinal relationships as "paths" among several eastern Indonesian societies. Indeed, given the widespread use of the title of this volume as a description of marriage in these societies, it is worth noting that it could just as easily have been called "the path of life." Here and elsewhere in the literature, we find Kodinese "paths" (*lara*) of exchange goods (Needham 1980, 37), Mambai "paths" (*dan*) blazed by ancestral marriages (Traube 1986, 81), old Anakalangese alliances that are a "smooth path [*lara*], worn-down trail" (Keane 1997, 54), and the characterization of an Atoni mother's brother's daughter as the "woman of the path" (*fe lalan;* Schulte Nordholt 1980, 235). Other writers also speak more generally of alliance paths (Barnes 1974, 240; Forth 2001, 104–105) or pathways (McKinnon 1991, 124), or note the "movement" involved in the relationship between alliance groups (Barraud 1990, 214). These works are primarily concerned with metaphoric representations rather than the active movement involved with marriage relations. While, in a later edited collection on Austronesian ideas about place, Fox calls for a comparative study of "pathways," he still envisages them as "an active *mode of representation* of relations and their transformation" (1997a, 17; my emphasis).[1] In contrast, this chapter shows how connections of marriage between different houses and villages are not simply "represented" by the paths crisscrossing the Manggarai landscape, but are in a very real way experienced as travel along these paths.

In the previous chapter, I showed how houses, as a key feature of the Manggarai landscape, become places of value through a range of everyday and ritual activities that create the house as both a node in a mobile milieu and a center for "liveliness." In this chapter, I concentrate on some of the paths that fan out from and back to these permeable houses, and the various journeys by which these paths are made. The paths I focus on are marriage paths, and the journeys I describe are emotional ones made by women, but also by men. Outlining the ways in which these paths contribute to an environment entangled with kinship will show how, as much as it can be said to be "house-based," Manggarai sociality is also "path-based."

The importance of focusing on movement as well as (more or less fixed) place has been particularly stressed by James Clifford, who argues that in common assumptions about culture, dwelling is understood to be "the local ground of collective life," whereas travel is conceived as a mere "supplement" (1997, 3). Clifford's polemic is addressed to a discipline that has imagined fieldwork as a "dwelling practice" rather than a "travel practice," and he thus tends to play down the significance of those studies—from Malinowski's descriptions of *kula* trade to the literature on pilgrimage—which have focused on "local" travel. Indeed, within the ethnography of southeast Asia alone, Rosaldo (1980) has very persuasively shown how Ilongot kinship is fundamentally constituted by movement through the landscape. However, what I take to be most useful in Clifford's work is the tension or relationship that he identifies in any one society between routes and roots, calling for an examination of "everyday practices of dwelling and traveling: traveling-in-dwelling, dwelling-in-traveling" (1997, 36). In this chapter, I go beyond such a vague, if tantalizing, expression and show how journeys are very practically involved in the creation of Manggarai marriage connections, and of gendered identity throughout the life cycle.

WOMEN, PIGS, AND CHICKENS

In the hours immediately after a birth, a Manggarai baby is declared to be either a female "outside person" or a male "inside person." These declarations of the future location of children doubly express travel and fixity. Because they are destined at marriage to move away from their natal home, girls are "outside people," the counterpart to their "insider" brothers (cf. McKinnon 1991, 197; Sugishima 1994, 154). However, there are some respects in which this pattern of gendered movement is an ideal form not always matched by reality. For instance, some men will move permanently away from their natal village, either to seek work or to settle and receive land in their wife's village. There are also a number of women who, for a variety of personal reasons, never marry, instead remaining in their natal homes, often to become heads of dispersed households, or weavers of great renown (see Allerton 2007c). Thus, the description of children as "insiders" or "outsiders" is to some extent contingent and dependent on later circumstances.

Framing this pattern of residence and movement is a division of a Manggarai person's social world into three main groups. These are kin (*ahé-ka'é*), and the two alliance categories of *woé* and *iné-amé*. The latter are best translated, respectively, as "sister or daughter" and "mother-father."[2] Although it is tempting, following most analyses of eastern Indonesian marriage systems, to translate these two categories as "wife-takers" and "wife-givers," I prefer here to use glosses of the local terms. This is because, first, the conventional analytical terms lack the complex familial meanings of *woé* and *iné-amé*.[3] As elsewhere on Flores, terming the partners in a marriage alliance "sister/daughter" and "mother-father" encodes their relationship as a kin-like connection between a female "child" and a senior, generative couple (Barnes 1974, 250–251; Sugishima 1994, 152; Forth 2001, 117). Second, the conventional terms exclude from membership the very women who move between groups after marriage. As feminist critics of Lévi-Strauss' conception of "woman-exchange" have argued, women in such alliance systems are not simply the "conduit of a relationship" (Rubin 1975, 174), but are centrally involved in the imagination and practice of marriage alliance. As this chapter shows, Manggarai women are involved with and constitute the landscape of relatedness as much as men, and are recognized as doing so by men.

Perhaps the most important conception underlying ideas about marriage alliance is the fact that the two alliance categories should never be confused. A man should never marry a woman from a family into which one of his clan branch "sisters," "father's sisters," or "grandfather's sisters" has married in the past. Manggarai people often express this by reference to the livestock that should pass from one group to the other, declaring that "what is a pig is rightly a pig, what is a chicken is rightly a chicken" (cf. Traube 1986, 92). Marriages that are perceived as reversing this "flow" of life and goods are forbidden or "not legitimate" (*toé kop*). If the couple is determined to marry and the link between the two groups is rather distant, fines and a procedure of tracing other kinship links, called "looking for a mother-father," may make the marriage possible. However, in other forbidden cases, couples who decide to live together will have no bridewealth, no marriage rituals, and may be disowned by their families. One woman in Kombo had apparently never spoken to or played with her three grandchildren, even though they lived in a hut some two hundred meters from her house. This was because her son had chosen to remain in a forbidden relationship, a situation that was blamed for various deaths and illnesses in his family.

FOLLOWING OR FORGING A MARRIAGE PATH

Manggarai people distinguish a number of different contemporary and historical types of marriage, from "kidnapping" (*roko*) to "looking after orphans" (*tinu-lalo*) whereby a woman married her sister's widower.[4] However, the main contrast that people draw is between *sangkang* marriages that create a "new path" of alliance and a form of cross-cousin marriage called *tungku*—"joining" or "to join." The purest form of *tungku* is marriage of a man with his mother's brother's daughter (MBD), often referred to as "joining the path" (*tungku halang*). However, as in Anakalang on Sumba (Keane 1997, 54), the broad definition of cross-cousins, together with the complex histories of marriage between different families, means that men and women always have a number of possible "joining" partners. There are therefore a number of different paths that any one person could "join" with a *tungku* marriage.

In Manggarai, marriage between couples with close genealogical links has been forbidden by the Catholic church. Nevertheless, despite this ban, and helped by occasional dispensations from the regional bishop, marriages described as *tungku* continue to be contracted, perhaps accounting for one-fifth of all matches. This persistence can be explained by a number of factors. In the first place, people are seeking "joining" links by tracing more distant alliance connections, often through a parent's same-sex sibling (known as *néténg nara,* "each brother"). Second, and like other Austronesian peoples (Fox 1997a, 9), those in Manggarai place great importance on remembering their origins to ensure health and success in life, saying they want their sons to contract "joining" marriages because they are "scared of forgetting our mother's path." However, perhaps the most important reason for the persistence of *tungku,* and one rarely noted in the eastern Indonesian literature, where preference for MBD marriage may be seen as "almost solely ideological" (Barnes 1980, 84), are the currents of mutual attraction running between potential *tungku* partners. From early childhood, they will be teased about playing with their "husband" or "wife," and as they grow up, their relationship is one framed by the possibility of marriage. Just as cross-cousin marriage is a "romantic ideal" in southern India (Trawick 1992, 151) so, under the right circumstances, Manggarai "joining" partners are thought to be irresistible to one another.

As noted, such marriages are conceived of as following the path of the father's sister or another female relative who went before, while marriages that create a new connection are thought to forge a fresh path of relatedness. Although there are many similarities between the practices constituting such marriages, there are also inevitable differences in experience between old and new pathways, a subject to which I shall return. For now, I want briefly to outline how Manggarai marriages are initiated and created, while again pointing out that the process sketched here is something of an ideal type that some marriages will subvert.

Over the past decades in Manggarai, there has been a gradual though not complete change from a custom of parents finding marriage partners, usually subject to the approval of their children, to young people initiating the process, subject to the approval of their parents and older kin. This change is often reflected on humorously in conversations. People told me that, in the past, a girl felt *jejé*—she "trembled with fear"—when a man was announced as her "guest" or prospective husband. They stressed a contrast with the contemporary situation, wherein it is parents who now feel *jejé* when they are told that a young man visiting is their daughter's "guest." Marriage proposals, which were once made formally to the bride's kin by a spokesperson or "bridge," today are usually made via a letter from the young man to his prospective bride. If she accepts this proposal, both sides will meet in the young woman's house and the couple will exchange rings (*tukar kila*). I was told that in the past rings were not exchanged but the girl was often given a "bracelet to fix things in advance." The bride may also receive a number of other gifts of clothing, and the date will be set for the *kémpu,* the ritual at which the bridewealth (*bélis*) is negotiated.

The bridewealth negotiations tend to be rather drunken and protracted, following which the previously hidden bride is "accompanied" (*karong*) into the front room of the house, where she and her prospective husband sit together slightly awkwardly on the main guest-mats. Things may grow rather rowdy and occasionally arguments break out, with either side launching into competitive singing.[5] There is then likely to be a wait of between six months and a year before the church wedding and final marriage ritual (*wagal*). During this time, the couple will pay numerous visits to the church, in particular to attend a marriage course, in which they are given religious instruction and taught the basics of "Christian family life" (cf. Smedal 1994, 271). Depending on the priest, these recently instituted courses may also involve discussion of the couple's relationship, though many of my informants told me that they thought such questioning ("Why do you like her?" "What do you talk about together?") was embarrassing and unnecessary.

In rural parishes, the church wedding is often a lengthy affair, with a large number of couples being married by the priest in one go. The preference is for the bride to wear a white wedding dress, lacy gloves, and makeup, and for the groom to wear a suit (usually borrowed and ill-fitting) and white gloves.[6] After the ceremony, the bride and groom process back to a house of the bride's kin, where coffee and cakes are served and villagers come to shake hands with the newly married pair and cry with the bride. That night, if the bride's family is well-off or have connections with town, a "wedding party" (*pésta kawin*) may be held, but in most village weddings there is simply a meal for the family and guests. Some time later—perhaps the next day or after a few more weeks to make preparations—the final marriage ritual is held. This is a large-scale event involving further financial negotiations, ritual speeches, and meals of specially killed pig. At the end of this event, the bride departs on her *padong,* the ritually significant journey to her groom's home, on which she is accompanied by numerous friends and relatives. At the end of the *padong,* the bride is met by a party of gong-banging women, come to "greet the young girl" (*suru molas*). She then, ideally at the base of the short house ladder of the groom's home, "treads on an egg" (*wegi ruha*) held in special leaves by an elderly female relative of the groom. Later that evening, after receiving the greetings of villagers, the couple's new status is finally marked by the ritual of "blood on feet." Those who have accompanied the bride will

FIGURE 3.1   Leaving the church after the wedding

usually leave the next morning, and she will begin her new life as a member of her husband's clan and household.

SPATIAL "SYMBOLISM" AND MARRIAGE PRACTICES

The events outlined above could be called the bare skeleton of Manggarai marriage. What fleshes out this skeleton are journeys, ritual actions, displays of tears and laughter, and, in particular, numerous images of place and movement. Marriage events, gifts, and negotiations are spoken of variously as "climbing houses," "treading over thresholds," "entering," "bridging water," "opening doors," and "sheltering." Such spatial symbolism is common to eastern Indonesian marriage (McKinnon 1991, 137; McWilliam 1997, 113; Keane 1997, 189) and, in Manggarai, combines images of both dwelling and movement, particularly through the idea of the threshold. Thus, men described their initial approach to their wife's family as "climbing the house" and often reported back its acceptance with the ritual phrase, "The door is stepped over, the mat is spread." Later, when the groom's kin return for the bride-wealth negotiations, they might say to the bride's family, "Your door is going north to our village, and our door is coming here to your village." In such phrases, and in line with van Gennep's (1977 [1908]) analysis of the symbol-ism of thresholds in rites of passage, the coming together of doors illustrates the union of two worlds, in which all boundaries have been reduced.

The spatial symbolism of ritual speech is echoed in the names of various textiles presented by the bride's to the groom's kin in exchange for cash. A "sarong to place," "sarong to accompany," and "sarong to shelter" may all be given at the final marriage ritual to ensure the bride's protection in her new home. Indeed, these crucial motifs of "sheltering" and "accompanying" are particularly stressed in the "accompanying" (*karong*) that takes place at mar-riage rituals, when the bride is brought through from the back to the front of the house. The "accompanying" is an example of the kinds of "ransoms" that van Gennep (1977, 119) saw as a frequent feature of marriage rites, and it is significant that what seems to be held to ransom is the bride's free passage from her natal kin to the groom's family.

At the "accompanying" of Edis, the bride was first dressed in a shiny pink blouse, her best, embroidered sarong and scarf, and a metal headdress (*bali-bélo*). She then had an open umbrella[7] held over her by a small group of female kin as they took her into the front room, filled with the smoke and conversation of male guests. Once in the front room of the house, Edis sat with her husband on a newly woven "mat to accompany," with the women grouped around her. There then followed a negotiation over the amount of "money to accompany" that the women should receive from the groom's kin. It is not until this money has been paid that the women can return to the back of the house, having safely handed over the bride. Since it is normally men who negotiate and handle money at alliance events, the demands of these accompanying women are viewed rather humorously. The women them-selves often play up to this, eschewing the formulaic language of negotiation, nonchalantly asking for extra cash as they spit red betel juice between the cracks in the floor. At one final marriage ritual, a woman rejected the first amount of money that she was offered with the blunt phrase "It's not much" (*toé dod*). This was met with hoots of derisory laughter from the young men in the room, who shouted "It's enough, mother!" Nevertheless, she refused to budge, and soon received all the money she had requested.[8]

What are we to make of such ransomed journeys within rituals, or sarongs that "place" and "accompany" brides, or talk about climbing houses and treading on thresholds? And how can these examples, which employ images of place and movement, help us to understand the way Manggarai people conceive of marriage as a "path"? By concentrating on the rich language of ritual speech or the names of textiles, one might be tempted to see these images in a wholly symbolic light. Indeed, Manggarai people themselves take great delight in uncovering the meaning of the riddles (*bundu*) of ritual speech. However, despite this, there is an additional element at stake with regard to marriage events. For example, the spokesman who reports back that "the door is stepped over, the mat is spread" is using these simple images of house visiting as a metaphor for acceptance by the bride's family. Yet, at the same time he is also describing actions that he has performed. The process of Manggarai marriage does not simply involve symbolic language of paths and thresholds, but also the actual performance of a series of bodily practices involving place—rooms, houses, churches—and travel between places. If we concentrate on these practices, we can begin to understand the significance of referring to marriage as a "path."

When I first started to think about paths in Manggarai, I carried in my mind an image of the muddy trails that I had walked on from highlands to lowlands, from house to washing spring, from village yard to field. If you travel frequently along certain paths, your body gets to know them well, anticipating a sudden dip, grasping with feet for roots to grip onto, knowing that you are coming round a corner to a viewpoint. But, of course, these paths do not preexist in the landscape. Rather, it is in the very process of travel, pounding the ground with bare feet, that paths are made. This is particularly noticeable when one is walking along paths through the forest, as men cut back new plant growth with machetes, or women clear fallen branches and prickly leaves from the trail. However, even the lowland roads that have brought new trucks between southern villages and the town are by no means permanent. Owing to the high levels of rainfall in Manggarai, they are periodically washed away, and these sections need to be rebuilt by those wishing to travel.

Just as the marriage process involves a series of practical actions, so too are paths made by action, by people travelling along them. Thus, the journeys that are central to Manggarai marriage actually blur the boundaries between "real" and "metaphorical" paths. My argument here is much stronger than that of writers who see eastern Indonesian marriage paths as simply an "image" or "reflection" of real paths (McWilliam 1997, 111,114) and explains why, when walking to other villages, Manggarai people will point to forks in the trail that lead to "Wihel's path" or "Kata's path." The action of travel creates both a physical trail and an alliance relationship: the two are fundamentally entwined. Moreover, just as a forgotten forest trail becomes overgrown and impassable, so too can alliance paths become neglected when people no longer travel them to renew the connections between families.

To consider these complex marriage paths in more detail, I now turn to the most significant marriage journey—the bride's *padong* to her new home. I focus on married women's *padong* recollections, and on the emotional intensity experienced by those on a *padong* journey. As mentioned, the traditional literature on eastern Indonesian marriage has tended to focus on marriage categories as a pivot to classification (Needham 1958), or on describing the ritual speech idioms that surround alliance relationships (Fox 1971). However, little attention has been paid in such literature to how people talk in a non-rule-like way, or how they relate their own experiences. Including such accounts here is crucial if one is to give a more nuanced account of the marriage process, and if one is to include the voices of women and young people as well as those of male ritual "specialists."

THE *PADONG*

The Manggarai word *padong* can be literally translated as "to lead by the hand," and is overwhelmingly used to describe the accompanying of the bride to her new home. *Padong* journeys may be long or short, they may involve transferring possessions from one village house to another, walking for miles through forest, or taking a cramped and bumpy ride in a wooden passenger truck. The bride is accompanied by young friends, siblings, and older relatives, all of whom receive a small amount of "money for accompanying" from the groom's kin. Fathers will often accompany their daughters; but mothers, even for a *padong* within the village, should always stay behind, "rooting" (*wu'at*) their daughter's journey. I was prompted to consider the significance of this journey after interviewing a number of older, married women, all of whom gave it a central place in their life stories. In addition, the cultural salience of the *padong* is evident in rituals for the construction of a drum house, when the central ridgepole is carried into the village and "met" (*suru*) in the same way that a human bride would be after her *padong*.[9]

Padong journeys are marked by emotional leave-taking and by the crying of the bride and her natal kin. Indeed, the bride's wailing—which also occurs after the church wedding and when she is left behind in her new home— is considered a central motif of the marriage process. This crying, common throughout Indonesia (Rodgers 1990, 328–329), has a songlike quality to it, a rising and falling refrain of "Oh, mother, ehhhh..." echoing the ritual crying of women after a death. On the day of a bride's departure, the sound of her crying affects the mood of the whole village. Female relatives may lament how far away the new village is or talk of other women who have moved away from their house. Women also reflect on their own *padong* journeys. One young mother, prompted by a bride's wailing, confided that when she left her own natal village she had thought, "If I die, where will my mother and father be? Not on the same land as me." During interviews with older women about their lives and marriages, they all dwelt, with both laughter and sadness, on their crying. For example, Iné Kris told me about her *padong:*

> Oh dear, I really cried! Until I got to the hill down there [she describes exactly where the hill is]. And that was where I stopped crying. Ai, because until then I could still see the village to the west. [I say, "You loved your village?"] Yes, I had forgotten to eat with my father, that was why I cried.

Iné Kris' distress at forgetting to eat with her father is typical of these *padong* stories. Feeding people and eating together are crucial means of constituting closeness in Manggarai, and not eating implies emotional upset. Moreover, autobiographical memories in Manggarai are not structured by objects or domestic animals (Hoskins 1998) but by the eating of food and shedding of tears. Iné Kris went on to describe how she felt at the *padong* of her own daughter, Min. Although Min had married within the same village, Iné Kris still felt sad that they would no longer eat together as one "room" or household:

> The reason why I cried, it was because she was going from eating all together with us, struggling and chaotic, and after that, I would be alone, that was why. [I ask, "But she was still in the same village?"] Yes, she was in the same village, but she had changed her room. Eh. Changed her room. [She describes how she came back from the house where the wedding was taking place and cried.] I felt as if she had married into a village far away. And starting with lunch, I couldn't eat.

The crying of the bride and of her relatives could, of course, be seen simply as a cultural convention rather than a sign of real emotional distress. However, it is worth noting that some brides, despite feeling great sadness, do not cry at their *padong.* Older women in particular, who tend to be rather scathing about what they see as the excessive crying of contemporary brides, may believe that crying places one in spiritual danger. Several told me that they had been given "medicine" at their *padong* so that, in spite of their emotions, they could not cry. Iné Aga, for example, told me that, despite the crying of her mother, she herself was given medicine to ensure she would remain "dry-eyed" until she reached her new village. Brides may also be given medicine to protect them from the strong emotions of others. Iné Kata said she was given coconut medicine before her final marriage ritual to prevent her being "held onto" by a man in her home village who had wanted to marry her. She told me that various "old people" were afraid that the love this man still felt for her would cause "unripeness" (*ta'a*), whether in the form of illness, infertility, or even death.

Grooms as well as brides may also be considered to be at risk (of strong emotions or harmful intentions) during the journeys of marriage. Iné Aga described "medicine" that her son, Simus, wore in his sarong during his wedding to protect against the possible witchcraft of those in his bride's village. Mateus, a young man from Wae Rebo, also wore protective medicine under his shirt during his church wedding and final ritual. The *padong* of Mateus' bride, Anita, was an interesting case of the emotions of the marriage process threatening to expose hostility between the bride and groom's families. Anita's village, Rotok, was to the east in the lowlands, and Mateus' wedding party set off in the afternoon, travelling by truck for the hour's journey from Kombo. The next day, after the "accompanying" ritual, the truck arrived in Rotok to take the *padong* party back to Kombo. Mateus' friends and relatives crammed themselves onto the hard wooden benches, some men sitting on the roof or hanging onto the outside of the truck. Anita was then led out of her house, wailing, as she said goodbye to her widower father and younger siblings. It soon became clear that there was little space left in the truck for Anita's friends, and tempers flared on both sides. Anita's relatives shouted that if the bride's friends could not accompany her there would be no *padong*. A rather drunk Wae Rebo man then shouted back, "We are the owners of this person" and "She's already been paid for." This shouting continued for some time, Anita becoming more distraught, until space was eventually made in the truck for her and a few friends.

Although Anita had recovered from this incident by the time she arrived in Kombo, her reception there still betrayed a sense in which the two sides were struggling over ownership of the bride. At the edge of Kombo, as happens at the end of all *padong* journeys, Anita was met by a party of women come to "greet the young girl" (*suru molas*). In a house nearby, they dressed Anita in a blouse and sarong of their own, brushing her hair into a differ-

FIGURE 3.2 Bride
and groom about to
enter the village at the
end of the *padong*

ent style and decorating it with a metal headdress. This re-dressing recalls
a similar, more violent, ceremony among the Merina of Madagascar, where
the bride is taken over by women of the groom's party, partly stripped, and
reclothed in finery with a different hairstyle (Bloch 1978, 27). Bloch explains
this "taking over" with reference to the division of the bride's status between
two places, which are "awkwardly juxtaposed" in the wedding ceremony. In
Manggarai, the wedding process and the *padong* journey also involve tense
juxtapositions, as a bride moves from one room and family to another. The
re-dressing of the bride may sometimes be rather brusque, but it can also be
tender, a chance for a groom's female kin to turn his new bride into one of
their own. Indeed, people say that the egg that the bride must crush with her
foot as she climbs into her new house is an explicit mark of her new land.

Significantly, a bride's post-*padong* sadness is often experienced as a longing for the "land" (*tana*)—village, fields, and general environment—of her natal home. Indeed, travelling a long marriage path dramatically transforms the landscape of a woman's daily life. Iné Aga, a woman in her sixties, told me:

> Eh, child, I was sad after my *padong*. My thoughts were sad, if I looked to the side and around me [she pauses]. Well, everywhere [in Wae Rebo] there were mountains! But when I lived in the west, we were open to the sky above. In the lowlands. If I looked to the south [in my natal village], there was the sea, and if I looked to the west, I could see all the villages to the west. [She describes a particular village in the west, and I say, "But here, all mountains"] But here, just mountains. "Oh," I said, then, "I would run away, if I could see the path."

Although people feel great sadness as a bride leaves on her *padong,* marriage events also have a rather contrasting emotional tenor—one focused on the children or "growth" (*beka*) that the couple's sexual relationship will produce. Indeed, among the young people accompanying a bride on her *padong,* the rather sexually charged atmosphere is something to be revelled in, and the drunken teasing indulged in by young men, in particular, is in sharp contrast to female tears.[10] As one bride's *padong* party departed from her new village, a crowd of young men gathered to laugh raucously at the crying of the young women. Grooms themselves may occasionally join in this laughter, although their bride's sadness often leads them to shed a tear, to the merciless delight of their friends.

The presence of large parties of unmarried young people, often visiting a village for the first time, means that *padong* journeys have always provided an excellent opportunity for meeting a potential spouse. One woman recalled attending her sister's *padong* in the 1970s:

> We went to accompany Anna in the past, accompany her west to Wiko. When we arrived there, all these men came! They came to look at you! You couldn't go alone to go outside [to the toilet]. That's what men from Lembor[11] are like. [She laughs.] If it is the first time they have seen you, that's what it is like. They all flap their hands! Ai, they really look, ooh! Some of them come, and they really disturb you by sitting with you! [She laughs.] [I ask, "So are people here different, they don't do that?"] People here are different. [She pauses.] Maybe they look here, but they are not really staring. These people to the west, they do it until they just eat you![12]

Today, this atmosphere of excited flirting is particularly seen as people walk along together or squeeze next to each other on trucks, and on occasions when a tape player is found and an impromptu party takes place late into the night.

I have quoted a few *padong* stories in an attempt to show the emotional significance of the bride's move away from home. This journey marks the final transformation in a bride's status and is a key reason why Manggarai people refer to marriage as a "path." Indeed, like a pilgrim journeying to a sacred site, it is in the very process of travel, framed by departure and arrival, that the bride is transformed (cf. Turner 1973, 204). At the end of the *padong*, the "blood on feet" ritual literally marks the young woman's assumption of her new status as she is incorporated into those who her natal kin refer to as their *woé*. She must now relate to her natal kin, not only as close relatives to whom she may return if her husband dies before the couple have children, but also as an alliance group who are owed appropriate gifts and respect.

OLD AND NEW PATHWAYS, PLANNED AND HASTY JOURNEYS

Although the *padong* is one of the defining features of the "path" of Manggarai marriage, it is important to consider how a bride's initial experience of married life is profoundly influenced by the type of path she travels. In Manggarai, a relatively egalitarian place that does not classify people into "commoners" or "nobles," different types of marriage are not associated with upholding or undermining hierarchy as they are in the Tanimbar islands (McKinnon 1991, 17). However, it is certainly the case that *tungku* matches are particularly favored by poorer families as they are less costly than "new paths." Of greater significance is the fact that a woman travelling a new path of marriage faces many more unknowns in her husband's village as compared with the bride whose marriage "joins the path" of a father's sister or other female relative.

For a *tungku* bride who follows an old path, the trauma of the *padong* may be quickly forgotten as she settles comfortably into the routines of a familiar house. Indeed, although the *padong* ideally is a woman's first bridal journey, many of those embarking on "joining" marriages will have spent much of their childhood visiting their "aunt" (*inang*), of whom they are usually extremely fond. For marriages within the same village, the bride faces an even easier transition period. One woman remarked that "Things are different if you marry within the village. It's the marriage of one community," adding that she hadn't cried, since "It's not as if I was far away." However, for a bride forging a "new path," the negotiation of new household arrangements, and of relations with her mother-in-law, may be rather more fraught. Ideally, a newly married couple should be incorporated into the husband's natal "household/room," sharing resources and labor with his parents. However, as we saw in Chapter 1, this kind of arrangement is often difficult to manage practically, and tensions frequently focus on if and when a new bride will start to "eat separately" from her mother-in-law. Significantly, from my observations, it would seem that a "joining" bride is far more likely to "eat together" with her mother-in-law than an unconnected bride. Sia, whose marriage was a "new path," complained that her husband's elder brother's "joining" wife was more accepted by the family and acted rather snootily towards Sia, the "outsider" bride.

The lack of familiarity that may make a "new path" a source of tension is particularly pronounced in two forms of marriage involving a more rapid movement of the bride along her marriage path. These are the past "stealing" (*roko*) of the bride and its modern equivalent, "running away" (*wéndol*). *Roko*, which can be compared with other forms of "marriage by capture" in eastern Indonesia (Barnes 1999, 57–59), involved the kidnapping of a girl, either because she could not be persuaded to marry the man in question or because her family did not agree to the match. Although I heard no reports of recent "stealing" marriages, this practice still holds great imaginative sway over people's minds and leads to endless rumors of bridal capture, whether by humans or spirits. Whereas a *padong* bride knows that she will be allowed to visit home sometime after her arrival in her husband's village, "captured" brides are always portrayed as panicking after their arrival and running away. In one story told to me, it was significant that the unwilling bride only became "calm" once her male relatives had found her hiding in their house and escorted her back to her husband in a more "official" (*resmi*) style.

By contrast with the violence of marriages by capture, *wéndol* refers to a more recent type of marriage (growing in frequency throughout Manggarai) where the bride simply moves in with the man, either without the knowledge of her parents or before the correct procedures have taken place. Such "running away" denies the normal marriage practices of slow house climbing, protective "accompanying," and processing. While *padong* brides are "led by the hand," people say of *wéndol* brides that they "just went." During my fieldwork, a young woman called Sisi ran off with a man while attending the final marriage ritual of her own brother, Pius, shocking her family, who had only just become reconciled with Pius' own "running away" marriage. A month or so after this event, Sisi visited Kombo with her new husband and his family, presenting gifts to "praise the patience" of Sisi's father, and organizing a hurried bridewealth negotiation. Significantly, Sisi began to cry loudly as soon as the truck drew up outside her parents' house. Unlike the bride who leaves on an official *padong,* the *wéndol* bride weeps not as she departs but as she returns, as she never officially "left" in the first place.

These less orderly forms of marriage still indicate the significance of marriage as a series of journeys, for they are primarily described and experienced as overly hasty movement along a path, rather like pushing through the forest undergrowth without carefully cutting a trail.[13] Nevertheless, however a marriage begins, the relationship it creates between alliance groups should continue to be marked by journeys between their respective houses or villages. It is these journeys, as much as the emotionally intense *padong,* that lead those walking through the forest, or taking a truck up to town, to point out a particular woman's "path" to their fellow travellers.

OTHER JOURNEYS ALONG MARRIAGE PATHS

One of the first journeys in which a marriage path is retrodden, an alliance relationship remembered, is a woman's initial visit home after her *padong.* Such visits are both emotional reunions and a solidification of the woman's transformation into an out-married "sister or daughter" (*woé*). Interestingly, when recalling return visits, many women dwelt on the kinds of foodstuffs they had taken back along their path to their parents. Thus, Iné Aga told me:

> "…if we had harvested rice, we pounded it well, and took it to give to mother. It was always like that, if I went to the west. And if not, child [referring to me], [she pauses] if I was just going to visit, I took a chicken [slight pause]. Ehh, that was all that I took to do a good turn for the old people who had looked after me in the past. When mother was ill again, when she was near to death, I took that again. I took rice, child, I took a chicken, and I took dried meat."

In later years, probably after having a number of children, women will make these visits less frequently. Iné Kata told me that after the death of her parents she didn't travel back much to her home village, because, "If you don't have a mother and father…you aren't motivated to travel." Instead, retravelling a path to visit a woman's natal kin becomes a more formal process, often undertaken by the woman's husband or sons. For example, when a man is preparing to marry, his family will make "requests for money" (*sida*) from their various "married sisters/daughters," just as they make them before the final death rituals described in the previous chapter. After a meeting to determine what sums are to be requested, the groom's "brothers" set out along the paths of these married women. Here, the landscape of social relations is seen in the webs formed by these journeys outwards from a center along paths of alliance. Later, these webs are retraced as male representatives of the "married sisters/daughters" travel back along their path, bringing the requested sums to a large ritual called "collecting up" (*ongko*). As guests crowd into a house where a "collecting" ritual is being held, the hosts start to count how many "paths" are attending.

For those women who are married *within* Wae Rebo-Kombo, and who may live very near to the houses of their fathers and brothers, the retravelling of a marriage path is achieved as much by formal etiquette and spatial arrangements inside the "collecting" house, as by their self-conscious walk there. This is spoken of, often rather humorously, as "becoming a guest" (*pandé meka*), as it involves re-creating a more formal, alliance relationship out of the everyday, informal processes of shared village life. For example, at one collecting ritual, I watched as one old man greeted his married daughter extremely formally, as one would someone who had travelled a long distance. The fact that this woman, married to a Kombo man, was a frequent informal visitor in her father's house, where she often helped with cooking or chatted with her unmarried sisters, made this greeting particularly striking. The woman was ushered through into the central corridor of the house, seated on the guest-mats, and ceremoniously handed coffee and a plate of banana cakes.

People seem to find such displays of hospitable politeness between those who, in daily life, are very intimate both touching and amusing. As they are served coffee and cakes by those well known to them, women often make a point of taking extra helpings, saying, "Me, I'm a guest now." Indeed, it is significant that from an early age young girls appear to appreciate the importance of "becoming a guest" in their natal home. Joking within the village reinforces this: men will often ask girls if they have brought a chicken (the usual gift from out-married women) to give them, and (as we saw in Chapter 1) sisters will mockingly call one another "sister-in-law" (*ipar*) as they cook together. Passing by a house one day, I saw three small girls, aged between three and five, sitting in the doorway playing. They had oversized sarongs wrapped around their small bodies, and at their feet were three wooden bowls filled with earth. When I asked them what they were doing they of course replied, "Auntie, we are becoming guests."

Although people travel to a "collecting" ritual in response to a formal request, men will also make more spontaneous, emotional journeys along marriage paths. I once walked with Talis and Odi, the parents of five children, to a village northwest of Wae Rebo. Talis was visiting his deceased father's sister, envisaging his journey as that of a loving nephew rather than a "mother-father" (iné-amé) member with a specific request. As we climbed up out of Wae Rebo on an overgrown path, Talis stressed that this was a journey he made only rarely, although he was extremely fond of his aunt. He said that since he had no sisters there had been no "joining" marriages in his generation. However, he hoped that one of his own daughters would in the future contract such a marriage, in order to maintain links with this aunt and so that he could continue to travel along this favorite path. This demonstrates how Manggarai men feel the paths of various womenfolk as emotionally resonant trails in their own kinship landscapes.

Although apparently spontaneous, Talis' journey was made at a time after harvesting when he was able to take an appropriate gift of rice. As with Iné Aga's recollections of taking chickens to her mother, or the money taken for a "collecting" ritual, this shows that it is not only people who travel along marriage paths but also exchange goods. When I walked with one woman through the forest to her natal village, her father-in-law recalled a time in the past when he had helped to bring a buffalo along the same path. Today, one often sees people walking along carrying a live chicken in a basket or strapping a trussed-up pig onto the back of a truck as they set off for a marriage event. As described earlier, such livestock are often used to represent groups related through marriage. Moreover, preparing such goods is as much a part of journeys along marriage paths as are the actions of departure, walking, and arrival. When married "sisters and daughters" are due to return from a visit to their natal home, they are always cooked small bundles of rice intricately tied up with palm leaves. These are called *supak* and are a key gift from a woman's natal kin, and are often eaten by the woman, her husband, and children as they stop for a rest by the path on their journey home.

Throughout eastern Indonesia, such movements of exchange goods, whether valuables or perishables, are often considered to be as significant as the movement of people. For the Kodi of Sumba, "path" primarily refers to the direction of exchange goods: the "path of beasts and ear pendants" goes to wife givers, while the "path of cloth and pigs" leads to the wife takers (Needham 1980, 37). Similarly, in the Tanimbar islands, male and female valuables flow in opposite directions along exchange pathways (McKinnon 1991, 113). However, in Manggarai, paths are overwhelmingly imagined as being travelled by people, as it is human movement that makes a trail. This is not to say that people in Sumba or Tanimbar do not also pay attention to the movements of persons along paths of exchange. Rather, it is a matter of emphasis: Manggarai paths are always conceived of as paths of people rather than exchange goods. Moreover, the main exchange goods given—rice and livestock—connect with the importance of commensality in Manggarai social life. Memories of pathways are quite literally fed by communal meals of rice and meat. Indeed, as women's recollections of their marriages showed, such acts of ingestion are closely connected with acts of release, particularly the shedding of tears.

The flow of tears along marriage paths is particularly apparent after a death, when affinal ties are reactivated by a series of mortuary rituals. After the death of one young child, groups of affines began to gradually arrive in Kombo to join in the ritualized crying. The most poignant of these arrivals was that of the child's maternal grandfather, who wailed loudly as he entered the village. Not only did this man's journey mirror his daughter's *padong* to Kombo, but his tears echoed her own crying when she had left her natal village long ago. For Manggarai people, travelling creates and renews paths of alliance, and arrivals and departures lead to communal meals and tears.

Of course, the significance of marriages being paths that are formed by travel is that sometimes they may become overgrown and neglected. When news reached one woman that her father had died, she refused to attend his final death ritual, claiming that her brothers had "forgotten" her and her path, never travelling to see her or inform her of family events. Such amnesia can occasionally have dangerous consequences, as when one "new path" bride died shortly after her *padong* to her husband's village. Many saw this as the responsibility of the groom's kin, who had failed to "root" the marriage journey with the groom's mother's natal kin in Wae Rebo. Although not contracting a "joining" marriage, the groom's kin should still have respected the origins of their family's blood by returning to sacrifice a chicken with their original "mother-father." Such rituals to "root the feet" in an origin village are also common before marriage rituals or (as described in Chapter 6) before a young person goes away to study.

These "rooting" rituals raise the issue of how the images and actions of movement that I have described here relate to the botanical idioms common in eastern Indonesian kinship talk. Across the region, metaphors such as "planting" prevail (Fox 1971): the mother's brother may be called the "trunk"

(Barnes 1974, 249) or "ground" (Beatty 1990, 464) of his sister's children, who are in turn conceived as shoots or "sprouts" (McKinnon 1991, 111). In Manggarai, botanical images of "rooting" connect with the significance of origins. A woman is rather like a forest climber as, however far she may travel along her marriage path, the source of her reproductive capacity and labor always remains in her roots of origin. Failing to "feed" and remember these roots will inevitably damage the prosperity and fertility of the woman, her husband, and their children. Thus, because the notion of a path implies both a beginning point and an end point (Parmentier 1987, 132), journeys along marriage paths by affines acknowledge the (hierarchical) connection of "roots" and stretchy plants.

GENDERED MOVEMENT AND THE LANDSCAPE OF RELATEDNESS

This chapter has shown how the Manggarai concept of a marriage "path," a concept widespread in eastern Indonesia, blurs the boundaries between real and symbolic trails. The Manggarai marriage process is surrounded by the spatial symbolism of ritual metaphors, with textiles presented to "place" and "accompany," and ransomed journeys held at alliance events. However, it also involves a number of actual journeys, including the *padong,* journeys to death rituals, and informal visits to remembered aunts. These journeys constitute marriage paths as both trails through the landscape and historical connections between families. Such paths are kept open through active remembering, and those involved in an alliance connection must travel, bringing with them stories, gifts, and foodstuffs.

Ethnographically, it is worth noting that path imagery also appears in other contexts of Manggarai life. For example, goods that open up lines of communication at rituals—most notably money and chickens—may be described as "paths." More intriguingly, elders sitting down with chickens, ready to begin a ritual, will sometimes say "Well, let's find the right path!" Here, paths are avenues of communication that have to be found, suggesting the existence of a number of possible routes, some more correct than others. Such a use of path imagery connects with the more risky aspects of alliance relationships in Manggarai. For, though travelling an old, *tungku* path is relatively easy, forging a new connection is more difficult: the twists and turns of the way remain unpredictable, as do the kinds of gifts that might be appreciated. Moreover, no marriage path can be assumed to be fixed and unchanging. Despite dire predictions of the fatal consequences of doing so, alliance relationships are often neglected or forgotten, the undergrowth reclaiming a route to history.

By arguing that travelling paths constitutes kinship and marriage, this chapter has challenged those approaches that would see eastern Indonesian marriage alliance as constituted only by rules and classifications (Needham 1966; Hicks 1984). Moreover, by contrast with the cosmological stress of traditional Leiden School ethnography, this chapter has revealed more individual, nuanced, and informal aspects of eastern Indonesian life. Such an approach to marriage is crucial if one is to show women as more than simply the channel for male relationships, and men as more than simply the givers or takers of women. However, this is not to deny that there are key differences between men and women with regard to mobility and identity throughout the life cycle. When newly married, women divide their time and allegiances between two places and two sets of kin, as they struggle to establish a new household while travelling back with gifts for their parents. In Marilyn Strathern's (1972) apt phrase, newly married Manggarai wives could be said to be "women in between." By contrast, once a married woman has reached old age, she will have become very much an "insider" in her husband's village, such that when her own children marry, she does not travel with them but stays behind to "root" their journey. Thus, an older married woman no longer appears "in between." Indeed, this is why it is important to translate the Manggarai term iné-amé as "mother-father," rather than "wife-givers," since when a daughter marries, her mother is considered a core member of the clan branch that ensures her safe passage to the groom's kin. Although other ethnographers have described the asymmetries involved in the relationship between groups described as "mother-father" and "sister/daughter," they have not focused on the transformative power of time and reproduction in this way. With time, an outsider bride becomes a mother who is central to the figuration of alliance relationships.

Unlike women, and following a common southeast Asian pattern of male travel and migration (Rosaldo 1980, 192; Tsing 1993, 127–128), Manggarai men have more freedom to travel beyond the local to gain access to outside power. They may work for cash on regional road-building projects, or even travel as far as Malaysia, seeking wealth and experience. Their "outsider" sisters, by comparison, may choose to show independence by not travelling in marriage, perhaps receiving land in their natal villages. Such unmarried women sometimes say that they have not married because they "love the land." Indeed, in day-to-day life, it is literally "outsider" women who keep the home fires burning, who provide the domestic anchor that allows a village to negotiate a balance of dwelling and travelling, tapping into outside powers while retaining a land-based identity.

If Chapters 1 and 2 emphasized the entanglement of people with rooms and the movements of households between different houses, this chapter has focused on the experience and memory of marriage as a path connecting dwellings and villages. The significance of paths to the constitution of Manggarai kinship and marriage demonstrates the problems with taking for granted the "house-based" nature of eastern Indonesian sociality. A Manggarai dwelling makes little sense (and indeed is sterile) without the paths of married women leading to and away from it. Similarly, affinal ties are not free-floating connections, but are "rooted" in an origin place. Manggarai kinship and marriage is intimately connected with the landscape, but this landscape is not separate from travel or movement. As we have seen, relationships between a husband and wife or between a mother-in-law and her son's bride, as well as a woman's ability to bear healthy children, can all be influenced by the agency of household rooms. However, the potency of the landscape as a realm of kinship is not simply a product of the agency of such key places. It is also produced by everyday practices in and out of houses—calling out to children in a neighboring house, cooking cassava in a saucepan, sharing a cigarette while sitting on guest-mats—and by a historical sequence of movements along a marriage path. These activities all give the cumulative landscape of kinship a potent role in evoking memories of births, deaths, and marriages. Throughout their lives, people feel, and engage with, the power of a lively house or an old, well-trodden path. Yet the landscape is not only one of lively sociality; it is also a fertile maze of past, current, and future fields where crops are grown. As we shall see, this agricultural landscape also evokes memories—of raising children, pigs, and chickens, or of escaping from noisy (and nosey) village life. In addition, and as the next chapter will reveal, this "land" has its own concerns, its own desires, and its own dangers.

4

Earth, Stone, Water
The Animate Landscape

In March 1999, a young man called Lorens went missing in the forests around Wae Rebo after going there to gather rattan. News of his disappearance emerged on the evening of my own leaving party, when villagers had gathered in my house for food, songs, and dancing. Someone coming in from outside reported that they had seen flames on the mountain slopes to the east. At first, there was alarm that one of the garden-huts in a far-off field was on fire. A woman whispered that it might be the *api-ja,* a kind of spirit that appears as a walking ball of fire on paths through fields or forests. It then emerged that the flames were from the torches of villagers who had gone to look for Lorens. Those sitting near me in the house stressed that when a person becomes lost in the forest it is often the work of a spirit. Such a spirit changes the direction of the land, so that when you think you are walking towards the mountains, you are actually walking towards the sea. The more the spirit does this, the more disorientated one becomes, walking round and round in a circle. An older man thought such disorientation was the work of forest spirits (*darat*), who often kidnap human children, later depositing them at the top of a cliff or in some other inaccessible place. Someone suggested that the only way to make the spirit leave such areas of the forest might be to build a church there, but others were not sure this would be effective. One woman said that the spirit that had caused Lorens' disappearance was probably the "land-creature" (*kaka-tana*). As the discussion broke up, a number of people stated that the reason for such disappearances, as well as for other mysterious phenomena, was "really/actually the land" (*tana muing*).

The story of Lorens' disappearance (happily, he returned to the village the next day) is just one example of a range of narratives and practices by which people in southern Manggarai reflect on and engage with a landscape that to them is profoundly animate.[1] In the previous three chapters, I have explored the ways in which rooms, houses, and paths are connected with pro-

cesses of kinship and marriage. These connections follow a common Manggarai logic, but may also be personal and contingent. I have also considered the
ways in which ritual performances make aspects of place that may not always
emerge in everyday practices explicit. Thus, we saw how both "blood on feet"
and "praising" rituals create the presence of rooms as ancestral agents, while
rituals for "living in" (*wéé*) a house explicitly ask the land's help in making a
house a protective shelter. In this chapter, I turn my attention to the wider
landscape, the "lived-in environment" (Ingold 2000, 168) of fields, forests,
water sources, and stone platforms. Such an environment gains value and is
enlivened by everyday activities such as planting and weeding crops, picking
coffee, fetching water, or gathering forest products.

Yet, as with rooms, houses, and paths, this environment also gains value
from the performance of ritual, the marks of which accumulate in fields and
on stone platforms. Rituals are significant in explicitly acknowledging the
existence of a spiritual landscape beyond the visible land, both to ensure the
ongoing presence of beneficial forces and to protect human activities from
amoral or malevolent energies. What is striking in southern Manggarai is
that, despite the importance of Catholicism to other areas of life (such as
marriage practices), it has had relatively little influence on understandings
of the animate landscape. In the next chapter, I trace out some of the links
between people and the land, as well as the wider impact of state resettlement
policies, through a consideration of the differences between Wae Rebo and
Kombo. Here, after describing the agricultural and other activities that give
value to the land, I discuss how best to analyze people's engagements with
the land as a powerful agent, and how this is connected to understandings of
Manggarai "custom" (*adat*).

FIELDS AND THE AGRICULTURAL CYCLE

Like the overwhelming majority of Manggarai people, the inhabitants
of Wae Rebo-Kombo continue to depend for their livelihoods on agriculture.[2] This is largely subsistence cultivation, although coffee and other crops
including cloves, candlenut, and vanilla are sold in markets for cash. The split
of the village between two sites, together with the ownership of government-
donated wet-rice fields (*sawah*) in Sebu near the coast, means that most
households farm a variety of crops in a variety of locations. In dry fields in
Wae Rebo, families plant red hill-rice, maize, cassava, sweet potatoes, yams,
various beans, cucumbers, pumpkins, ground nuts, and leafy vegetables. They

may also maintain, in fields or small gardens near to houses, coffee, cloves, bananas, sugar palms (*tuak*), orange and lime trees, papaya, marquisa fruit, and vanilla plants. In Sebu, families farm small plots of *sawah,* while a number also grow hill-rice, maize, and vegetables in dry fields near to Kombo and have jackfruit and mango trees near their Kombo house. In general, crops grow more quickly in the hot lowlands, but more frequent rains and cooler temperatures in the highlands support coffee, citrus fruits, and a wider variety of tubers and vegetables. Therefore, one important ecological benefit of a two-placed village is that people are able to grow a wide range of different plants and crops.

Fields (*uma*) fan out in all directions around Wae Rebo, some a good hike away from the village center, others near houses. These fields, of varying shapes and sizes, all have permanent names, such as "crab water field" and "boil a pig field." Some fields near Kombo also have names, though these are less well known by residents, partly because most farming efforts in the lowlands are concentrated on the rice fields in Sebu. Ownership of individual gardens within these fields is based roughly on a system of patrilineal inheritance, with fathers dividing up their gardens among those sons who remain in the village. Historically, this "ownership" entailed a sense of people belonging to certain plots of land but lacking the right to alienate that garden. However, in recent years, a number of people based fairly permanently in Kombo have sold highland gardens to villagers based in Wae Rebo, a development that has made many nervous and has brought to the fore the difficulties of maintaining interests in both highland and lowland sites.

When a dry field is due to be reopened, it is first cleared and then, following the appropriate ritual procedure, carefully burnt off. A newly opened field is referred to as an *uma rana* in its first year of planting and, enriched by wood ash, can be used to plant a wider variety of crops than during subsequent years of farming, when it is referred to as an *uma lokang.* People say that it is the "heat" of a new field that makes it fertile, and that by the time of its third or fourth years it has become "cold." The planting of coffee trees, however, means that small sections of highland gardens will continue to be visited in order to pick coffee fruit, even when the surrounding field lies fallow.

The system of shifting cultivation in Wae Rebo-Kombo is referred to as *olo olo lodok, kolé lingko,* which can be roughly translated as "wherever there was a *lodok* before, there will be a *lingko* again." Traditional Manggarai fields are called *lingko* and form a circular, "spider's web" pattern on the land. At the center of this circular field is the *lodok* or ritual center, around which carousel the individually owned, wedge-shaped gardens (*moho*). Throughout Manggarai, the shape and layout of circular *lingko* fields are explicitly compared with circular *niang* houses (Erb 1999, 55–56): not only are fields circular, but they have a communal ritual center and are divided into individual gardens, just as houses have a central house-post and are divided into individual rooms. The local description of shifting agriculture creates a sense of the *permanence* of ritual centers, around which fields will be periodically reopened and then left to become fallow again. Indeed, the system of shifting cultivation, and people's experience of it, fundamentally influences local understandings of time.

In a classic ethnography of southeast Asian shifting cultivators, George Condominas described how the Mnong Gar of Vietnam designate years with the phrase "We ate the forest of…" followed by a place-name (1994 [1957], xxxi). Because the cycle of cultivation meant that Mnong Gar returned to cultivate a field after ten or twenty years, Condominas states that "the same term serves to denote two years separated by one or two decades," made more specific by reference to hamlet locations or unusual events (ibid., xxxi). In a similar manner, Wae Rebo people designate years by reference to which named fields were opened and farmed at that time. A mother will talk about her child being born "at the time of the *likop* stone field," or a man will describe his father dying "at the time of the prosperous field." However, the cycle of shifting cultivation influences not only how people describe the past but also how they reexperience it, and how they view the changing nature of their surroundings.

When people talk about past events, they often do so not simply by reference to fields that were open at the time but also by indicating the appearance of crops in those fields. For example, Amé Lodo described how he first went to school "when the maize was flowering in the new field." Similarly, Iné Anas described how her eldest daughter was born "at the time of the *ketang* plant field," as the tops of the rice stalks were beginning to droop. The marking of time specifically according to the *appearance* of the land, not simply the work one happened to be performing at the time, can also be seen in two further instances. The first are the old names for the seasons or months of the year, which a number of older people in Wae Rebo continued to use but which have gradually been replaced by the calendar months. In general, these old names refer to the flowering of particular trees or plants. Thus, the time around September was called *rasi,* owing to the flowering of areca nut trees.

The second instance of marking time according to the changing appearance of the land is something that occurs extremely casually, and on a daily basis, in Wae Rebo. Owing to the village's location in a dell, it is surrounded on almost all sides by mountains. This gives the village a rather snug feeling, termed "living in a saucepan," that is always commented on by new brides. It also means that sunlight hits the mountains to the west before it hits the village, and lingers for longer on the mountains to the east after sunset. Although people often commented to me that they could tell the time of day according to the calls of chickens and other birds,[3] I noticed that they also frequently looked at the length of shadows on the mountains around them before deciding whether it was time to visit their gardens or if they could go to bathe before boiling water for early evening coffee. Of course, during the dense, low clouding of the rainy season, it becomes difficult to see very far at all, let alone to the slopes of far-off fields. Nevertheless, people packing up a weaving loom, feeding pigs, or returning to their houses after visiting, will sigh, "Afternoon land!" (*Mané tana!*). This conveys a real sense that it is the land that reflects the time of day, just as the changing appearance of crops or trees, and of new fields as they are burnt, planted, and harvested, structures the year.

The agricultural cycle, and in particular the process of reopening fallow fields after a period of perhaps twenty years, has a profound effect on people's recalling of their pasts. In particular, they experience "topophilia" (Tuan 1974), an intense, affective bond, with old, often dilapidated garden-huts. When a couple in their fifties reopened a garden in a field far from Wae Rebo, they were reminded of and spoke about the last time they had lived in and farmed that field, when their (now grown-up) children were small. In this instance, the very process of physically being in the field—rebuilding the hut, reestablishing the field boundary, fetching water from a nearby stream—brought back memories of this time to them. This is very similar to Küchler's description of people in New Ireland reencountering places of memory, whereby "a nut or fruit tree, a plant or a piece of wall, like an odour, may trigger a recollection of social relations and of past social conditions" (1993, 100).

Garden-huts or "monkey-huts" (*hékang kodé*)[4] are the focus for intense place-attachments not only because of their connections with the opening and closing of fields but also because life in garden-huts has a rather different tenor or flavor to that in village houses. We have already seen how such huts can be places to escape both the stresses of sharing in communal houses and tensions with other villagers. Iné Sisi told me it was better to raise a young family in a garden-hut because you were close to all kinds of vegetables and didn't have to carry heavy loads back to the village, where seasonal produce might be claimed by others. The equivalence of "room" and dwelling in huts makes them a focus for household intimacy. Jokes about couples who spend

FIGURE 4.1   Sitting outside a mountain monkey-hut

more time in their garden-huts than in shared houses, as well as comments
that some unmarried women made about being visited by suitors in huts, suggest an association between these small buildings and sex. In both symbolic
and practical terms, huts are also associated with fertility, particularly since
(as the next chapter will show) monkey-huts constructed some distance from
a village always carry the potential of becoming a new village site.

The character of huts also owes much to the kinds of objects used in
them. Owing to the reduced storage space, as well as the need to keep good
crockery in houses for receiving guests, people in monkey-huts eat out of
gourd bowls (*sewak*), and drink from easily transportable tin or plastic cups.
When I visited people in their fields, they always made a big show of apolo-
gizing for these old-fashioned implements, while at the same time appearing
to take a certain nostalgic comfort from using them, stressing that such bowls
were what were used in the past, and were what you ate out of when going to
work cooperatively. This kind of self-deprecating language is also a common
way of discussing agricultural produce. When visiting one another in garden-
huts, people tend to downplay the success of their crops, saying "really, we

should have cucumbers, but the monkeys have had them all," even when I knew they had already eaten many cucumbers, or "we only have a little produce," even before presenting me with large bags of beans to take back to my house. This is not to deny that sometimes wild animals do destroy crops, but to point to a style of speaking which, as I shall show, is partly concerned with acknowledging unseen presences in the landscape.

AGRICULTURAL RITUAL AND SPEECH-OFFERINGS

In the context of a discussion of hunter-gatherers' perceptions of their environments, Tim Ingold has problematized the conventional anthropological separation of "practical-technical" activities, understood as concerned with "subsistence," from "mytho-religious" activities, understood as part of the cultural "construction of the environment" (2000, 56). By contrast with such an analytical separation, Ingold stresses how *both* subsistence activities *and* "singing, storytelling and the narration of myth" are "ways of dwelling" through which the environment "enters directly into the constitution of persons" (ibid., 57). Ingold's argument is extremely pertinent to an understanding of Manggarai agricultural activities, in which fields gain value, not only from weeding, planting, and harvesting, but also from numerous ritual procedures that are considered essential to the production of a successful crop (cf. Freeman 1970, 159).

Because respect for "custom" (*adat*) and rituals "has varied very much from priest to priest" (Erb 2006, 210), there is wide variation throughout the Manggarai region in the frequency and manner of sacrificial rituals. In parishes to the west of my fieldwork sites, many religious teachers (*guru agama*) are said to practice a form of Catholicism known as *karismatik*. Such "charismatic" Catholics might kill a chicken for a life-cycle ritual in a house, but they will not inspect its stomach or throw food to ancestral spirits, and they are said to hold agricultural rituals that lack sacrifices and focus mainly on prayer. In Wae Rebo-Kombo, the most common way to refer to such charismatics is as people who "don't eat medicine," as they usually reject the efficacy of healing practices that involve "blowing" spells into roots or water. However, in the area of southern Manggarai with which I am familiar, only a few people are rumored to be charismatics. Most others, including regular attendees at the Dengé church, still speak of the fertile power of spirits and ancestors, and the necessity of holding agricultural and other rituals. The previous, highly respected, priest of the parish appears to have had few problems with *adat* ritual procedures so long as people also attended church and had their children baptized. Indeed, many people told me that this priest had encouraged them "not to forget" such ritual practices. The current priest, though he is less encouraging and does not attend the sacrificial element of communal rituals, also seems to have a rather tolerant attitude. Thus, as in other contexts where Christianity has not been adopted "under exclusivist constraints" but has become "a matter of enculturation and education" (Anderson 2003, 128), people remain open to and interested in a variety of understandings and practices.

Communal agricultural rituals are particularly important in ensuring the success of a new field. Opening up and burning the scrub of a fallow field may involve anti-rain magic (*toka*), and is surrounded by prohibitions, including a ban on women washing saucepans (associated with fire) in the stream. The burning of the field is called "the big machete" rather than "fire," one of a number of riddles that, as we shall see, acknowledge the unseen presence of spirits. Once the field has been burnt, individual garden owners will come together to clear it (*bula*), led by the "head of the *teno* stake" (*tu'a teno*). Though a ritual position, the *tu'a teno* is aptly described as a "land manager" (Moeliono 2000, 111), since the holder makes decisions about the dividing up of fields, as well as the timing of ritual events. To re-create the *lodok* ritual center, the field leader plants a thick stake with a rounded top in the ground. This "*teno* stake" marks the exact center of the circular field and is the point from which calculations of individual gardens are made. Next, a large flat "offering rock" is placed on the ground for the ritual presentation of betel quids. The wedge-shaped gardens of individual men are then worked out according to how many "fingers" of land they have. A man with "three fingers" physically measures this at the stake at the ritual center. He then traces lines all the way to the edge of the field, marking the boundary of his garden with sticks laid out on the ground (*landér*). In line with the parallels drawn between circular fields and houses, these sticks are explicitly compared with the supporting struts of a conical *niang* roof.

This "making of the *lodok*" marks the beginning of a series of rituals held before each stage in the agricultural process. For example, at the time of planting, a large ritual called *males* is held to "thrust in" the crops, while *wus* is a ritual, held once crops have started to grow, to "root the land." As the majority of Wae Rebo fields are on extremely steep slopes, there is a very real risk of soil erosion through heavy rain, or damaged crops through falling stones and minor landslides. Indeed, it has been estimated that 70 percent of all arable land in Flores is found on mountain slopes and hillsides with over a fifty-degree incline (Prior 1988, 59). This is certainly the very practical context to this emphasis on "rooting" in agricultural rituals, though as Chapter 6 will discuss, "rooting" is also a key trope of Manggarai kinship and of procedures connected with journeys.

As with rituals in houses, those held at the field center involve a ritual speech (*tura*) before the sacrifice of chickens or a small pig. This is followed by the presentation of eggs as substitute "palm wine" and of rice and cooked meat as "food for the ancestors," and then by a meal for all participants. Thus, fields are not only connected with houses through spatial arrangements but also through practices of commensality that stress the coming-together of equals (whether individual gardens or rooms). Moreover, a key aspect of agricultural rituals is that they involve leaving marks on the field center, signs that steadily accumulate with the progress of the agricultural year. Just as the appearance of a field changes as crops grow and are harvested, so a ritual center looks very different during the various stages in the planting and growth of a new field. At the reopening, the field center receives a *teno* stake and offering stone; at later rituals, further bits of ritual apparatus are placed there: a tall, wooden dedicating post, more offering stones on a shelf, two bare "trees" with spindly branches, and a largish piece of wood hung from the offering shelf and used for attaching chicken wing feathers and pig ears. Like the offering platforms hung inside houses, these signs gradually accumulate on the field center, evidence of human endeavor and the correct performance of ritual.

Thus, the accumulated evidence of various platforms and offerings is what marks out (to both humans and nonhumans) the ritual center of a field. These offerings, and the temporary or stone platforms on which they are placed, are closely connected with ritual speech, because in many respects such platforms plant ritual speech in the ground. Indeed, in order to understand the links between ritual speech and the materiality of the field center, it is worth considering the "semiotic ideology" that may be at play in the context of Manggarai agricultural ritual. The notion of "semiotic ideology" has been developed by Webb Keane to describe "basic assumptions about what signs are and how they function in the world" (2003, 419). Keane's own recent work (2007) analyzes a historical clash between the semiotic ideology of Dutch Calvinism—which saw speech and materiality as utterly distinct—and that of ancestral ritualists on the island of Sumba, for whom words and things were not so radically separate, and who were therefore less concerned with maintaining clear boundaries.

In the Introduction, I noted the important role of phenomenological perspectives in criticizing "representational" or "constructionist" approaches to place and landscape.

Tilley, for example, argues that a methodological focus on how land-scapes are "synaesthetically experienced through the body" (2004, 28) steers the analyst away from regarding landscapes as "systems of signs, or as texts or discourses" (ibid., 31). Such a phenomenological emphasis on the body is also seen in Casey's exhortation to "get back into place" through our lived bodies (1996, 21). However, this phenomenological privileging of bodily experience over speech threatens to replace one Western ideology (the separation of nature and culture) with another (the separation of words from things and subjects). This is why Keane's notion of "semiotic ideology" is so helpful for understanding the role of speech in the making of place.

In his earlier book, Keane (1997) described how followers of ancestral rituals in Anakalang, Sumba, thought that ritual words gained efficacy by resting on the "base" provided by material objects. While the Manggarai people I know do not express a "semiotic ideology" as explicit as this, it is nevertheless the case that talk frequently involves a distinctive materiality.[5] During rituals, speech is always accompanied by the placing of offerings. These usually consist of betel quids and small amounts of rice and cooked meat ("food for the ancestors"), although offerings may also include eggs, wing feathers of chicken, or a pig's foot. In houses, offerings are placed on bamboo platforms that hang from the rafters, and after rituals in fields they are placed on specially constructed tripods of sticks and stones[6] or, in the case of communal rituals, on the *lodok*. I was told that these platforms and offerings provide "material evidence" to ancestral and other spirits that the correct rituals have been held, the correct speech spoken. Moreover, before the throwing of "food for the ancestors," ritual speakers usually speak at the same time that they mix up the rice and meat mixture with one hand, as though their words are literally being mixed into the food.

Ritual speech is therefore not separate from the material offerings it involves. Rather, such offerings *emplace* speech: they are "speech-offerings" that actively and materially constitute ritual sites in the landscape. This is seen most obviously by the steady accumulation of markers and offerings on the field center as the agricultural year progresses. By creating hybrid speech-objects in this way, Manggarai people ensure that their conversations with ancestral spirits have what Latour calls "temporal and spatial extension" (1996b, 239). That is, even once the ritual participants have returned to their houses, the objects they leave behind continue to influence ancestral actors. Of course, unlike stone platforms, most offerings are fairly impermanent: betel quids rot or are blown away, "ancestral food" is soon eaten by dogs and cats, wooden tripods in fields eventually fall apart, and platforms hanging in

FIGURE 4.2   Throwing the "food for the ancestors" at an agricultural ritual

houses must be continually replaced. However, Manggarai people see such speech-offerings as acknowledging and ensuring the continued presence of ancestral and other spirits. Indeed, ritual speech is primarily conceived as addressing nonhuman "interlocutors." As Andie Diane Palmer stresses with regard to Secwepemc discourse, the term interlocutor "refers to one who is engaged in conversation, as a speaker, a hearer, or both" and may involve "others considered to be Persons, albeit of the non-human sort" (2005, 17). In Manggarai, ancestral and other spirits are "interlocutors" in this sense, listeners to both formal and informal talk, and viewers of emplaced offerings. Let us therefore now consider such spirits in more detail.

SPIRITS AND THE SPIRITUAL LANDSCAPE

Most Manggarai people I know take seriously the existence of a range of spirits and invisible energies, though, as we shall see, spirit-beings merge with spirit-places and are often a shorthand for discussing the power of the land. Nonhuman persons are often referred to as "people on the other side" (*ata palé-sina*) and, as such, are thought to occupy a different dimension, the counterpart to human life on *this* side. People say of such spirits that "they can see us, but we can't see them," a form of definition common throughout Southeast Asia (Barraud 1990, 218; Rafael 1993, 111–115; Cannell 1999, 83–87). Such everyday invisibility is the case even though, as one middle-aged woman put it, spirits "live as close together with us as a maize leaf and a maize cob." One may become aware of spirits through sound and smell, but they can only be safely seen in dreams, the "other side" of our daily existence (cf. Scott 2007, 173). In line with this, "magic" (*mbeko*) is thought to be passed on from ancestral or other spirits in dreams, and a number of people told me stories about dreams in which a spirit had tested them by trying to give them "bad magic."

People mostly use the generic term *poti* to refer to spirits, including ancestral spirits. However, at other times they are more interested in speaking of specific types of beings, such as dwarves associated with rocks (*jing*) and spirits who travel at night in search of heads (*empo-déhong*).[7] *Darat* are spirits of the forest and sea, thought to live in places uninhabitable to humans, but also often represented as living in cities, with all manner of modern conveniences. They are also believed to have once lived together with humans, but various myths tell of how human actions led these spirits to choose to live separately, and invisibly, from humans.[8] These spirits retain a curious, amoral interest in human beings and may sometimes kidnap human children, or seek to turn human adults into their spouses. However, a human person must die in the human world in order to live with a *darat* spouse on "the other side."

Spirits, conceptualized as unseen interlocutors, animate and merge with a material landscape of energies, effects, and practical consequences. Thus, rather than focusing on spirit classification as part of an overarching Manggarai cosmology, I want to draw out the ways in which spirits and spirit-places are entwined in a distinctive spiritual landscape (Allerton 2009), with various hidden realms lying beyond, behind, or immanent within the visible earth. Talk about spirits may often be a kind of front, or a shorthand, for talking about an energy that belongs to the land itself. For, just as the land gains value from human activities like agriculture, so it is also believed to have a potency in and of itself—a potency that can be both beneficial and harmful.

The boundary between spirits and spirit-places is not clear-cut. Certain named fields, particularly those through which streams flow, are rather generally associated with harmful spirits and, as among the Nagé, can be said to have "acquired a reputation" (Forth 1998, 66). Fear of offending these spirits or spirit-places often necessitates avoidance behavior such as not exclaiming or shouting loudly, not drinking water from the stream, and not letting children play there. At times—for example when a woman is pregnant, or when a place is thought to be particularly potent—it may be best to avoid such sites altogether by taking detours that "carve out a negative space" (Munn 1996, 452). However, what is significant is that, having described the kinds of precautions that should be taken against such spirits, many people went on to stress to me that they were "really/actually the land" (*tana muing*).[9] For example, in 2001, two schoolgirls drowned in a relatively shallow lowland stream. Their deaths were universally interpreted as the result of the actions of the stream's spirit. However, the teacher who discovered the children, a devout Catholic who often leads the hymns in church, told me that this spirit was "really the land," implying that the land and its places have a force of their own. To understand Manggarai engagements with spirits, then, it is important not to separate "spirit-beings" from the wider landscape of places and pathways.

This spiritual landscape of seen and unseen realms has everyday consequences for humans who engage with it as a lived-in world. As in many societies, the relationship with such a landscape is not one of thoughtful reflection or "idle cosmology" (Atkinson 1989, 38), but is instead pragmatic and practical (Harvey 2001, 199; cf. Povinelli 1995, 509). A Manggarai person who accidentally injures a wild animal—particularly an eel—is always encouraged to confess this to a healer, who will then make protective medicine. Though I never received an explicit explanation of this, people seemed to be suggesting that an eel might be the temporary material form taken by a particular place-spirit, and therefore harming it would put a person at risk of spiritual attack.[10] Similarly, a person who becomes tired or ill after visiting certain fields, or going to the spring at dusk, is often said to have had a "meeting" (*sumang*) with an unseen forest- or other place-spirit. Such spirits may have their own paths through fields that require ritual blocking at harvest-time. When we were resting during one exhausting walk to the highlands, my friend Nina told me not to sit right on the path but to one side, so that spirits could still walk along it without disturbing us.

Connections between variously defined or acknowledged spirits (who might sometimes be said to "really" be the land) and the landscape are also seen with regard to different kinds of ancestral spirit. Both the recent dead and distant ancestors are described as "people on the mountainside" (*ata belé*), and in Chapter 2 we saw how death practices begin the process of orienting the deceased to the side of the mountain (*lé*). In rituals, speakers sometimes addressed "the ancestors on the other side of the mountains, the ancestors on this side." One man told me that the former were those who had been dead for a long time, while the latter were the more recently deceased. It is as though, as time passes, and there are fewer ties of memory with a deceased person, they move farther towards the interior of Manggarai.

Human ancestors (*empo*), then, tend not to be named individually but are a generalized category connected with the mountains, the protection afforded by certain places such as rooms, and the fertility of the land. As such, they frequently become blurred with spirits known as the "ancestors of the land" (*empo de tana*) or the "owners/lords of the land" (*mori de tana*). These spirit owners are addressed in rituals held in fields and forests or near water sources. One young woman, Regi, told me that the "ancestors of the land" were different from "ancestors who are dead people" but that she didn't exactly know how. Her brother remarked on another occasion that the ancestors of the land were rather like "officials" (*pegawai*) who "guard" key sites in the landscape. This use of the language of the state to describe guardian spirits is intriguing, particularly as there is almost no use of the language of the church in such contexts.

Spirits similar to Manggarai "ancestors of the land" are found throughout Southeast Asia (see Hicks 1976, 25; Gibson 1986, 173–174) and are one form taken by the phenomenon of "founders' cults," described by Kammerer and Tannenbaum as "part of the Southeast Asian matrix of cultural possibilities that reflects widespread beliefs in spirit ownership of territory and control of fertility and prosperity" (2003, 8). During certain phases of the Manggarai agricultural cycle, it is felt important to use riddles or code names (*bundu*) as a sign of respect for the spirit owners of animals and the land. Particularly when harvesting, or during other significant phases, one should be careful not to "call the exact name" of an animal. To do so might be interpreted as arrogance by the spirits and result in negative consequences, most obviously the death of any domestic livestock. This necessitates calling goats "on-top-of-a-stone," horses "round foot," pigs "unspun rope," and chickens "wing" in order to show that one is both humble and "polite." Such speech demonstrates the speaker's awareness of a landscape beyond land, of the unseen spirits and agents to whom one is advised to pay respect, and can be compared with deference and avoidance in taboo languages or ritual speech found elsewhere in the region (Dix Grimes 1997, 126–127; Keane 1997, 108–109).

STONES, WATER, AND POTENCY

Two kinds of places in particular are most often associated with spirits and potency in Manggarai; these are water sources and stones (whether large boulders or stone platforms). Water is intrinsic to the Manggarai landscape; the word *tana* (land) refers not simply to earth and rocks but also to rivers and streams. Similarly, Fox (1997a, 7) argues that Austronesian societies regard water as "fundamental to, and in many instances coterminus with, any specification of a landscape." Like paths, streams and rivers draw our attention to the flows and movement of the landscape, as does the sea, the source of many "powerful beings" in other, more seaward-oriented eastern Indonesian contexts (Pannell 2007, 86; cf. Spyer 2000, 144–146). Moreover, in Manggarai, water (*wae*) is associated with a kind of life-giving "oil" (*mina*). When discussing ritual events at water sources with me, one old man asked, rhetorically, "Where do people come from?" and then answered, "We are alive because we drink water, and the oil of that water becomes human beings." Yet despite the life-giving nature of water (cf. Barnes 1974, 61), its fertility—like that of the earth—requires ritual recognition and renewal.

In the lowlands, to the southeast of Kombo, and at the side of the river of Wae Awéng, a large cross marks the site of a small concrete dam and channels. Here, water flowing down from Wae Rebo is diverted towards the wet-rice fields constructed in a 1970s state development project and today shared among various lowland villages. In April 2001, these villages gathered livestock, rice, saucepans, and personnel for a large communal ritual to renew the fertility of this water source following years of declining productivity in the rice fields. Upstream from the cross and dam, a group of male elders, joined by the Camat (head of the subdistrict, *Kecamatan*) and other state officials, listened to a ritual speech and witnessed the sacrifice of a buffalo, several pigs, and a number of chickens. They were watched by a large crowd of villagers standing on the banks of the river.

Like other rituals in fields or forest, this event was described as being "what the land wants" (*ngoéng de tana*). According to my informants, when work was first begun on the Wae Awéng dam in the 1970s, a large boulder obstructed the proposed path of a water channel. This unwieldy object could only be moved after the original (human) owner of the land promised to sacrifice a buffalo in the future. In 2001, many felt that this debt was finally being called in by the land. This was shown by a number of "signs," such as the descendants of the original owner being repeatedly bitten by ticks and the leaders of the different rice fields falling ill. These "signs" convinced various ritual leaders of the need to honor the earlier promise of a buffalo sacrifice. The declining productivity of the rice fields was directly linked with the failure in the past to hold this ritual. "We've been eating food from this land for a long time," one man told me, "now we need to give respect, or we fear the land will be dry and hot."[11]

Procedures for the Wae Awéng ritual engaged with a spiritual landscape of multiple agents and energies. Chickens were sacrificed in the rice fields to invite the "spirits" from the individual plots to attend the ritual at the river. Elders and ritual speakers who came from Wae Rebo described themselves as bringing down with them "the souls of the old ancestors in the past" and stressed that, although these ancestors are buried in the mountains, they will travel to the lowlands for significant events. The night before the buffalo sacrifice, small rituals were also held outside family rooms in each house in the villages involved. The purpose of these was to "collect together souls," to ensure that no human souls followed the spirits or the buffalo to "the other side." People were also warned not to kill any eels in rivers or streams at this time, as these might be ancestors on their way to the ritual. In addition, for the three days after the ritual, it was forbidden to enter the rice fields, because during this time ancestral and other spirits would be "going to do farming work."

This water ritual, the significance of which I will return to, shows the clear links that are drawn between the fertility of the land and of water sources. Such sources are also linked with stones, particularly during the annual festival of *penti*. This is a large-scale ritual event, previously held at the end of the agricultural year, but now more frequently performed at the start of the new calendar year. *Penti* involves a series of sacrificial rituals at key village sites culminating in an evening of drumming and dancing in the drum house. In Chapter 5, I stress the significance of *penti* in reestablishing the drum house, and its rooms, as a place of origin. Here, I want to stress the way in which *penti*, as a ritual *performance,* both renews the potency of key sites and reproduces their presence as agents. As such, *penti* can be compared to other rituals, including "praising" events in rooms, that ostensibly focus on the renewal of ancestral potency, while also ensuring the continued presence of various place-agents.

Penti in Wae Rebo begins with a procession of formally attired men and women to the "offering stones" near to the main water source (*wae*). Here, men sing and perform a short, swaying dance before placing a betel quid on top of the stones and singing a kind of trilled chorus (*renggas* or *piak*) to awaken ancestral and other agents. Although women do not always take an active part in other, site-specific rituals for *penti*, it is considered important that they should attend the ritual at the *wae*. This is partly in recognition of their daily roles in collecting and transporting water, but also of the spring as the source of health and fertility. The latter association is most strongly apparent in one of the many meanings of *wae*, which is "child, descendant, or generation," connecting with the pan-Austronesian significance of "sources" and water (see Lewis 1988; Thomas 1997). It was perhaps because of the importance of springs and sources that a number of people, though recognizing the improvements they brought to village health and women's work, expressed uneasiness about the standing-pipes that are slowly becoming a feature of Manggarai villages, including Kombo. Iné Anas told me that in her natal village to the west, *penti* no longer involves a "report at the spring," because the advent of a standing-pipe means that people "don't precisely know" the source of water.

Following the ritual at the main water source, *penti* continues with a succession of other speeches and sacrifices performed at key sites around Wae Rebo. These are the *oka*, a large stone up on a hill associated with the past grazing pastures of horses and cattle; the ancestral graves; the "offering stones" on the village yard where "sins" were once discussed; and finally, and most significantly, the *sompang*. The latter is a large, circular, stone platform found in the center of all old Manggarai villages. Like the *liké*, a stone platform extending out from the entrance to the drum house, the *sompang* is thought to have a mysterious, unspecific potency, perhaps because it was built by spirits or slaves, or because it contains "secrets" or ancestral graves.[12]

As in Belau, Tahiti, and other Austronesian societies, the association of these stone platforms with a distant or mythic past makes them what Parmentier (1987, 11) calls "signs of history." They are like "monuments" in the Wae Rebo landscape, which, even when climbed over by children or used for practical purposes like drying coffee, nonetheless connect with the past actions of ancestors and other, vaguely conceived figures. The history of Wae Rebo describes how the village's ancestors planted the founding stone of Todo, the village whose leaders were appointed to the position of raja of Manggarai in the nineteenth century. Whenever I was told this history, the speaker would stress that the Todo stone was still standing, thereby making a claim to ancestral connection with this important village. Michael Scott has described how among Arosi in Southeast Solomon Islands even a "spontaneous partial allusion" to a matrilineage narrative "performatively reproduces a lineage as inseparably wedded to a particular territory" (2007, 163–164).

FIGURE 4.3   Collecting on the stone *sompang* platform at *penti*

Similarly, for Wae Rebo-Kombo residents, speaking of their ancestors' role in the creation of topographical features in other villages, particularly when these features are heavy and immobile stones, reiterates their claim to "precedence" over these villages.

However, like "history objects" in Kodi, Sumba, the Wae Rebo stone platform is not simply a "sign of history" but can "even help to *make* history" (Hoskins 1993, 119). During the new year ritual performance, the *sompang* platform is addressed as an agent with the power to protect the village from conflict and bad luck. I was told that the purpose of the ritual speech and the offerings left on an elaborately decorated, woven platform is to "persuade" (*reku*) the stone *sompang* itself. Indeed, a number of people told me that at the end of the site-specific rituals at *penti*, the whole community of Wae Rebo-Kombo—including platforms and other sites—is invited into the drum house. The *sompang*, like other spirit-places, is thus at times spoken of as a material place, a sign of history, and at other times is personified as a kind of place-agent that may join in lively events in the drum house.

In a discussion of the significance of megalithic stone monuments to the

Zafimaniry of Madagascar, Bloch argues that these monuments construct a permanence that, in contrast to the "growing" permanence of human life in villages, is absolute (1995b, 73). He portrays the Zafimaniry as having a rather ambiguous view of megaliths that is based on what he considers to be a common Austronesian contrast between stone, which is eternal but has never been alive, and wood, which originates in a living thing (ibid., 73). However, it is not clear that all Austronesian societies follow the Zafimaniry in denying vitality or agency to stones. Bonnemaison, for example, has described how the first inhabitants of Tanna, Vanuatu, were thought to be magical stones who travelled noisily about the island, waging war with each other and, in so doing, creating the land and its roads (1994, 115–116). In Manggarai, stone platforms have a kind of animate energy that connects with the wider fertility and potency of the agricultural landscape. Moreover, as we have seen, the steadily accumulated ritual paraphernalia of the center of a new field—including a flat stone—aim to "thrust in" and "root" crops into that field. As with stones in Gawan fields, these mini-monuments produce a certain (ritual and physical) "heaviness" (Munn 1986, 80; cf. Kahn 1996, 180) in Manggarai fields that are forever shifting, changing, or slipping down the mountainside.

ENCULTURATION, LAND, AND ANTISYNCRETISM

It should be clear by now that inhabitants of Wae Rebo-Kombo imagine and engage with a landscape full of spirits and energies. The landscape bears the marks and signs of human history in its garden-huts, field centers, and stone platforms. However, these places are more than simply signs of history; they but have the potential to make history. In the case of garden-huts, this may be by helping nurture and mend troubled relationships away from the prying eyes and ears of co-villagers. In the case of field centers, this may be by helping to plant ritual speech in the land, to minimize the displeasure of spirits and ensure the future flow of fertility. One further named place in Wae Rebo is the grotto (*gua*), a small, fenced patch of land planted with trees, and containing a stone platform housing a statue of the Virgin Mary. Although the grotto is admired by young people for its prettiness, and occasionally has candles lit inside it during the Months of the Virgin Mary (*Bulan Bunda Maria*) in October and April, it is not the focus for any large gatherings or prayer meetings, and is certainly never incorporated into events at *penti*. This raises the issue of what influence Catholicism has had on people's understandings of the animate landscape, and whether, beyond the existence of the lowland church, Catholic signs have been incorporated into the wider landscape.

The missionaries who first converted the population of Manggarai were members of the SVD (Societas Verbi Divini, or Society of the Divine Word), a missionary society noted for its study of local languages and cultures, and its promotion of printing "as a serious business" (Huber 1988, 61). Steenbrink's history of Catholics in Indonesia describes the SVD as "pragmatic organizers," who put less emphasis than other missions on a "specific type of spirituality" (2007, 558). In Flores, the SVD fathers considered what they called the "traditional religion" to be "a deficient religion, but not...a completely negative factor" (ibid., 143), since its study would lead to traces of belief in the "Supreme Being." For example, Paul Arndt, an SVD priest and disciple of Pater Schmit, the founder of the journal *Anthropos* (Dietrich 1992, 112), claimed in a number of books and papers to have "proved" the original monotheism of various Florenese people, thus allowing for the use of local divinity terms for the Christian God (Prior 1988, 36). This theme was also central to the writings of Father Verheijen, who conducted extensive research on the many dialects of the Manggarai language, and was equally keen to demonstrate the monotheism of his parishioners (see Verheijen 1951). The most notorious utilization of local culture to translate and make meaningful Catholic practices was the "Buffalo Mass" instituted by Monsignor Wilhelmus van Bekkum, the first Bishop of Manggarai, which fused Catholicism with traditional sacrifice. He was, however, part of a "radical minority," and other priests were more forthright in viewing sacrificial practices as "un-Catholic" (Erb 2006, 212–213).

Since the 1960s, the impact of Vatican Two has seen a number of initiatives by the Catholic church on Flores to "deepen the faith" through processes of "inculturation" or "contextualization," integrating the Gospel with local "culture" (Barnes 1992, 171; Graham 1994a, 125–126; Erb 2006, 213). Such initiatives mirror post-Vatican Two strategies throughout the Catholic world (Cannell 2006, 25), involving a complex series of conversations with notions of culture, ethnicity, and locality (Orta 2004). Missionary projects of "inculturation" on Flores attempt to be "more accommodating and tolerant towards local customs and practices" (Molnar 1997, 403). Nevertheless, "inculturation" is still "an ideology of conversion," involving the "pastoral pruning" or "purifying" of local practices (Orta 2006, 176). In Manggarai, the most successful initiative has been the production of a book of Christian songs, *Dere Serani,* which use the Manggarai language and follow the rhythms and cadences of traditional singing (see Kartomi 1995, 167). More contentiously, there have also been moves to create Catholic places that draw heavily on local material culture. For example, in the coastal village of Borik in southern Manggarai, a chapel has been built in the style of a traditional, circular house, complete with drums hanging from a central post. Though this chapel interests local people, many of my informants seem puzzled by the presence of drums in a Catholic place, since drums are used in communal rituals to awaken ancestral and other spirits. In addition, crosses have been built at some key sites, such as water sources, and when I visited the village of Lamba, young people told me excitedly of their plans to construct a Catholic grotto on top of their stone *sompang* platform.

In Wae Rebo-Kombo, people have so far resisted any such attempts to create syncretic places. Indeed, some people told me that they wished to build a separate chapel in which to hold prayer meetings, because they feel uncomfortable holding these in the drum house. The ritual leader (*tu'a adat*) of the community, Amé Dorus, has very strong opinions about the mixing of religion (*agama*) and "custom" (*adat*) in this manner. When I talked with him about the plans in Lamba, he reacted angrily and unfavourably, arguing that the Lamba villagers would regret such a move in the future. He implied that they were putting themselves at risk of illness and infertility engendered by the displeasure of ancestral and other spirits. What is interesting is that Amé Dorus is a relatively devout Catholic, who regularly attends prayer meetings and was once also a "religious teacher." However, like many others, he sees Catholicism as "coming from outside" and, therefore, as not applicable to practices concerned with the land, its energies and fertility.[13] This is why he also rejects changes to ritual practice that have occurred in other villages, such as pronouncing "Yesus Kristus; Amin" at the end of rituals, rather than the usual, affirmative chorus of *Ehhhh*.

As Stewart and Shaw discuss, the concept of syncretism has a somewhat contentious history within religious studies, since it has often been used to imply either confusion or "deviance" from a "given" tradition (1994, 5–6). However, embracing the term's contentiousness, they suggest the recasting of syncretism as "the politics of religious synthesis," of which Catholic "inculturation" strategies are clearly an example. Moreover, Stewart and Shaw argue that we should give as much emphasis to what they term "anti-syncretism," or the opposition to religious synthesis shown by those "concerned with the defence of religious boundaries" (1994, 7). This notion of "anti-syncretism" is extremely helpful in understanding the attitude of Amé Dorus and others who, unlike the East Timorese villagers described by

Bovensiepen (2009) have *not* integrated Catholic figures into their spiritual landscape. Though he enjoys Manggarai hymns, Amé Dorus abhors the use of Catholic language in rituals held in fields and houses.[14] His rejection of syncretic practices, such as placing crosses on old stone platforms, is not a question of policing the boundaries between two "religious" traditions but, rather, maintaining a separation between "religion" (Catholicism) and practices of ritual and naming that are pragmatic and rooted in a historical landscape. *Adat,* for Amé Dorus, references a holistic phenomenon that is part of the very land itself. Thus, as I will describe in more detail below, sacrificial rituals are said to be held because they are "what the land wants." If such rituals were stopped, people would become ill since they could no longer count on the protection of the ancestors and of the powerful "energy of the land" (*ghas de tana*).

Amé Dorus once described to me a church meeting in the past at which the then priest and various teachers had called for what he described as a "Catholic Organisation." This Organisation was to have demanded an end to certain ritual practices, such as throwing food for ancestors after a sacrifice. Amé Dorus was opposed to such a move and described his opposition as follows:

> What I said at that meeting, child, was this, "I will agree with a Catholic Organisation," I said, "if you change the name of this land of Manggarai, this area of Manggarai. Change the name of this area of Manggarai, change all the villages, change the flat lands, change the names of the rivers, then I'll agree with a Catholic Organisation. But if not, then I will not agree. The reason why it was called Manggarai in the past," I said, "was because of all those customs. That's why it is called Manggarai. If you cannot change that, teacher," I said, "no, don't do it."

Here, Amé Dorus explicitly connects the name of the "land of Manggarai," as well as the names of its many villages and rivers, with the practice of ritual sacrifice. To have a fully Catholic landscape, according to Amé Dorus, one would not only need to stop throwing food for the ancestors, but would have to change the names of the land, therefore making it a completely different (non-Manggarai) landscape. Again, we must not underestimate the significance here of clashing "semiotic ideologies" regarding the "real" relationship of words to places and persons. For Amé Dorus, the name of the land connects with the potent agency of the land, which demands recognition.

Many authors have argued that the politically constrained definition of "religion" (*agama*) in Indonesia has led most of the country's ethnic groups to reconceptualize ritual practices in terms of a folkloristic, aestheticized category of "tradition" (*adat*) (Acciaioli 1985; Kipp and Rodgers 1987). However, in southern Manggarai, *adat* practices retain a strong moral and spiritual force. In keeping matters of *adat* separate from those of "religion," people have not necessarily accepted an aestheticized (or purified) version of the former. Some people I know, aware that Catholicism does not encompass all aspects of their life, call themselves "half-half people." A few others take the separation of Catholicism and *adat* to imply that there are actually "two religions" and that, in the words of one older man, "We must use them both!" Another man, somewhat unusually, spoke of the "pagan religion" (*agama kafir*) and "the religion of only a few days." Further east in Flores, the northern Lio are said to "creatively embrace the tripartite categorization of socio-political life" into the domains of "religion," "government," and "tradition" (Howell 2001, 145). Indeed, Howell (p. 148) describes one man, Martinus, a retired schoolteacher, devout Catholic, and traditional priest-leader, who seems to personify the "scrupulous" attempt at maintaining the boundaries between such domains. Martinus clearly has much in common with Amé Dorus, and such boundary-maintenance may partly explain many Manggarai people's distaste for attempts to integrate Catholicism with *adat* practices.

The rejection, among most of those I know, of overt attempts at synthesising "religion" and *adat* means that Catholic rites are often simply added-on to events concerned with the spiritual landscape. Indeed, one man told me that separating *adat* speech from Catholic talk was right since priests taught that "you must not mix pagan talk with that of the angels." Following the Wae Awéng ritual described above, crowds of villagers walked to a large clearing, where chairs and benches had been lined up beneath a temporary structure of bamboo and tarpaulin. Here, the local priest, who had not attended the sacrificial ritual, held an open-air Mass, which included a speech by Amé de Sana, the descendant of the original owner of the lowland fields. This speech gave thanks to God for water, and for all that we receive from him each day. Amé de Sana also presented the priest with a white chicken, rice, and some money in gratitude for holding a Mass at such an event. However, what most engaged the attention of those I was accompanying was not the Catholic thanksgiving, but the section of Amé de Sana's speech in which his eyes filled with tears as he remembered his father. They told me that this was no doubt because being at the dam site evoked strong memories of his father, who had overseen the dam's construction, but had died before the buffalo sacrifice could be held.

Though this kind of structured event, in which *adat* talk is followed by Catholic speech, maintains an anti-syncretic boundary between "culture/tradition" and "religion," in non-ritual contexts such a boundary is not always considered important. Thus, an attitude of anti-syncretism is neither universal nor clear-cut. We have seen how the southern Manggarai landscape is one that, to its inhabitants, almost seethes with spirits and energies. What is interesting is that Catholic prayers and objects are included in practices protecting people from harmful place-energies. Before my friend and I embarked on a journey through the forest to the west, her father ensured our spiritual protection by infusing ginger with his "magic" for us to eat, but also by marking our foreheads with the sign of the cross. Meren, who lived by herself in a field-hut, stressed the potency of her bible and rosario as protective devices. In particular, she believed these objects would protect her against various spirits, and saw them as more appropriate and more powerful than traditional medicines prepared by healers. She and other informants were fond of telling me the story of a European priest who had been involved with the building of the stone road connecting this area of Manggarai with the "Trans-Flores Highway." They described one area of rocks that had been impossible for the workers to get through, and that only became passable after the priest held a Mass at the site, placating the evil spirits who had been obstructing the work. This story does not question the existence of land spirits, but confirms both the personal power of priests (who are often said to have strong magic) over spirits, and the more general power of Catholicism as a highly-effective means of protection against the spiritual dangers immanent in the landscape.

Significantly, ideas about the potency of water that influenced the Wae Awéng ritual have been particularly ripe ground for Catholic reinterpretations and blessings. As described in Chapter 3, children entering a house for the first time are often subject to an informal house baptism, their foreheads marked with water as someone intones "this is your house." Earlier, I described how the main spring is one of the key sites for sacrifice at the new year ritual of *penti*. Surprisingly, Amé Dorus, the same man who so vociferously rejects syncretic practices, told me that the *penti* ritual was held at the spring so that God would not forget to bless (*berkat*) the water that the village uses every day. Though water sources are often places associated with malevolent spirits, villagers told me that the main water source in Wae Rebo was safe since it had been blessed by a priest. These and other cases show both the influence of Catholic notions regarding holy water and the power of Catholic blessing as protection against spiritual harm.

AGRICULTURAL ANIMISM AND THE ENERGY OF THE LAND

Villagers in southern Manggarai do not hold one point of view on such issues as the relevance of Catholicism to agriculture, the existence or nature of spirits, or the consequences of failing to hold sacrificial rituals. As in the rest of this region, a diversity of attitudes and practices exist. Though many of the people I know reject explicitly syncretic places, at other times they utilise the power of Catholic blessings to protect them from spirit-places. Nevertheless, I think it is clear that theirs is a resilient, dense, and powerful spiritual landscape that has only marginally been affected by their Catholic identity. For example, though people find Catholic holy water powerful, it is hard to imagine its substitution for chicken blood in communal rituals, as has occurred in Lamalera (Barnes 1992, 175).

Recent anthropological approaches to the resurgent topic of "animism" have urged a shift away from earlier, intellectualist understandings towards both a more phenomenological approach and a focus on the environmental sensitivities and relationships that animism implies. Just as phenomenological approaches to landscape critique the notion of landscape-as-representation or cultural construct, so the new theorists of animism stress that animism is "best analysed as an active way of being in the world, and not merely as a passive representation of it" (Pedersen 2003, 243). For Bird-David (1999, 77), animism is a kind of "conversation" with the environment, a "two-way responsive relatedness" with trees, elephants, rocks, or whatever else has "relational affordances" for the people concerned. David Anderson has described the "mutual interrelation" of Evenki people and place in terms of a "sentient ecology" by which hunters act in a manner that is conscious of the reactions of both animals and the tundra itself (2000, 116). Similarly, arguing against the characterization of animism as a "system of beliefs," Ingold (2006, 10) describes animism as a "condition of being *in*" the world, of being sensitive and responsive "in perception and action, to an environment that is always in flux." This work has stressed how distinctions between nature and culture, or between human agents and animals (or objects), fail to comprehend hunters' conceptions of the world (Nadasdy 2007) and, in the case of fourth-world communities, have particular political implications (Povinelli 1995).

Rather than seeing Manggarai understandings of the spiritual landscape as a matter of what ethnographers of other societies on Flores call "traditional religion" (e.g., Molnar 1997), I prefer to follow some of the leads afforded by this literature on animism, and stress how both everyday and ritual activities imply an openness to conversation with the environment as an animate realm of multiple agents. Among many Manggarai people, the landscape is thought to communicate signs or omens of impending human misfortune (cf. Harrison 1979, 60), as when one woman interpreted the strange swaying of a tree as a sign of her husband's impending death. In addition, the landscape gives signs of its own needs. For example, an elder who is the leader of a particular field, might notice a spider appearing on the field's ritual center. Here, the spider proceeds to walk round and round in a circle. This spider is one form taken by the "lord/owner of the land," and its circular movements are a "sign" that the land wants to have an *uma randang*, an agricultural festival involving significant sacrifices and the opening up of new fields. I was told that fields should be regularly planted "in case the land should cry." Similarly, if the land is dug in order to build a new house without the appropriate rituals being held, it might cry, "What are you doing? Why are you injuring me?" When I asked Amé Dorus if the land could really talk like this, he emphatically replied, "It *can* talk. Its *appetite*. The appetite of the land. Don't let anyone say this, that the land doesn't have an appetite. It *does*."

For Amé Dorus and others, the land has agency, expressed here in terms of its "appetite" (*nafsu*), as well as its ability to "talk." At times, people also described a kind of intrinsic potency of the landscape, something that they usually called the "energy of the land" (*ghas de tana*), although on a couple of occasions this was called the *rang* or "exalted spirit" of the land (Verheijen 1967, 528). As we have seen, talk of spirits often turns into talk about the power of the landscape. People initially explain places such as a hot spring, or a forest where people get lost, in terms of a spirit. However, they often later state that such spirits are "really the land." By contrast with the beneficial aspects of the fertile landscape, humans need to be vigilant to this more dangerous "energy," avoiding it at key times (such as dusk at water sources) or attempting to stem its flow. After an agricultural ritual in Wae Rebo called *oli*, small platforms (*hanggar*) for offerings were set up on the paths into the field. These speech-offerings are spiritual barricades, their purpose described as to "impede" (*kepet*) "all the spirits and ghosts" that might "go into the field" and disrupt the growth of crops. During a ritual for planting the posts of the new Wae Rebo drum house, a small hole was dug into which both betel quids and an egg were put. Afterwards, Amé Dorus told me that this egg was to prevent people becoming "hot," since the land has "an energy that is no good." He added that, in the past, a number of people had died after eating a particular "earlobe fungus" growing on timber they had felled. He stressed that this fungus is "the vegetable of that energy" and eating it makes people fatally "drunk."

However, whilst people need to pragmatically guard against the harm that the "energy of the land" can cause, the potency of the landscape is central to its fertility, something on which humans rely, and which they must also renew. An understanding that the land has agency is seen in people's descriptions of sacrificial rituals, including that for Wae Awéng, as "what the land wants." People say that if they don't hold rituals, they will be "scared of the accusations of the land," accusations that could take the material form of human sickness and death, or of weak crops and a poor harvest. By contrast, if humans *do* maintain a conversation with the "land" (which includes its water sources and stone platforms), if they do satisfy its specific wants and needs, they will receive health and good harvests. Following the sacrifices at the Wae Awéng ritual, buffalo horns, pig feet and chicken wings were left on a post by the river, as communicative offerings, or material signs of the ritual speech spoken. Moreover, in the days after this ritual, various forms of ancestors were said to be doing "agricultural work" in the rice-fields. In contrast to people's conversations with this energetic landscape of spirits, the concrete cross next to the dam seems somewhat static. The problem for many Manggarai people with the idea of a "Catholic landscape" is that Catholicism does not acknowledge the (beneficial) agency of the land itself. Rather, it assumes an essentially passive environment in which protective signs and symbols can be planted, without ensuring the continued potency of the land.

This Manggarai focus on the *land* and its fertility offers a Southeast Asian agricultural contrast to relationships between animals and hunter-gatherers, which have tended to be the default focus of recent work on animism. Bird-David has herself acknowledged that "[a] diversity of animisms exists, each animistic project with its local status, history and structure" (1999, 79). In contrast to the hunter-gatherer animism her own article outlines, Manggarai "conversations" with the environment constitute what might be called a kind of "agricultural animism." Though rituals are occasionally held for forest spirits, the primary conversations that take place in this context are focused on the fertility of land and water, and the connected health of humans. Moreover, when people do engage with wild animals, it is predominantly as manifestations of ancestral or land spirits. The *ancestral* element to this agricultural animism is worth stressing: because the ancestors are buried in the ground, and because clear distinctions are not always made between *human* ancestors and "ancestors of the land," agricultural fertility flows when all forms of ancestors are remembered. One old man explicitly told me that it was because the souls (*wakar*) of the ancestors were in the ground that they were asked, in rituals, for their help in ensuring agricultural fertility. It is therefore noteworthy, given the "anti-syncretism" of the spiritual landscape, that the church has left matters of death and burial largely to villagers (cf. Howell 2001, 49). There are no church graveyards, and the priest has little involvement with most death practices. The church is, therefore, left out of the reciprocal relations between the living and the dead that are necessary for fertility. This situation offers a strong contrast to the Sasak village described by Telle (2009), where Islam is central to the places and processes of death, and where the ancestral landscape cannot, therefore, be so easily separated from "religion."

Though Manggarai "agricultural animism" remains strong it does, as Bird-David's comment suggests, have a specific history, which involves not only anti-syncretic responses to Catholicism, but also accommodations with state-sponsored resettlement and agricultural development. As mentioned, the Wae Awéng ritual was held to renew the rapidly declining fertility of lowland, wet-rice fields. These fields, and the dam which ensures the flow of water into them, were constructed by the local Manggarai government in a development project in 1972.[15] This project was connected with the earlier resettlement program in the mid-1960s, when Kombo was established. Both because lowland villages are *resettled* villages, and because wet-rice cultivation (as a recently introduced technology) lacks the ancestral connections of upland, swidden agriculture, ritual events have been relatively rare in lowland fields. The Wae Awéng ritual, for many people, marked a turning point in ritual activity in the lowlands. However, this ritual was also attended by several, high-ranking, uniformed state officials. Does "animism" explain their presence?

John Bowen (1993, 180) notes that for many modernist town-dwellers in the Gayo highlands of Sumatra, agricultural rituals are "best construed as entirely social and technical, with the goal of coordinating farm labor." Though rituals in southern Manggarai, unlike in Gayo, are never conducted in Indonesian, there were aspects of the organisation of the Wae Awéng ritual that would support a view of it as a technology of cooperation and coordination. Formal "letters of invitation" were typed for all teachers and other officials in the local area. Participation in the ritual, both through attendance and through financial and other contributions, was compulsory for all families with wet-rice fields fed by Wae Awéng. Even those "charismatic" Catholics who would not normally organise their own sacrificial events were still required to contribute to the event. At their speeches (in Indonesian) following the Mass, the Camat and other state officials stressed the need for harmony and cooperation between those farming the wet-rice fields. People were told not to block water when it was scheduled to flow into a neighbor's field. They were also told to be very careful about accusing others of stealing land, since such accusations have led to violent conflict in other areas of Manggarai.

For these state officials, though they were respectful towards its participants and interested in its "cultural" aspects, the Wae Awéng ritual was clearly a chance to re-educate the local population in the techniques of *sawah* farming, the importance of cooperation and the avoidance of conflict. However, for most villagers, the ritual has a rather different significance and shows how perceptions of the landscape and its needs are not unchanging, but may involve the *reassertion* of ritual procedures (cf. Bowen 1993, 194). The inspiration for the ritual came after a number of "signs" appeared to the original owners of the land. It was felt that if these signs were ignored any longer, the land would become "hot," and the fields would dry up. Thus, fields, the ownership and agricultural techniques of which had their origin in a government development project, and that had to a great extent been devoid of ritual, now appeared to be undergoing a reevaluation. The Wae Awéng ritual not only asserted the ability of ancestral spirits to travel from the mountains, it also constituted a new conversation with the land and the "ancestors of the land" in the lowlands. Moreover, in continuing to assert the potency of the land, villagers are mounting a subtle, political and moral response both to the issues posed by resettlement, and to the (church and state) view of ritual as a matter of "traditional culture."

The "land" in southern Manggarai is linked in innumerable ways with the people who drink its water, plant its soil with crops, and bury their kin in its ground. This is seen by a number of ritual phrases that men and women quote even outside of ritual contexts, such as "the fate of the land, the fate of the people" and "bodies are healthy, land is healthy." Though the somewhat mysterious "energy of the land" can cause human illness and death, human actions can in turn have consequences for the health and "fate" of the land itself. In particular, disputes over land are thought to make it "hot," something that has worrying implications for human health, which relies on the cultivation of "coolness." Though there have been no serious land conflicts in southern Manggarai during my fieldwork visits, my informants are aware of more violent disputes elsewhere in the region (see Erb 2007, 263–269; Moeliono 2000, 1–2, 29–30). During a visit to his married daughter in Wae Rebo, one elderly man told me of how he had recently gone to a subdistrict office elsewhere in Manggarai to act as a witness in a land dispute. He described how, as he walked towards the office, he was preceded by a number of "ances-tors of the land," who walked slowly in front of him. This accords well with the understanding of many Manggarai people that the power of the land and its spirits remains relevant to the contemporary context. The agency of the animate landscape has long explained the desirability of holding sacrificial rituals, but it is also central to understanding and dealing with both land con-flicts and involvement with state officials.

5

Drum Houses and
Village Resettlement

Amé Dorus, the ritual leader of Wae Rebo-Kombo, cuts a stern and imposing figure, but when he plays the drums or sings tales of past warfare between villages, he becomes lively and animated. As we have seen, Amé Dorus has strong opinions about the connection between rituals and the land, and about the necessity of keeping such *adat* matters separate from those of "religion." As in much of eastern Indonesia, authority in southern Manggarai is traditionally divided between a political leader known as the "head of the hill/village" (*tu'a golo*) and a ritual leader known as the "head of the drums" (*tu'a gendang*).[1] Drums are potent ancestral heirlooms used to awaken and communicate with spirits and spirit-places. For the Wae Rebo-Kombo community, all drums are stored in the highland site, the clan "drum house." Although the community's political leader lives in Kombo, it is in Wae Rebo that Amé Dorus, its ritual leader, spends most of his time and where one of his sons lives. The traditional division of power therefore now has an added spatial element, the ritual leader being located in the highlands and the political leader in the lowlands. Nevertheless, Amé Dorus does occasionally travel to Kombo, the home of two of his other sons, where he sees his grandchildren and visits old friends before returning to the mountains.

In his occasional movements between highlands and lowlands, Amé Dorus contributes to the constant flow of personnel between Wae Rebo and Kombo, the constituent sites of a single community. Most Wae Rebo-Kombo people have houses in both sites, and many have become adept at exploiting the various economic opportunities in each. However, despite villagers' everyday movements between them, Wae Rebo and Kombo are very different kinds of places. Amé Dorus may visit Kombo regularly, but he once vehemently insisted: "When I die, wherever I die, I must be brought back here to Wae Rebo to be buried. Because Wae Rebo is the land that feeds me and that fed my father. Don't bury me in Kombo, don't. The food that we get from Kombo just fills our stomachs, but we can't live on it. It is just a monkey-hut."

In this chapter, I consider this and other such statements in order to draw out people's perceptions of the differences between these two sites. As we shall see, the history of village expansion and movement in southern Mangga-rai, combined with a state program of village resettlement, means that people engage seriously with questions concerning the meaning of villages as places or the connections between land, identity, and authority. By what means do people make villages into valued places? Do all settlements permit the same kinds of activities? More specifically, given the potency of the named land, can people create a thriving *adat* community on land that has been donated by others? As we shall see, it is in many respects the existence of a drum house that marks a settlement as an independent ritual community. Yet what factors influence the decision to build a drum house? How might the significance of such a house be transformed when its building is sponsored by the local government?

Like Amé Dorus, many Wae Rebo-Kombo inhabitants describe their lowland site as "just a monkey-hut," a hut in a field from which to guard crops. However, perceptions of villages as places are individual and nuanced, partly dependent on personal connections and biographies. Not everyone would say that the food in Kombo is less nurturing to their own or their children's bodies. Many people are happy to live in Kombo and say that they feel rest-less in the highlands. Many have also buried their relatives in Kombo and express no desire to be buried in the highlands. As we shall see, the history of this community, its movements between two sites, and its views of the differences between highlands and lowlands, have been—and continue to be—heavily influenced by state development policies. Yet state policy alone cannot explain the contemporary significance of Wae Rebo and Kombo as settlements or the various ways in which people respond to the dilemmas of being split between two sites. Like many places dense with history and poli-tics, these two villages are "multilayered" and "multivocal" (Rodman 1992), their significance shaped by a range of factors.

MOVING VILLAGES

In the mid-1960s, at the start of Indonesia's "New Order" regime, many villages in southern Manggarai were encouraged to move down from their highland sites to specially built sites in the lowlands, near to church, school, and coastal market. All of Kombo's nearest neighbors—Lenggos, Paka, Nikeng, and Wongka—were established from the mid- to late-1960s, when these communities gradually abandoned previous highland sites. A number of people told me that construction of Kombo as the new lowland site for Wae Rebo villagers began in 1965, and that the village was "made official by the government" in 1967. In 1972, the government opened up wet-rice fields in an area near to the coast known as Sebu, giving a standard-size plot to all adult males and further orienting people in this area away from the highlands and towards the lowlands.

The new villages in this area all consisted of two lines of houses (not supposed to house more than two families) on either side of the rough lowland road.[2] These new sites were then incorporated into one administrative village, Desa Satar Lenda. The *desa* is the smallest unit of bureaucracy and governance in the Indonesian state, and one *desa* area often contains a number of settlements that might be called "villages." In Manggarai, the term *béo* is used to refer to a named "village" community with its own ritual and political leaders, while the Indonesian term *desa* refers to the local administrative area with an elected "head" (*kepala*). It is partly because of the link between the establishment of Kombo and the creation of a new *desa* unit that some people talk of the move to the lowlands as being initiated by the need to "hear the talk of the head." When I asked the political leader of Wae Rebo-Kombo the reason behind the village move he said: "Ai, looking for flat land. So that we Wae Rebo people were on the flat lands. Ai, that was what the government did in the past. Ai…they were scared of going to the mountains, the government. They only came here to the lowlands." Talk of the government being "scared" to hike up the mountains to Wae Rebo is a common way to describe this history. People continually stress the government's insistence that villages should be built on "flat land," though when I asked why this should be better, most shrugged their shoulders and said "Who knows?" I have also heard a number of people describe this resettlement as "transmigration."[3]

The establishment of Kombo and other lowland villages, with the focus on roadside houses and a move away from the inaccessible forest, appears to be a classic exercise in state surveillance, an attempt by the state to, in James Scott's terms, "make a society legible" (1998, 2). Such resettlements followed a pattern established by the Dutch colonial government in Manggarai, for whom (as we saw in Chapter 2) village "renovation" involved the dismantling of large housing structures and the building of new forms to be occupied by a maximum of three families (Nooteboom 1939, 224). Across Flores, Dutch colonial policies aimed at "pacification" and implicated in the creation of the island's forest reserves often involved the resettlement of villages in valleys, away from cosmologically important hilltop sites (Metzner 1982, 54). This continued a long southeast Asian practice, often initiated by Christian missionaries, of regrouping highland villages in the lowlands (Reid 1988, 16). Since Indonesian independence, but particularly during the early years of state expansion under the New Order, local governments have continued these practices of sociospatial transformation. Dispersed populations from Kalimantan to Flores have been settled in so-called model villages (Erb 1987, 41; Lewis 1988, 330–331; Tsing 1993, 45; Duncan 2002, 348–349), while highland communities have continued to be resettled in the lowlands, near to the economic and bureaucratic advantages of lowland roads (Gordon 1975, 65–66; Atkinson 1989, 2; Graham 1994, 125).

However, although the establishment of Kombo can be seen as part of a strategy of "legibility" by the local government, and although such strategies have often been backed by force in Indonesia, I want to make two initial points that should caution against an overly simplistic analysis of the implications of resettlement. First, all Wae Rebo-Kombo people talk of the establishment of Kombo in a generally positive manner, stressing the advantages of having houses near to the school, of being able to access roads more easily, and of farming wet-rice fields near the coast. As we shall see, the resettlement does pose some problems with regard to ritual authority, but in many respects Kombo's existence has been normalized. The second point to stress is that, in the specific case of Wae Rebo, though not in the case of other villages, the government's relocation strategy partially failed. Although Kombo was built, and although a number of families moved there, state officials were unsuccessful in their attempt to persuade residents to abandon Wae Rebo entirely. Some people told me this was because of brave opposition from local leaders. Amé Dorus himself claims to have argued strongly against pressures to move away or burn the houses of the ancestors. Some say that the isolation of Wae Rebo (which became more pronounced as other villages relocated) made it hard for state officials to enforce complete resettlement and easier for the people there to "endure." Amé Gaba told me that, in the 1970s, the local government became worried about preserving the forest around Wae Rebo and about preventing the drying up of a river feeding lowland rice fields. Pressure on Wae Rebo residents to move was therefore reexerted, but again failed. According to Amé Gaba, this was partly because he himself argued that it would be better to kill all of the residents of Wae Rebo than to move them from their lands.

Whatever the specific reasons for Wae Rebo's continued existence, Kombo is the only lowland site in this administrative area that has retained its highland site as a place to live and work, and whose residents travel regularly between highlands and lowlands.[4] Initially, some old people from other villages remained in their highland sites, a situation similar to that among the Atoni of Timor, where elders remained in sacrificial sites following colonial resettlement (Schulte Nordholt 1971, 94). However, today these former sites are simply places to harvest fruit from old trees or to open up an occasional, distant, garden. People in Nikeng, Paka, and other lowland sites refer to their lowland villages as *real* villages, using the Manggarai word *béo*. In contrast, Wae Rebo-Kombo villagers only ever speak of Wae Rebo as a *béo*. Kombo, as we saw in Amé Dorus' description, is referred to as a temporary dwelling, a "monkey-hut." Indeed, the taken-for-granted use of these terms in daily life continues to constitute each site as a very different kind of settlement. While Wae Rebo's continued existence in the highlands is in many respects a kind of victory over earlier, zealous policies of relocation, the constant movements of its residents between two sites appear to have left it in a position very different from those of other relocated communities. One of the major differences between the sites—a difference with significant implications—is that only Wae Rebo has a drum house.

DRUMS AND DRUM HOUSES

The drum house is the largest and most significant dwelling of any Manggarai village or, since some villages may have more than one such house, village section. Wae Rebo's village yard is dominated by its imposing drum house, the ridgepole of which is decorated with wood carved in the shape of buffalo horns. Whatever its architectural style, the central house-post of a drum house is always hung with a collection of drums and gongs. These drums give the drum house its name but are also what animate it. Drumming and drumming songs (*mbata*) are described as the "voice of the village," or the village's "spirit" (*semangat*). Drums are the most significant form of "heirloom" object in Manggarai, referred to both by the Manggarai word *mbaté* and the Indonesian *pusaka*.[5] Ritual authority is seen to derive from, and be invested in, drums, hence the designation of the ritual leader as the "head of the drums." More than any other material artifact, it is the drum that is most closely associated with the ancestors. Indeed, drums are in many respects like ancestral agents, and are rumored to play by themselves. One woman in a relocated village to the west told me that it was not only a government resettlement program that had led her community to abandon its old site but also

FIGURE 5.1   Dancing around the drums at *penti*

the highly disconcerting way in which the village's drums would often beat by themselves in the middle of the night. Gongs, which are played and stored together with drums, also have a spiritual potency. If a child is kidnapped by forest spirits, he or she can be found by banging a gong loudly in the forest and calling out "O-o-oh, have you seen our child here?"

Drums are so closely connected with the drum house that they may not be taken out of it without the correct ritual procedures. Before the old, rectangular drum house in Wae Rebo could be dismantled, the drums had first to be moved temporarily to a neighboring house. As the drums were taken down, some men asked whether any spiders could be seen inside them, creatures whose appearance may, as we have seen, be interpreted as an ancestral "sign." However, far from being treated with reverential delicacy, the drums in Wae Rebo were frequently taken down for a spot of impromptu drumming, particularly on rainy days or Sunday afternoons. On such occasions, older women, the acknowledged mistresses of the art, would coax youngsters into practicing, sitting cross-legged, cradling the drums across their laps, and hitting them forcefully. These hand-played drums are referred to as *tembong,* while the *tambor* is a roll-drum beaten with sticks. As Kunst noted in his mid-twentieth-century survey of music on Flores, drums are used everywhere in Manggarai "to add lustre to festivities and celebrations" (1942, 124). Drums make events lively for both humans and nonhumans (cf. Moeliono 2000, 113) and are played when a new bride approaches Wae Rebo at the end of her marriage journey. When they hear drumming, women and men engaged in domestic tasks come out of their houses, shout to neighbors, and look up at the hillside to see who might be coming into the village.

Drum houses share some features with the kinds of "great houses" that are central to Lévi-Strauss' theory of "house-based societies." Certainly, the symbolism of the drum house, as revealed in its construction, recalls his comments about the centrality of marriage to great houses (Lévi-Strauss 1987, 155; cf. Bloch 1995a). When the central ridgepole (*ngando*) of a new drum house is carried into a village, it is ritually greeted as a "mountain bride" in exactly the same manner as is a human bride at the end of her marriage journey. Significantly, the pole is a *captured* (*roko*) bride, whose spirit companions are instructed, in a triumphant song, to "return to the mountains." Later, as the drum house is constructed and the house-posts are raised, the ridgepole is said to become the "head" (*ha'i*) of the village, a protector of its land and inhabitants.[6]

Yet, although the ridgepole is initially personified as a mountain bride, the drum house as a collective institution is not in fact central to the organization of human marriages. In her characterization of the "Exchange Archipelago," Errington argues that the eastern Indonesian House functions as a "node to mobilize valuables to exchange at marriage" (1989, 236). In other words, according to Errington, eastern Indonesian societies contract marriages *between* Houses (1989, 241). However, in Manggarai, marriages occur between fluidly organized but ideally patrilineal groups. Within Wae Rebo-Kombo, a community that is united as one drum house, certain marriages can and do occur. Such in-House marriage is clearly not "sociologically impossible," and neither, judging from the happiness of many such couples and their families, is it "mythologically horrifying" (Errington 1989, 269). Errington's characterization of eastern Indonesian Houses is therefore overdrawn, and unsuited to west Flores in particular. Similarly, Howell has argued that among the Lio of north-central Flores, "patri-groups" and "Houses" may sometimes "overlap," but they "do not do the same thing" (1995, 152). Her characterization of Lio Houses as "life-promoting communities" (ibid., 154) is a more revealing and appropriate description of Manggarai drum houses than Errington's "Exchange Archipelago" House.

A Manggarai drum house also has a significant role (both real and symbolic) to play in social organization. Such houses are the collective property of one or more clans—large, broadly patrilineal groups known as *wa'u,* whose members share a single food taboo (*seki*). In many Manggarai villages, the right to ritual authority, or to "hold the drums," can only be claimed by those descended from the village's first or original clan. Indeed, many villages have more than one drum house, reflecting complex histories of clan origin and migration.[7] Wae Rebo, somewhat unusually, considers itself a single-clan village by virtue of the community's common descent from Empo Maro, the founding ancestor. Its drum house has eight rooms, which represent the eight ancestral branches of Empo Maro's descendants. At *penti,* the annual ritual of renewal, each Wae Rebo household sacrifices a chicken outside the drum house room of its ancestral branch. These rooms are occupied as dwellings by branch representatives, ideally the eldest son of an eldest brother (known as *wae tu'a*), though practical circumstances often make this impossible.

Yet, although the drum house is presented as a place of unity through patrilineal descent, many Wae Rebo residents are members of the drum house through relationships of marriage alliance. One elderly man, Amé Sebas, sacrifices a chicken at *penti* in front of the ancestral room of his deceased sister's husband, because as an orphaned child he moved to Wae Rebo to live with this married sister. In common with other "great houses," then, a drum house encompasses people connected through a range of kinship relations. Such principles of membership are (as Lévi-Strauss argues) "incompatible" only if we "expect to classify societies by consistent 'kinship' 'types'" (Errington 1989, 238; cf. Lévi-Strauss 1983, 184; Carsten and Hugh-Jones 1995, 19). I only knew of one man, Huber, whose family did not seem to have a room in the drum house, and, perhaps revealingly, it was difficult to gather information on why that was. Some said that Huber's family were not original clan members but had moved to the village. Others said that he had no room because his descent line was "extinct" and he was the only member left. However, Huber's daughter had recently married within the village, and it looked likely that in the future his family would sacrifice a chicken outside the room of her husband's family.

At *penti,* after holding sacrifices outside their ancestral room, people immediately return to their individual household room to offer a chicken to their ancestors. It is as though, having reaffirmed their origins in the clan house, they are propelled outwards, retracing their subsequent moves to individual rooms and houses. People say that they take their ancestors with them from the drum house to show them their house moves, thus demonstrating the growth of the family. Later that evening, the drum house comes alive with a series of songs and dances that lasts all through the night. The last, and most communal, of these is the *sanda*. In this dance, people form a large circle and move in a kind of "conga" around the central house-post and the hearth, shuffling from side to side and edging slowly forward. As is the usual pattern with Manggarai songs, a male or female leader sings a refrain asking for growth and fertility, and is answered by the crowd. At dawn, a group of men take the dance out onto the stone platform (*liké*) in front of the drum house, where they mark the end of *penti* by performing a trilling call for the ancestors.

These events for the new year demonstrate the significance of the drum house as a building that can potentially house all members of the community, both human and nonhuman, living and dead. The noise of the drums is believed to awaken the ancestors and the spirits associated with key places. Moreover, as we saw in the last chapter, these places themselves—such as stone platforms and the village spring—are invited *into* the drum house to join the celebrations. However, in daily life, the Wae Rebo drum house is used as a normal home by those who occupy its rooms. It is also the place where any community meetings are held and where, on Sunday mornings, people gather for Christian prayers. More widely, drum houses are also crucially implicated in processes of village growth and in the transformation of temporary settlements into permanent sites. Closely observing and considering such processes will allow us to further understand the challenge that partial resettlement in Kombo presents.

ORIGINS AND VILLAGE GROWTH

As an old village, Wae Rebo not only is connected with Kombo but also is the origin site of a number of communities farther to the west. The movements of these communities away from Wae Rebo are spoken of in terms of people who "went to find maize and rice" and therefore built a monkey-hut in a faraway field. Over time, these huts became houses, and eventually each community sought to establish itself as a real village by founding a new drum house. However, even before this building can be constructed, the new community must begin a ritual separation from its village of origin by holding a "praising" ritual (*mora*) in Wae Rebo's drum house. Like the family *mora* described in Chapter 1, this ritual ensures future growth by "rinsing the plates" of the ancestors outside the relevant room of origin in the drum house. Moreover, the connection between building a drum house and establishing a new

FIGURE 5.2   The mountain village of Wae Rebo

village emphasizes the necessity of linking the ethnography of the house with that of the wider landscape.

Village "praising" rituals enable a new village to celebrate the new year on its own terms but are also part of a process (termed "chopping up same-sex siblings") that allows particular clan branches to change bonds of siblingship into relationships of marriage alliance. Crucially, though, it is the descendants of an older sibling in the origin village who become the "mother-father" (source of brides) to the descendants of a younger sibling in the new village. For example, following a "praising" ritual in the village of Nandong, a number of Wae Rebo women married Nandong men. While Nandong people still acknowledge their origins in Wae Rebo, they have gained almost total ritual independence from the origin village, and most of their involvement with Wae Rebo is now structured by relationships of marriage alliance.

Throughout eastern Indonesia, ethnographers have described similar processes of community expansion and historical relationships between satellite and origin villages. Traube described how, in East Timor, Mambai origin villages were "only intermittently inhabited" sites for performing life-cycle and agricultural rituals that united scattered group members in their origin place (Traube 1986, 71; cf. Dix Grimes 1997, 123). In Anakalang, Sumba, clans are based on "great villages" founded by the earliest ancestors and marked by accumulated tombs, with lesser settlements and garden hamlets conceived as "branches" of these ancestral sites (Keane 1997, 49). Members of "branched" settlements must return to the altars and house sites of the great villages for large rituals, and the lower status of the former is reflected in this "ritual dependence, historical recentness, and impermanence" (ibid., 50; cf. Smedal 1994, 8). Fox has argued that "analogic identification of life processes in a botanic idiom" is one of a number of distinguishing features of eastern Indonesian societies (1988, xii), and botanical imagery of a central "trunk" village and its "branches" is particularly significant for the description of the stratification of villages. The Weyewa of Sumba speak of lesser, offshoot villages as "tendrils" in contrast to the "source/base" that is the ancestral village, and Kuipers describes how these satellite villages remain in a position of ritual dependency and marginality, "even if people have lived there for decades" (1998, 27).

Although botanical metaphors are to be found in descriptions of the clan "branches" in Wae Rebo, or the need for "rooting" a journey in an origin place, once a Manggarai satellite village has built a drum house it does not remain in such a heavily subordinate position in relation to its origin village. In part, this is because Manggarai is a far less hierarchical society than many of those found on Timor and Sumba. In the early phases of founding a new village, the satellite might be seen as a kind of offshoot or seedling, as it is after all a "monkey-hut," a temporary dwelling in a field. However, once a "praising" ritual has been held and the hierarchical connection of siblingship with the origin village is "chopped up," a new site becomes a full "village" (*béo*) in its own right. Returns to the origin village after this time are, like family "praising" events, an acknowledgment of ancestral origin rather than an expression of a subordinate status. Of course, as these relationships are transformed into affinal ones, acknowledging a place of origin implies a certain element of hierarchy. However, paying respect to a "mother-father" group is rather different from the ritual dependence of one entire village on another, particularly since—as ethnographers of asymmetric alliance have long noted—that affinal group is itself in the position of "sister/daughter" to another group.

Wae Rebo has a number of offshoot villages, and while the precise nature of the genealogical connections with these communities may no longer be remembered, their names are. Representatives of this diaspora should be invited to all large communal rituals. For example, at the ritual to plant the posts of Wae Rebo's new drum house, the speaker made great show of listing these villages:

> Ai, this Wae Rebo has grown. The farming work that was started in the past. Langgur. The growth from Langgur, because it was crowded in Langgur, Wae Liang. Watu Weri. That's to the east. To the west! Nandong! Some in Pela. Some in Bea-Raja. They are all in on this. Don't you say, ancestors, "Where are some of those from the past?" That's what I'm saying, they are all in on this here.

In proclaiming "they are all in on this here," the ritual speaker reassures the ancestors that representatives of all their dispersed descendants are present. Moreover, just as calling the names of stone platforms summons them into the drum house, so does slowly pronouncing village names temporarily summon the souls of their inhabitants back to Wae Rebo.

Ritual pronouncements of the past growth of new villages away from and out of Wae Rebo further highlight the uniqueness of Kombo as a permanent "monkey-hut." Because Kombo is not really a separate community from Wae Rebo, it is unable to gain status as a "real" village, the name of which can be called in rituals. By contrast, the nearby villages of Nikeng and Paka both built drum houses on the new sites to which they were relocated by the government. The village of Lenggos had a rather different solution to its relocation by retaining a drum house in its old village site of Kondor. However, many of those I know in Wae Rebo feel rather uneasy about Kondor as an uninhabited ritual center. Although rituals are one important way in which a house—including a drum house—becomes "lively" (*ramé*), everyday activities and talk inside houses are equally significant, and it is these that the empty Kondor drum house lacks.

RITUAL ABSENCE, ANCESTORS, AND LAND "RIGHTS"

The 1960s development project to relocate Manggarai communities has left Wae Rebo-Kombo villagers in the unusual position of continually moving between highlands and lowlands. Moreover, Kombo's unique situation makes following older processes of village growth and ritual fission difficult. Because members of the community travel frequently between Wae Rebo and Kombo, and since they maintain houses in each site, Kombo is still closely connected with Wae Rebo. As such, Kombo continues to be described as a "monkey-hut," a temporary site of dwelling, and residents continue to travel to Wae Rebo for important communal rituals such as *penti*. However, there is another reason why Kombo cannot easily build a drum house and become a "village," and this has to do with the land on which it is built.

In the previous chapter, I described how Manggarai people often attribute agency to the land, an agency partly connected with the ancestors but also seen as a potent energy in its own right. Significantly, one of the state officials who visited Wae Rebo in the 1970s to try once again to persuade the community to move from its highland site was said to have later been killed by the "energy of the land" (*ghas de tana*)—an energy that took offence at his plans. Remembering this death, one old man told me that the official should have been more wary of the spirit that guards the village. Others connected his death with procedures for building a drum house, saying that this is why the song for welcoming the central house-post and ridgepole asks them to "bite angry people."

As an ancestral site, Wae Rebo's land is closely associated with its founding ancestors, as well as with the many people who have been buried in its graves. In general terms, and so long as the correct rituals are held, the land protects and provides, both spiritually and materially, for the Wae Rebo people who live on it as their "decreed/inherited place" (*baté pedé*). However, when Kombo was built in the 1960s, it was constructed on land given by Lenggos, a lowland village standing in a relationship of younger "siblingship" to Wae Rebo (based on a now-forgotten ancestral connection). Although Kombo residents own their land in the legal sense of it being their property, Lenggos people are still considered to be the "owners of the land" (*ngara tana*). *Ngara* is a term that can simply mean "owner" but most often refers to a particular kind of ancestral connection, original link, or ritual ownership. The *ngara* of an area of land has to be acknowledged in ritual, even if that land has been sold or given to another person or group. For example, one teacher had built a house on land he had purchased near to the school where he taught. When the ritual was held for moving into this house, he made a point of inviting "those who are the owners of the land." As we saw in Chapter 2, the "moving-in" ritual establishes a connection between a house, its occupants, and the land. Acknowledging the "owner" of the land helps make this connection. Thus, the notion of "owner of the land" further evokes the agency of the land, which is able to recognize those who are most legitimately connected with it. Although Kombo people have built houses on the land and live there with their families, they are not considered to have any ritual "rights" (*hak*) over the land, as it was not originally the land of their ancestors.

In other words, Kombo people are living on donated land, on which they have property but over which they have no "rights." This is why a drum house cannot be built in the lowland village, because the "right" to do so is only held by people from Lenggos. I think this also explains why Amé Dorus does not consider the food from Kombo as truly nurturing (because it is not grown in ancestral land), and is why he wants to be buried, like his ancestors, in Wae Rebo. Indeed, he once explicitly told me that there were not any ancestors associated with the site in Kombo because Wae Rebo-Kombo people do not have the "right" to the land. Although many members of the community live in Kombo more or less permanently, and although Kombo has seen many births and deaths, the lack of a more profound connection with its land has certain ritual implications. *Sasi* whip fighting—a traditional contest often played at alliance rituals and connected with the power of the drums—can only be played in Wae Rebo.[8] After a corpse is buried in Kombo, some of the soil from the grave should always be taken to Wae Rebo, although the reverse

FIGURE 5.3   The road through Kombo in the lowlands

is not required. This seems to be a way of merging this soil with the ancestrally charged land in Wae Rebo—a way of burying a person's spirit in Wae Rebo, even if his/her corpse must remain in Kombo. A new bride arriving in Kombo can be introduced to her room and land there but will soon be taken to Wae Rebo to "see the village," where the welcoming rituals are again performed. In contrast, a new bride who first arrives in Wae Rebo does not need to be ritually introduced in Kombo. However, this is not to say that ancestral spirits (who are used to walking) cannot be called down to the lowlands to attend specific events, or that such spirits cannot appear to Kombo residents in dreams.

The lack of ancestral connection with the land in Kombo is one of the reasons why, when I first attempted to conduct a survey, every person stated that they didn't have any land in Kombo. Subsequently, it emerged that nearly every household had wet-rice fields down near the coast, and several also had swidden fields near to Kombo. Nevertheless, the story that people tell is that Kombo is just "the government's house," a place where there are no fields, no ancestors, and no communal rituals. Although Kombo was founded at the government's insistence, and although the local *desa* office keeps records of who owns which house plots or other plots of land, some Kombo residents nevertheless have a sense of the village as relatively temporary. Despite the importance of the lowland wet-rice fields and the school that Wae Rebo children attend, concepts of the powerful agency of ancestral land pose a challenge to the state's legalistic understandings of land rights.[9]

BUILDING THE BUPATI'S HOUSE

It should now be clear why Kombo is a rather different site from Wae Rebo, why its establishment had certain ritual implications, and why, despite having been inhabited for over forty years, it is still described as a temporary "monkey-hut." However, understandings of the differences between these two sites continue to change and develop, both as the local government has become more interested in Wae Rebo and as certain families have established a more permanent base in Kombo. Though Wae Rebo and Kombo have different historical and ritual significance, we must avoid any easy juxtaposition of these two sites in terms of what Barbara Bender describes as the common "opposition between a rooted sense of belonging and the alienating forces of modernity" (2001, 7). It would be easy to write of Wae Rebo as a traditional, authentic place and Kombo as an example of imposed "colonial space." However, to do so would be to ignore the subtle influence of outside interest in Wae Rebo, as well as what can be called the normalization of life in a two-placed village. As Edward Casey has stressed, a place is not "a mere patch of ground," it is "something for which we continually have to discover or invent new forms of understanding" (1996, 26).

In November 1997, just one month after I had arrived to undertake field-work in Wae Rebo-Kombo, the highland village was visited by the Bupati or district head of Manggarai. Alerted by previous foreign visitors that Wae Rebo still contained four old *niang* houses, the Bupati arrived with a large group of over forty state officials and teachers to see for himself what he and his staff immediately began to call the most "authentic" (BI *asli*) of Manggarai villages. The fairly explicit reasoning behind the visit was that, if Wae Rebo had retained traditional housing it must, de facto, have preserved other "traditional" aspects of Manggarai life. The foremost newspaper in this region of Indonesia, *Pos Kupang,* reported the visit and the Bupati's aims as follows:

> According to Bupati Ehok, one of his reasons for visiting Wae Rebo is that it has many of the customs of Manggarai people which have already changed as a consequence of recent development. "I wish to discover again the authentic culture of Manggarai people in Wae Rebo. I don't want Manggarai people to lose their authentic culture. It is for that reason that I am trying to give a warning about culture," states Ehok.
>
> Ehok hopes from his visit to obtain symbolic values which have begun to disappear in Manggarai. "I am expecting from my visit there, that there are still left-over authentic Manggarai values," is his hope.
>
> In addition, he also wishes to see the potential for what could be developed for Wae Rebo. Tourism, for example. Maybe it is just right for "hiking" or "adventure," but all of this is dependent on the results of the visit. (*Pos Kupang,* 3.1.98)

An official visit on such a scale was an extremely unusual event for a remote village such as Wae Rebo, and preparations—including a frenzied race to dig latrines—took up much of people's time and energy. However, of more significance for the village's future was the development project conceived in the aftermath of the Bupati's visit. No sooner had the local government "discovered" Wae Rebo and become interested in the values that might be "left over" in the village, than it became anxious about certain incomplete aspects of its authenticity. In 1997, at the time of the Bupati's visit, the drum house of Wae Rebo was a large rectangular building raised up on stones. Some three weeks after his visit, news reached Wae Rebo of his plans to sponsor the rebuilding of the drum house in the *niang* style. Another *niang* house was also to be built in place of a large, rectangular house in the village yard, the new and shiny roof of which was thought to produce an unattractive gleam in photographs of this cultural curio. The remodelling of Wae Rebo, while intended to preserve its uniqueness as a place of authentic architecture, thus clearly had what Urry (1990) calls the "tourist gaze" very much in mind (see Allerton 2003).

The rebuilding of the Wae Rebo drum house began in 1998 and was completed in 1999. This was not the first project in Manggarai to rebuild traditional housing. A few years earlier the drum house of Todo, a village whose leaders had been appointed to the position of *raja* or king of Manggarai by the Dutch colonialists, was rebuilt as a *niang* house. The Todo project had been instigated and funded by Westerners, notably the Polish parish priest and a Swiss development agency involved in road construction throughout Manggarai (see Erb 1998). However, by contrast with Todo, the rebuilding of the Wae Rebo drum house not only took place against the backdrop of four preexisting *niang* houses but was entirely funded (to the sum of 30 million rupiah) by the local Manggarai government.[10] Although 1998–1999 was a time of acute economic and political instability in Indonesia, paradoxically, the rebuilding project meant that during this period, Wae Rebo-Kombo people continued to experience the state as both *strong* and *local.* Moreover, although the building of the Wae Rebo drum house was completed after the fall of Suharto's government with its appeals to "traditional values," it was a classic "New Order" cultural project (Hitchcock 1998, 127).

One key catchphrase of Suharto's New Order was "the preservation of national culture" (BI *kelestarian kebudayaan nasional*).[11] However, what the state chose to preserve—houses, ritual costumes, handicrafts, and other marketable "objects"—was only a small part of what anthropologists would term "culture" (Kipp, 1993, 111–113; Picard, 1997, 197). In particular, "customary/traditional houses" (*rumah adat*) have enormous importance in state-sponsored representations of Indonesia, appearing in school atlases, maps in provincial offices, and tourist brochures (cf. Adams 1984, 476). Within Manggarai, pictures of traditional *niang* houses appear, in rationalized form, on the shoulder patches of local officials and teachers. Most explicitly, at Jakarta's "Taman Mini" theme park, twenty-six *rumah adat* representing the "genuine customary architectural style" of Indonesia's twenty-six provinces present an ahistorical image of Indonesia's "Unity in Diversity" (Pemberton 1994, 152).

The project to remodel Wae Rebo as a tourist site showed the changing significance of such *adat* houses. Although the Indonesian word *adat* generally signifies "customs"—and is used rather robustly by many rural Manggarai people to refer to a range of practices—when used as an adjective it increasingly implies what is "traditional" in the sense of no longer regularly used but necessary to "preserve" as a mark of cultural identity. As the focus for kinship and ritual that I have already outlined, the old, rectangular drum house in Wae Rebo was a "customary" *adat* center. However, in architectural or aesthetic terms it was not "traditional." The Bupati's rebuilding project was thus an attempt to make sure that the drum house became an Indonesian *rumah adat* in the full sense of the term. In the process, though, the significance of the house as an institution was overshadowed, and emphasis was primarily given to *niang* architecture as a marker of Manggarai ethnicity. A few years after the rebuilding project, a Wae Rebo man who teaches at the school in Denge built an extension onto his house. This extension has a conical, metal roof, echoing the shape of circular houses, and contains three guest bedrooms. The teacher's intention is for his house to become a reception area for the occasional group of tourists who come to visit Wae Rebo, and he has therefore typed up information sheets about this "authentic Manggarai village."

Hutajulu has argued that Toba Batak tradition, reworked for tourists, serves to situate the Toba Batak "as a 'legitimate' ethnic group within the framework of Indonesian nationalism" (1995, 639). This is an important point with regard to the political significance of house building and echoes Wood's arguments that "touristic space can offer an opportunity for asserting local identities and rights against other groups" (1992, 59–60). Manggarai as a region has long been lacking in the necessary cultural "objects" to entice tourists off their buses as they travel from Komodo to the regency of Ngada, the old village sites of which are a highlighted feature in guidebooks on eastern Indonesia (see Cole 2007). With their rebuilding of traditional housing, along with staged "performances" of *sasi* whip fighting (Erb 2001), "the Manggarai" have a stronger claim to being considered a legitimate ethnic group within the "diversity" of the nation. Further, though the rebuilding project emphasized the particularity of Wae Rebo and Manggarai, one undoubted consequence is that it has stimulated greater local reflection on what it is to be "Indonesian" in a remote area.

Erb (2007) has described three ways in which *adat* has been "revived" in western Flores in the post-Suharto era of local autonomy: as material culture and display, as ritual, and in the context of institutions of political authority and control over land. She notes that a number of key intellectuals and figures from the town of Ruteng have long been interested in organizing cultural displays that create an idea of "pan-Manggaraian culture" (2007, 251–252). Indeed, the "nostalgia about culture and adat" (2007, 255) that she describes appears to be predominantly, though not exclusively, a town phenomenon (cf. Moeliono 2000, 247). Certainly, I have heard relatively few laments about the "loss" of culture in Wae Rebo-Kombo, where many people maintain a holistic (rather than aesthetic) and relatively unselfconscious understanding of *adat*. Nevertheless, town nostalgia clearly played an important role in the rebuilding of the Wae Rebo drum house, as did discourses on "pan-Manggarai" culture.[12]

Marsel, the Kombo man chosen to liaise with officials in Ruteng (primarily because of his fluency in Indonesian), is a somewhat controversial figure in the community, seen as an impatient hothead and rumored to practice a more charismatic style of Catholicism. On the day of the greeting of the ridgepole, Marsel acted as an official photographer, and indeed consciously rearranged ritual participants in order to create a more photogenic scene for his camera. He also insisted that key participants should wear carefully starched headscarves as part of the correct ritual costume. Amé Bertolo, the ritual speaker, was sporting his usual woven hat (*jongkong bila*) and therefore attracted considerable criticism from Marsel. Later, Amé Bertolo told Marsel that in the past there were only woven hats and hats made from gourds, not batik headscarves, and who was Marsel to say what was authentic when he was so young? On another occasion during the rebuilding process, people gathered together in one of the older *niang* houses to sing drumming songs. When visitors from another village suggested that their songs were different from those of Wae Rebo, Marsel became agitated, insisting that people "must not talk about differences," since Manggarai culture was all "the same." However, Marsel was also capable of criticizing state officials whom he saw as imposing their views and interpretations on villagers; when one of the Bupati's officials described how a particular ritual was performed differently in his home village, Marsel apparently became angry at what he perceived as a criticism of local knowledge.

Although the rebuilding project was in general positively embraced, there were inevitably tensions surrounding the work, and these often centered on a clash between town schedules and procedures and the understandings of village elders. A general feeling among the latter was that the rebuilding project was being rushed through too quickly. The Bupati's officials who liaised with representatives from Wae Rebo wanted the house finished, and the ritual inaugurations held, before the end of the Bupati's term of office in May 1999. This put both men and women (who had to take primary responsibility for agriculture during the rebuilding) under considerable pressure. Labor for the felling and transporting of timber was organized on the basis of eight work teams, and those who missed a scheduled day of communal work (often in heavy rain) without prior warning were fined a sum of Rp 5,000. The introduction of these fines, and of payments for certain tasks, not only created tensions between different households with greater or smaller pools of labor, but also went against the notion (stressed by elders) of a drum house being built with (voluntary) communal labour.

Henley and Davidson (2007, 32–33) argue that Indonesian notions of *adat* have always contained an element of "wishful thinking." That is, particularly in rural areas, *adat* is often a vision of the ideal, of how things "ought" to be done, rather than a description of everyday practice. They note that "city-dwellers looking outwards at the countryside" often confuse the ideal and the actuality of *adat,* leading to a certain romanticization. Certainly, during the Wae Rebo drum house rebuilding, it was state officials and educated young men who were most likely to pronounce on the meaning of the house or to become angry at poor ritual attendance. By contrast, village elders often argued for greater flexibility with work schedules, stressing the necessity of a willing, collective workforce, and occasionally cut short discussions of *adat.* Many were concerned that the frequent arguments and raised voices occurring in the course of organizing work and events might alarm the ancestors. A number of people also compared the drum house rebuilding with the *uma randang* festival held several years before, at which new fields had been divided up for the whole community. Significantly, some people told me that the *uma randang* rituals had been "more lively," and therefore more satisfying. This was because, while the drum house was being built on the orders of the government, the *randang* festival was held in accordance with the tempo and appetite of the land.

The state-sponsored rebuilding of Wae Rebo's drum house marked a new phase in the historical development of Wae Rebo-Kombo. Older inhabitants told me that when Kombo was first built it was referred to as the "government's house." However, since the rebuilding project, it is Wae Rebo, not Kombo, which has had closer dealings with the government. After the inauguration of the Wae Rebo drum house, a small plaque was erected above the door of the new *niang* bearing the inscription "made official by the Bupati of Manggarai, Dr G. P. Ehok, Ruteng, 13 July 1999." This sign, along with people's awareness of the large sums of money spent on the project, contributed to an uneasiness about the status of the new building, which several villagers referred to, not as the "drum house," but as the "house of the Bupati."[13]

Kombo may have been established so that Wae Rebo residents could be incorporated into a new, more "legible" village unit, so that they could "listen to the government's speech." However, the subsequent interest of the local government in Wae Rebo's *niang* houses means that people now see a need for greater government involvement in the highland site. In particular, many of my informants now regard *niang* houses as structures that can be built only with outside help, whether from the government, wealthy Indonesians, or (as emerged in a recent visit) money from foreigners. Thus, ironically, the very *niang* houses that are interpreted as a sign of Wae Rebo's authenticity have become something with which outsiders and the local government are necessarily entangled and involved.

As we saw at the beginning of this chapter, Wae Rebo's geographical isolation became pronounced in the 1960s when various other highland sites were relocated to the lowlands. This isolation is undoubtedly part of the reason for the survival of *niang* housing in the village. However, despite this, Wae Rebo residents were not isolated from wider processes of change in southern Manggarai. Their children moved to the lowlands to attend school, they farmed new wet-rice fields near the coast, and they researched new cash crops to plant in fertile highland soils. Yet with the rebuilding project, Wae Rebo's isolation becomes a sign of its apparent "authenticity," of being *asli*. This authenticity has nothing to do with local ideas about the agency of the land and its connection with people, but is defined by a fabricated notion of a true, original Manggarai culture.[14] In addition, this notion of authenticity ignores Wae Rebo's entanglement with Kombo, the site to which an earlier government moved many of its inhabitants.

NORMALIZING SPATIAL TRANSFORMATION

Even in the most intimate, spatially confined, geographically isolated situations, locality must be maintained carefully against various kinds of odds.
—Appadurai 1996, 179

The local government in Manggarai, and various tourist guides who now organize occasional trips to Wae Rebo, emphasize the village's "authentic" and traditional nature. Yet, as we have seen, its drum house and village center were in fact substantially remodelled in the Bupati's building project. Despite its round *niang* houses, Wae Rebo is no more "authentic" (for which read "unchanged") than are the lowland villages founded by the government.

Although the highland village was not abandoned in the 1960s, it has nevertheless been profoundly affected by the practical and ritual consequences of resettlement.

Earlier in this book, I argued that ordinary houses were made as particular kinds of valued places, not only in their construction, but through myriad everyday practices that were not explicitly concerned with "making place." However, places may also be made (and contested) through more self-conscious acts that reference larger projects of place making. As Stephan Feuchtwang has argued, phenomenological accounts of place have tended to remain at the micro-level of "small-scale events" and have tended to ignore larger-scale events that may "destroy and abstract" local places (2004, 3). While a phenomenological perspective is crucial to drawing out the significance of houses as centers of "liveliness," the experience of travelling marriage "paths," or people's dealings with an animate landscape, it cannot furnish a full understanding of what makes a village a meaningful place. There are different scales of entanglement between people and places, and Wae Rebo-Kombo residents' entanglements with their two village sites include their responses to state-sponsored resettlement and rebuilding. Indeed, it is possible to argue that one of the impacts of resettlement for this community has been a strengthened self-consciousness regarding connections with the land.

In a well-known article on the culture concept and the limitations of focusing on a bounded "field," Gupta and Ferguson critique the anthropological assumption of a natural connection between place and culture. Instead, they argue for increased attention to shared historical processes, and to the ways in which "spaces and places are made, imagined, contested and enforced" (1992, 17–18). As sites founded in contrasting historical circumstances, Wae Rebo and Kombo are imagined as very different kinds of villages, with different connections to *adat*. Such imaginings draw on local Manggarai discourses on the connections between place and culture. Thus, in the previous chapter, we saw how Amé Dorus emphasizes the connection between the places of the named land and the "custom" of ritual practice in order to reject explicit strategies of enculturation. In this chapter, we have seen how people are concerned with the historical connections between places and people, and with the ways these can be utilized or transformed to ensure future growth. A landscape infused with ancestral and other spirits has a particular potency or agency, but this can only be tapped into by those who are the true "owners of the land." This is why, though Kombo is a home to many people—a place where they are happy to bring up their children and plant chocolate or jackfruit trees—it has not been able to become a real "village," to build a drum house and hold a celebration of *penti*. This is also why, for some people, its health and fertility may be compromised.

This book has described how human rites of passage create or strengthen the entanglement of persons and places or pathways. Thus, birth rituals involve the temporary transformation of a room into a protective womb. Marriage rituals highlight the creation or remembrance of a path in the landscape and end by symbolizing the couple's entanglement with their marital room. Death rituals also acknowledge the involvement of the deceased with a house of origin and gently point their soul towards the mountainside of the ancestors. As Appadurai has stressed, rites of passage are not only techniques for the production of subjects but are also "ways to embody locality as well as to locate bodies in socially and spatially defined communities" (1996, 179). However, I think we can take the connection between places and rites of passage even further. Just as humans undergo rites of passage through the life cycle, so we might also say that places, in the course of their social lives, undergo such rites. Take, for example, a household room newly built for a married couple. Such a room is not yet the kind of origin place in which a patrilineal ancestor might be ritually "praised." To become such a historically dense place, a room must be transformed by various rites. Through birth practices it is made into a nurturing womb for babies; through marriage rituals it is personified as an entity that ensures fertility; through rituals to "collect up souls" it emerges as a place of spiritual shelter. It is only after living a life of such rites that a room becomes the kind of place where a "praising" ritual can be held. Similarly, in this chapter we have seen that for a village to emerge as a *béo,* and as a historically dense origin place, it needs to go through certain rites of passage. It must grow from a collection of garden-huts to a collection of houses; it must return to its origin village to conduct a large-scale "praising" event; and it must build its own drum house and hold its own new-year celebration. Though Kombo, as a place, has grown and developed, it has not been able to follow this ideal sequence through which it might emerge as a "village."

However, it is worth emphasizing that this ritual sequence for the emergence of a real "village" is an *ideal,* and that people continue to search for new ways to understand and develop the lowland site. During my first period of fieldwork in Wae Rebo-Kombo, I was told that building a drum house in Kombo was impossible. However, during my second fieldwork in 2001, I was surprised to hear the beginnings of a very different story. The impetus for this new perspective was the Wae Awéng ritual, described in the previous chapter. Partly as a consequence of the close involvement between Lenggos (as the original "owners of the land") and Wae Rebo elders in the run-up to this event, the ritual leader of Lenggos indicated that he might be able to give some of the drums from their drum house in Kondor to people in Kombo. This gift would have to be "answered" with a buffalo, but it would mean that a drum house could be built in Kombo. The lowland site could then become a real "village," able to celebrate *penti*. It would also mean (contrary to most previous discussions I had heard) that the ritual "right" to the land could be transferred to people in Kombo. Giving some of the Kondor drums to Kombo was connected with wider plans for land rituals in the lowlands. One old man told me that an *uma randang* (a large agricultural festival involving buffalo sacrifice) needed to be instituted in the lowlands to satisfy the appetite of the land. However, both he and others stressed that this ritual process would be lengthy and expensive, and would necessitate drawing distinctions between people who lived more or less permanently in Kombo and those who spend more time in Wae Rebo.

These tentative plans to honor the land in the lowlands and to build a drum house in Kombo show how the resettlement program of the 1960s, and the later construction of wet-rice fields, continue to pose challenges to understandings of land and village places. As Tim Ingold has stressed, "the landscape is never complete...it is perpetually under construction" (2000, 199). The resettled and rebuilt landscape of Wae Rebo-Kombo is the result of earlier state policies of "legibility" and more recent concerns with "authenticity." However, unlike more harmful state visions (Scott 1998), the creation of this two-placed village has in fact been mostly beneficial for its inhabitants, diversifying their economy and protecting them from some of the more violent land conflicts raging elsewhere in the region. Indeed, while many elders such as Amé Dorus continue to be concerned about the ritual emptiness in Kombo, in many other respects the differences between the highland and lowland sites have been normalized. This may explain why the plans for the Kombo drum house were not supported by everyone in 2001, were not mentioned to me in 2005 or 2008, and, indeed, have yet to come to fruition. As the next chapter explores, one key aspect of the normalization of difference between Wae Rebo and Kombo has been the incorporation of travel between highlands and lowlands, and of the movements of goods and news, into the rhythms of daily life.

6

Roots and Mobility

Tanta Tin is an unmarried woman in her late forties, unusually tall and with a reputation as a talented weaver. Like most older spinsters in southern Manggarai, she faces no stigma due to her unmarried state but is respected for her economic and practical contributions to her household and wider kin group. From her house in Wae Rebo, Tanta Tin runs a small business refilling bottles of paraffin for her fellow villagers. This paraffin is bought in a small town several hours' walk to the west and regularly carried through the forest by Tanta Tin's sister's son. Though Tanta Tin relies on the mobility of this nephew for their small business, she herself also spent much of her youth travelling between villages. As a child, she attended school four hours' walk away in the lowlands, living with various different relatives and returning to the highlands at weekends. After finishing school, she lived for a three-year period with her sister in the west, journeying to and fro with foodstuffs for her parents. After the deaths of her parents, and of her elder brother, she stayed in Wae Rebo more permanently. Now it was the turn of her brother's son, Maka, to travel, as he went to work on various road-building projects in Manggarai. Tanta Tin says that, as Maka has "replaced his father's face" in her affections, she can only cope with his journeys away from the village if he first takes his leave from her: "I'm like this with him.... if he is going far away and...I don't see him go, I feel very sad. That's how I feel when he goes. But if it is like this, if he goes anywhere, if he goes for a friend's marriage, if he first takes his leave from me, ai...I don't feel so sad when he goes."

People in Manggarai have always travelled, whether willingly or not. An area of present-day Jakarta is still called Manggarai, so named after the slaves taken from Flores to western Indonesia from the seventeenth century onward. Fear of slave raiding was one reason why, until Indonesian independence, Manggarai villages were built in the mountainous interior of the region. Resettlement during the New Order era relocated many highland populations to lower-lying areas, but in the case of Wae Rebo-Kombo has been only partial and has led to a kind of ritual inequality between the two sites. However, in many other respects, the existence of two economically and ecologically distinct sites has been quite advantageous for this community. In this chapter I shall explore how everyday and temporally defined acts of travel between these sites continue to normalize the condition of living in two villages. As we have seen, travel and "paths" are central to the process of Manggarai marriage. Yet mobility also plays a wider role beyond marriage journeys in constituting the lived-in environment. Both mythical and everyday journeys create a dynamic network of places and pathways, and necessitate various protective measures or ritual acknowledgments. Manggarai people also undertake more extraordinary journeys, whether in search of magical knowledge, schooling, or work as migrant laborers.

Travel, mobility, and displacement have become key themes in contemporary anthropology, as the discipline focuses increasingly on migration, borderlands, diasporic communities, and the theoretical and practical significance of "multisited" fieldwork (Gupta and Ferguson 1992). Scholars who emphasize mobility do so in part to challenge what Liisa Malkki describes as "taken-for-granted ways of thinking about identity and territory" that see "peoples" and cultures as naturally rooted in place (1997, 53). Malkki is particularly concerned with the implications of such ways of thinking for the study of refugees and others who are "chronically mobile and routinely displaced" (ibid., 52). Her critique of the bias towards "roots" inherent in the culture concept echoes the work of James Clifford, for whom common notions of culture assume that dwelling is "the local ground of collective life," while travel is a mere "supplement" to it (1997, 3). Moreover, Malkki draws explicitly on the writings of Deleuze and Guattari, whose philosophical project of "Nomadology" involves a similar rejection of rooted histories (1987, 25). In place of trees, roots, and genealogies, which, they claim, have dominated Western thought, Deleuze and Guattari propose devoting greater attention to the notion of the rhizome, or rootstock, which engages principles of "connection and heterogeneity" (ibid., 7).

In what follows, I consider Manggarai travelling practices and the ways in which these constitute not only the paths and roads of the landscape but also its apparently stable places. However, I also describe how Manggarai people are troubled by the dangers posed by certain journeys and seek to overcome such dangers in part through events that "root" people's travel in a place of origin. This "rooting" is of a rather different kind to that imagined by Deleuze and Guattari or criticized by those anthropologists who are influenced by their "Nomadology." Though the notion of "roots" may in various places lead to ethnic violence and chauvinism, or to the classification of "uprooted" refugees as people "torn loose from their culture" (Malkki 1997, 65), we cannot prejudge its implications or significance in any particular context. As we shall see, what Manggarai people are eager to "root" in origin places is not culture or history but their feet.

ORIENTATION AND MOVEMENT

In the first months of fieldwork, when my efforts were mainly devoted to learning the local language, Bahasa Manggarai, I often became frustrated by my inability to utter even the simplest of sentences, such as "I am going to the village center" or "I am going to my house." I soon found a focus for this frustration: the Manggarai direction terms that must always be used when referring to the position of, or direction of movement towards, a place.[1] Like similar terms in other eastern Indonesian languages, these terms for direction function as adverbs, adjectives, and prepositions (Forth 1991b, 139). Moreover, since the use of these terms relates both to topographical features and to the movements of a person, they are very different from cardinal points that remain the same no matter where a person is.[2]

In southern Manggarai, four main axes or pairs of direction terms can be discerned. In common with other inhabitants of mountainous Indonesian islands, the most fundamental of these is the distinction made between "upstream/mountainward" (*lé*) and "downstream/seaward" (*lau*). Along the coast of southern Manggarai, *lé* roughly denotes "north" and *lau* "south." In contrast, in the town of Ruteng and along the northern coast of Manggarai, *lé* roughly corresponds with "south." The terms *awo* and *halé*, which correspond to "east/sunrise" and "west/sunset," provide a second axis of direction. These terms have a shifting and contextual connection with the mountainward/seaward axis, and people are fascinated by the appearance of the sun and the way it seems to travel differently in relation to different topographical features. This explains why I was constantly being asked to describe how the sun rose in England and how it travelled across the sky, and why people stressed that the sun appeared differently on the plains of Lembor to the west. A third direction axis is the opposition between "up/above" (*éta*) and "down/below" (*wa* or *hili,* sometimes combined to create *hilwa*). These terms are used to refer to a place within the village, such as a field or stream, but also to refer to other villages occupying a relatively lower or higher position.

Table 6.1. Manggarai Directional Terms

lé	mountainward/upstream
lau	seaward/downstream
halé	direction of sunset
awo	direction of sunrise
éta	up, above
wa or *hili*	down, below
oné	inside
péang	outside

These three pairs of direction terms are those used most commonly to refer to places and movements in Manggarai. Within Wae Rebo, people living on the hill up from the village center talk of going "mountainward down to the stream" or "down east to the likop field." People also use direction terms to locate those living in other towns and villages in Manggarai—for example, "west down in Labuan" or "up in Ruteng." Indeed, direction terms often substitute for the place-names of frequently visited or well-known locations. Thus, persons setting out from Wae Rebo to Kombo simply say they are going "seaward" (*lau*), while friends in Ruteng would ask me what I had been doing "below" (*hili*) in the Wae Rebo region. Though the use of direction terms as shorthands for place-names might imply a relatively fixed system of orientation, the essence of these terms is movement, or the imagination of movement, towards others (cf. Fox 1997a, 6). As noted with regard to the axis of sunrise/sunset, people become accustomed to using direction axes in specific combinations and with reference to a particular landscape. They gain knowledge of the use of these terms by moving about within such a landscape (cf. Ingold 2000, 230). This explains why, when in less familiar surroundings, people I knew often expressed disorientation or asked others to clarify particular directions. Some said they felt confused when they visited the town of Ruteng, finding it hard to remember locations or give directions (cf. Wassman and Dasen 1998, 693–694). This was because in Ruteng the "sunrise/sunset" axis was very differently oriented with the "mountainward/seaward" axis.[3]

A fourth and final pair of direction terms are used somewhat differently.

Rather than expressing directions of movement within a specific landscape, "inside" (*oné*) and "outside" (*péang*) are used to speak of entering and exiting houses, but also to contrast the land of Manggarai (which is "here" and "inside") with a range of "outside," mostly unknown, locations.[4] Thus, people speak of men they know who are working "outside in Kalimantan," while one man described his return journey to Manggarai from Malaysia in terms of "going inside." Whereas an unknown Manggarai person will initially be described as a "person from anywhere" (*ata bana*), those from other countries or other Indonesian islands are classified together as "people from outside." During the Indonesian political crisis of 1998, one woman asked where the demonstrators "from outside" were from and was shocked to be told they were "Indonesians like us." Many places in Indonesia, including Java, Jakarta, and Sumatra, are also described as "seaward" (*lau*), a term used to refer to unknown or faraway places. Significantly, some people, particularly the old and less educated, frequently assume that those lands that are "outside" of Manggarai must, by definition, be close to one another. One elderly woman once asked me "Is this Malaysia close to England or what?" to which her great-nephew replied, "No, mother, that Malaysia is towards here, England is farther outside."[5]

I have described direction terms in some detail because they are a crucial starting point for understanding the ways in which people express and imagine travel within and beyond Manggarai. Direction terms are also used to describe the weather, as when one woman painstakingly described to me the directions of different winds, and the connected warmth or coldness, at different times of the year in the lowlands. Indeed, weather fundamentally changes the appearance and experience of the Manggarai landscape, as we shall see with regard to walking along paths. Direction terms are also central to everyday social interactions, in which questions about actions and direction of travel serve as greetings. Passing someone returning from bathing at the spring, one asks, "You're returning from the spring?" Meeting someone travelling on a path towards the coast, one might say, "You're going towards the sea?" Upon encountering a visitor from another village, the most frequent greeting is to ask something such as "When did you come downstream from the west?"

Questions and discussions about precise details of journeys, where other household members are, or when certain events are occurring take up a good deal of everyday conversation. In particular, people like to know as much as possible about the arrivals and departures of neighbors, kin, or guests. When somebody arrives unexpectedly in a village, their reception is often a little tense. They might be greeted with a question such as "You've arrived in the afternoon?" but usually there is no further attempt at conversation until they describe the reason for their visit, or until someone reluctantly asks, "There isn't any news?" "News" in this context always refers to bad news, whether of illness or death. Indeed, this is why unexpected arrivals are greeted nervously, for such a visitor may sometimes be an "informing person" (*ata wéro*) bringing news of a death. It also explains why, when tuning in to their radios, people search (often in vain) for "Ruteng," as this station carries telegram-like news of local deaths and other events.

Daily life for Manggarai people, as is evident in most greetings, always involves an awareness of the positioning and movements of others, and of how to move towards them. The rarity with which my informants (compared with myself) used the directionless term *sina* demonstrates their considerable ability to remember the various directions of, for example, other people's fields or coffee trees. The people who *don't* have a precise location are various spirits, often described as "people on the other side" (*ata palé-sina*), whose unknown positioning accords well with their ambiguous nature.

However, despite everyday uses of direction terms, when meeting someone on a path or seeing someone walk past one's house the most common greeting is the simple question "Where are you going?" (*Ngo nia?*). This form of greeting is ubiquitous throughout the Austronesian world (cf. Gibson 1986, 33; Kahn 1990, 62; Forth 1991b, 139). Knowing where someone is going locates them in a dynamic and profoundly social landscape. Moreover, as I shall now describe, in the context of resettlement these questions have become central to social organization.

WALKING BETWEEN HIGHLANDS AND LOWLANDS

The difference between Wae Rebo, whose residents are also the "owners" (*ngara*) of the land, and Kombo, whose inhabitants are not, has important ritual and political implications. In particular, the notion of *ngara*, which emphasizes the profound connection between land, spirits, and original human occupants, lies behind the lack of a drum house in Kombo and the necessity for its residents to travel to Wae Rebo for large-scale ritual events. This has several implications for the temporal flows of persons between the two sites and explains why at the time of the new year ritual of *penti* the lowlands are almost empty. By contrast, the highlands often empty out at significant times in the Catholic calendar, such as Easter, when large numbers of people travel from Wae Rebo to attend services at the lowland church.

The local government's view of Wae Rebo as a fixed, isolated, and authentic village center ignores the actuality of the many journeys undertaken by its residents, and in particular their regular travels between Wae Rebo and Kombo. Indeed, in everyday life, the ritual or political differences between these two sites matter little when compared with people's practical needs and desires, whether involving journeys to attend first communions and wedding parties, to visit a sick relative, or to renew rice stocks in the highlands. In writing of the mobility of the inhabitants of the Meratus mountains in Kalimantan, Anna Tsing has described how state actors stereotype Meratus travel as free-ranging and "nomadic," neglecting the complex reality of differentiations between social landscapes and travellers (1993, 46). By contrast, the state focus on the isolated, localized, and static "authenticity" of Wae Rebo turns a blind eye to the (historical and contemporary) reality of travel to, and links with, a range of other places. In this respect, it is interesting that a frequent criticism of both church and state voiced by those in Wae Rebo is that their representatives are somehow unable, or too frightened, to travel. For example, I have heard people explain the lack of visits to the highlands by both the lowland priest and the health worker in terms of their "big stomachs" and "fear of walking." At the time of the Bupati's visit, a number of state officials were unable to complete the steep journey on foot, leading many villagers to comment gleefully that these officials were "not fit to walk." Indeed, the ability to "strongly walk" up the mountains, though hardly unusual in Flores, has become a characteristic that marks Wae Rebo-Kombo people in the local, resettled area.

From Kombo in the lowlands, the journey to Wae Rebo initially follows the road, climbing steadily past the villages of Nikeng and Paka, and passing the large concrete church, health worker's office, and school buildings at Denge. Here, the road ends and the journey continues along a stony pathway through land planted with coconut and clove trees. As the path climbs higher, it travels near to the sites of former villages, crossing the stream and rocks of Wae Ntijo, before eventually reaching the cool waters of Wae Lomba. This is one of the main resting-places on the path to Wae Rebo and is where women will stop to share betel nut quids, where young children will be given packets of rice to eat, and where people drink water and fill up small plastic bottles. From Wae Lomba, the path begins to climb steeply up through the forest towards the mountains. This section of the journey is hard work, particularly for those carrying heavy sacks, pigs tied up in baskets, or cradling children in a sarong on their backs. After an hour or more of climbing, the peak known as Poso Roko is reached, another resting-place and, since 2008, the best place to receive mobile phone reception (though only one villager had a phone at that time). From Poso Roko, the path continues to climb, with forested ravines to either side, until reaching a junction of paths known as Ponto Nao. From there, Wae Rebo, set in a dell surrounded by mountains, can finally be glimpsed. The path then descends into the village past fields and garden-huts.

As a villager walks into Wae Rebo they will be greeted with a number of questions, including the short but significant query "What have you brought?" (*Apa ba?*). Because of the ecological and economic differences between Wae Rebo and Kombo, it is rare for people to make the journey between the two sites without bringing something for other household members.[6] When travelling up from the lowlands, people bring coconuts, areca nuts, bags of sugar, dried fish, and, most important, sacks of rice. When travelling down to Kombo, people take seasonal fruit and vegetables unavailable in the lowlands, as well as supplies of coffee. Coffee has become the principle cash crop grown in the highlands, but transportation of coffee beans is entirely dependent on the strength of household members. Indeed, many Wae Rebo-Kombo households today rather cleverly exploit the economic opportunities of highlands and lowlands, moving their labor power down for rice planting, up for coffee harvesting, down for wet-rice weeding, up for swidden clearance, and so on. Knowing where different household members are, and when they are planning to travel, is crucial to the smooth operation of household affairs. Thus, those arriving from highlands or lowlands are given messages to pass on or are quizzed by others about the travel plans of their household members.

Travel between Wae Rebo and Kombo is thus highly productive, involving the movements of personnel, goods, and information along a historically significant path, replete with named stopping points. In particular, temporal movements of goods and people continually reproduce the highland and lowland sites as *different* kinds of places. In his recent history of lines, Ingold has argued that while places are often thought of as containers or, in their representation on maps, as nodes, they are better imagined as knots in a "meshwork" of trails (2007, 100). Because the trails that can be traced from these knots are "lines of wayfaring," movement along a trail is therefore always implicated in the making of place (ibid., 101). This is clearly evident in the case of Wae Rebo and Kombo, which are made as places in part through the movements of people and goods along paths.

Such productive, place-making travel is very different from one of the main kinds of travel that the local government acknowledges to Wae Rebo, the "hiking" of tourists through the forest. Wae Rebo-Kombo people in general walk fast, looking down at their feet, and rarely stop to take in "views." They enjoy jokes, songs, and lighthearted conversation as they move along. Men's walking is animated by the rattling of their encased machetes, which they frequently take out to cut back undergrowth or to fashion a walking stick for a fellow traveller. People enjoy identifying the calls of different birds and, if a monkey is spotted, will send dogs into the forest to chase it. Any edible fruit, fungi, or leaves are gathered and often consumed along the way, and as people draw near to the village they may collect some firewood. As Weiner has pointed out for the Foi of Papua New Guinea, such journeying is "never a matter of merely getting from one point to another" and often entails "casual, 'productive' acts" (2001, 17). People walk very close to those in front of them, and if a person trips or stumbles, others will immediately mutter *di'a di'a,* or "be safe." Despite this concern, the sight of a person falling over, even a pregnant woman, is usually met with laughter, as walking safely and sure-footedly is to some extent the mark of a "mountain person" (*ata poso*).[7] Certain sections of the path have a tendency to become extremely slippery, and when they do, or when it begins to rain, people will often take off their flip-flops, the better to grip the ground with their toes. Rain is one of the enduring problems of walking in the mountains, and during a prolonged shower people may look up to the sky and call out, "That's enough, earth." Once, when I was walking to the lowlands in the rain with a group of women, the rain clouds appeared to be beginning to lift, leading one of my companions to say, "That's right, earth, make it a little brighter, please!"

One of the key ways to prepare for a journey between highlands and lowlands, or travel farther afield, is to eat a full meal of rice. People worry a great deal about growing hungry while walking and never set off on a journey with an empty stomach or having had only a snack. Another way in which people prepare for walking is to change out of the sarongs they wear in daily life into smarter T-shirts and trousers, shorts, or a skirt. Indeed, in many respects, they dress up for travelling. When mothers of babies are called to the immunization clinic in the lowlands they all set off together, wearing blouses and skirts and carrying umbrellas, their babies cradled on their backs. During my fieldwork, Nina became (in her own words) my "walking friend" and would try to accompany me on my movements between highlands and lowlands. Over the months that I journeyed with her, I noticed that she kept certain possessions in one site rather than the other. In Wae Rebo, where she was mainly based, she kept older clothes for work in the fields, as well as her everyday sarongs and her clothes for walking. On the other hand, in Kombo she kept her smarter clothes and sarongs, including matching nylon tops and skirts for attending church, plus old photographs of her family. When we arrived in Kombo, and after a meal and a rest, she would often open up her wooden chest by our bed and bring out these smart clothes, carefully unfolding them, before replacing them in her chest. Thus, part of the normalization of the differences between Wae Rebo and Kombo is a somewhat differentiated material culture, with objects associated with church going and travel being stored in Kombo.

The complex and potent spiritual landscape with which people engage in agricultural practices (including rituals) is also encountered in travelling practices. For example, when stopping for a rest, one should always sit up on a bank or a tree root, to keep the path clear for passing spirits. There are also bridges, or paths over water, where a person should present a speech-offering to spirits in order to pass. If a smell of perfume or cigarette smoke is unexpectedly encountered along the way, this is always interpreted as evidence of travelling spirits. The fear of encountering such spirits is one of the reasons why, however well they know the path, people rarely travel alone. One elderly woman described how her son had once been frightened by spirits when walking in the forest. Anxious to delineate a separation between his travel and that of spirits, he addressed them directly with the words: "You who are going to Wae Rebo, this is your path below; you who are going seaward to Kombo, this is your path; and you who are going to the west, this is your path." Later, this unsettling encounter was interpreted as a "sign" (*alamat*) of his father's impending death.

In the previous chapter, we saw how, because Wae Rebo-Kombo people do not "own" the land in Kombo in a full, ritual sense, after a person dies and is buried in Kombo, some of the soil from the grave should always be taken to Wae Rebo. The return journey to Wae Rebo after such a death is rather solemn and processional. The family members are in many ways accompanying the soul of the deceased back to the mountains and, though they may rest by the side of the path, should not visit any other houses or villages along the way. In 1997, a very elderly man called Amé Beda died in Kombo after a long illness. Following his burial in Kombo, a large party composed of his sons, some of his brothers, their wives, children, and grandchildren walked from the lowlands to Wae Rebo. As we entered the highland village, it seemed unusually empty, and no one called out to us in greeting. Coming down the hill towards the village yard, a sound of wailing and sobbing rose from the drum house, where most villagers had gathered. The journey between Kombo and Wae Rebo, and the final arrival in either site, is therefore experienced quite differently depending on the context of travel. Moreover, as dirt from graves in Wae Rebo would never be taken to Kombo, this example again highlights how different kinds of journeys continually constitute the highland and lowland sites as different kinds of places.

Despite the common ways in which people travel between highlands and lowlands, not all people undertake this journey with the same regularity. Schoolchildren who live in Kombo during the week, depending on the weather, will walk up to Wae Rebo most Saturday afternoons in small, lively groups. They return the next afternoon, sometimes begrudgingly, accompanied by those heading down to the Monday coastal market. Men are more likely to take down goods such as coffee beans or oranges to sell in the market, though younger women sometimes go to buy cotton or to sell woven sarongs. Indeed, in general, married and older women travel far less regularly than unmarried or younger women, who in turn may not always be such frequent travellers as young and middle-aged men. Some men who pursue agricultural tasks in both villages are spoken of as "really swinging" between the sites, as are younger, unmarried women who spend equal amounts of time with, for example, their parents in the highlands and a brother and his children in the lowlands. Giving attention to the regularity of travel thus reveals how a "two-placed village" is maintained both by those who "swing" each week between the sites and by those who tend to remain fairly permanently in only one place.

ROADS AND TRUCKS

The argument that mobility and movement are central to the landscape as an ongoing, social process was central to the concerns of one of the pioneers of landscape studies, the American author J. B. Jackson. In a series of writings from the 1950s onward, Jackson analyzed the everyday significance of what he called America's "vernacular landscape." In particular, he focused on the significance to this landscape of roads, arguing that, for Americans, roads did not merely lead to places but were places *in themselves* (1997, 249–254). So, although roads served pragmatic purposes, Jackson also called attention to the ways in which they could stand for an "intense experience" of new relationships, new beginnings, or even freedom.

Certainly, if Wae Rebo is thought by many to be a more dense spiritual and ritual place than Kombo, then the latter's advantage over, and main source of difference from, the former is its road. This stone road, which starts at Dintor on the coast and reaches as far as the church at Denge, was gradually constructed by local labor, though it has never been of the same quality as the road from Todo to Dintor, which was constructed in a low-cost, Swiss-funded development project (see Beusch et al. 1997). Nevertheless, despite its potholes and boulders, both trucks and four-wheel-drive vehicles were able to travel along the Kombo road, and many Kombo residents describe how, when they are in Wae Rebo, they miss the sight of these movements. By contrast, many Wae Rebo residents are obsessed with the "problem" of how a road to the mountains could ever be built to help people travel more easily, and particularly to facilitate the transportation of the coffee crop to the town of Ruteng. One young man stated this succinctly, contrasting Kombo's road with Wae Rebo's many cash crops: "The problem with Wae Rebo is that it doesn't have a road; the problem with Kombo is that it doesn't have an economy." His friend added that "the only road you'll see in Wae Rebo is in a dream!" Over the years that I have been visiting Wae Rebo, the village has continually improved its path to the lowlands, gradually making it wider and routing it away from very steep sections that previously required one to climb by grabbing for roots with one's hands. However, as one of the attractions of Wae Rebo for tourists is presumed to be sporty "hiking," villagers have gradually realized that the local government is unlikely to pay for the construction of a road to the mountain village.

As road-building projects draw more asphalted lines across the earth, anthropologists are gradually turning their attention to the significance of roads and the vehicles that travel along them (Miller 2001; Colombijn 2002; O'Hanlon and Frankland 2003). Roads have been analyzed as a destructive influence (Fairhead 1992), as ambiguous technologies of control enabling the neoliberal economy (Wilson 2004), and as material entities that manifest both the presence and the absence of state power (Harvey 2005). In southern Manggarai, road building so far seems to have had a universally positive reception and has genuinely expanded people's worlds. The building of the stone road through Kombo in the 1990s enabled people to take coffee and other cash crops to town markets and stores, and has brought traders to the local market seeking good-quality sarongs or particular fruits or vegetables. Roads have also revitalized kinship connections with villages farther afield, allowing groups of people—particularly those who might not be strong enough to walk—to travel in trucks to attend alliance events. On several occasions, people have been able to commandeer trucks to drive very sick people, including women enduring difficult labors, to the hospital in town. Roads are also connected with mobility in less obvious ways, since road-building programs elsewhere in the region have been one of the main

FIGURE 6.1   Boys walking down the lowland road to school

"projects" (*proyék*) for which rural, male labor has been recruited. Far from complaining about the building of the stone road, most people say that its trucks make life more "lively."

Whereas life in Wae Rebo is often centered on the drum house, life in Kombo is centered on movements up and down the road. As most lowland houses are built on either side of the road, people enjoy watching others walking down to their rice fields near the coast or taking a buffalo to a new grazing spot. Children walk to school together early in the morning in large, usually single-sex groups, singing and joking, pointing out objects and animals. The middle-aged couple who lived in the house where I stayed in Kombo would often sit in the room at the front, looking out through their door, calling out to people as they walked down the road, and explaining to me any kinship or marriage connections with these travellers. Thus, the permeable houses that are a feature of Manggarai villages make it easy to observe the traffic of people, animals, and trucks along the road.

At least twice a day, a wooden truck passes through Kombo, and people will rush to see if they recognize any of its passengers. Young boys, in particular, love to guess which truck is approaching by the sound of its engine and music, and gather round to watch when anyone gets off, or when the driver calls to his young male helpers (*konjak*). When I asked various schoolchildren to draw pictures of Wae Rebo and Kombo, most boys drew a colorful truck on their picture of the lowland site. The drivers of these trucks, with their clove cigarettes and cassettes of Indonesian pop music, are romantic figures both to young boys and to young women of marriageable age. Trucks are often hired wholesale by people going to attend alliance rituals in other villages. Once, I sat with others in a lowland house listening to the gradual approach of such a truck on its way to a wedding in the east. The truck's roof was covered with jubilant young men holding a loudspeaker from which blasted taped Manggarai music. Whether the sound that moves through the landscape is such taped music or the crying of the bride, Manggarai marriage paths are therefore frequently *audible* paths.

Although the journey between Wae Rebo and Kombo, and those to many destinations to the west, is still undertaken on foot, people's "muscular consciousness" (Bachelard 1964, 11) of roads and paths through the landscape is also developed as they attempt to sit on wooden benches in trucks. When people recounted journeys to attend marriage rituals in far-off villages, they often dwelt on the length of time they were in the truck, or on the way in which a particular person couldn't endure the journey and kept being sick. Trucks going up to the town of Ruteng sometimes left Kombo as early as three or four o'clock in the morning. Nevertheless, before they left travellers would still be cooked a full rice meal by their relatives, then woken up and told to "eat until you are full." Inside trucks, seats on the wooden bench are given to women and older men, while younger men may have to hang off the sides or sit on the roof. Passengers are forced to put their feet up on sacks of candlenut or to endure the smell of dried fish being taken up to the market in town. As they travel along, people enjoy commenting on the condition of wet-rice fields or pointing out temporary awnings near to houses, evidence of large-scale "lively" events. Along the road, people may come out of houses to hand a letter to the driver, asking him to deliver it to another village or school. If people spot someone they know inside a truck, they excitedly call out "Where are you going?"

In September 2008, when I paid a brief visit to Wae Rebo-Kombo, the lowland road, for so long a bumpy stone track, was in the final stages of being asphalted. A couple of enterprising men from other villages had bought motorbikes and were charging to taxi people down to the market and rice fields and then back home with their produce. These motorbikes seemed to be changing people's relationship with the road. Previously, the road had been a place where children might play, as trucks could be heard slowly approaching long before they arrived in Kombo. Now, though, people fear for children's safety, because motorbikes travel far more quickly, and with less warning, along the road through the village. It seems likely that in the future, positive appreciation of the road's benefits may be tempered by fears of its dangers.

ANCESTRAL JOURNEYS

In addition to everyday travelling practices on foot or in trucks, narratives of ancestral journeys are also central to constituting the landscape as one of paths and mobility. The contemporary roles of roads and trucks should not tempt us towards the erroneous conclusion that mobility is a "modern" phenomenon. Rather, as in other contexts that emphasize ancestral journeys, the historical landscape can be described as "a network of places joined by various ancestral routes" (Munn 1970, 14), in which unusual topographical features provide evidence of past ancestral and spirit activity. Like many Manggarai narratives recounting the "origins" of a village, the story that describes the founding of Wae Rebo is one of ancestral movements from place to place. I recorded broadly similar versions of this story from both the ritual and the political leaders of the community, in addition to hearing versions from other villagers. The story tells of how the original ancestors first arrived in Manggarai from Minangkabau in Sumatra.[8] They moved from village to village, establishing a founding stone in one, a banyan tree in another, and escaping political intrigue, warfare, and ill health before eventually settling in Wae Rebo. This story is a narrative of a long, episodic journey from a place of warfare to an eventual place of safety. For example, after describing how the ancestors had to leave one site in the middle of the night because it was under siege, Amé Dorus' history continued as follows:

> That night, the ancestors slept on a mountainside and stayed there while they discussed which path to follow. Then they headed west, arriving in Wae Ntawang, sleeping in the forest and going from Wae Bangka to Besi to Deket to Perang. And then they arrived in Liho (Wontong), where they stopped safely for a time. They made shelters to live in, and discussed having a *lodok* [ritual center] for a field, and made a big house. Empo Maro was born in Liho, where the Wae Rebo ancestors lived for a long time.

Here, the names of sites that the ancestors travelled through, or where they "stopped safely for a time," are given particular prominence. Indeed, during my first weeks of fieldwork, I was given a shortened version of this history consisting of simply a list of place-names. Both this summarized version and the longer historical narratives that I recorded can be seen as examples of what James Fox has called a *topogeny,* an "ordered succession of place names" (1997b, 91; cf. Traube 1986, 30). Fox sees topogenies as "mnemonic devices," prominent means for ordering and transmitting knowledge among Austronesian populations and directly compares the recitation of a topogeny with the recitation of a genealogy. Significantly, Fox argues that in eastern Indonesia topogenies generally assume the form of a journey, whether of an ancestor, an origin group, or an object. He stresses that, while genealogy functions to establish succession in time, topogeny functions to establish succession in space (ibid., 101).

Topogeny is a particularly apt historical form for southern Manggarai, where there is very little interest in lengthy or elaborate genealogies and there is no clear boundary between ancestors and other spirits sometimes described as "ancestors of the land." It is noteworthy that in the narrative of the history of Wae Rebo, individual sites are named even if they were only passed through, whereas the ancestors are spoken of in mostly general terms, with the naming of only Empo Maro, from whom all Wae Rebo-Kombo people claim to be descended. This practice allows for an undifferentiated, collective group of ancestors connected with Wae Rebo as a named place. In addition, this lack of differentiation resonates with the relative lack of hierarchy in Manggarai as compared with other areas of eastern Indonesia that distinguish between nobles, commoners, and the descendants of slaves (Traube 1986; McKinnon 1991; Keane 1997).

While Fox sees topogenies as establishing succession in "space," I prefer to see the performance of topogenies as a practice constituting a temporal, processional landscape formed of both places *and* journeys. Moreover, the calling of place-names in the performance of a topogeny is significant because, as we have already seen, pronouncing such names can be a powerful activity. In recounting their history as an ancestral journey from place to place spurred on by fights between brothers and the actions of animals, Wae Rebo-Kombo people create a sense of a distinctive moral and historical landscape that can be continually reimagined and revisited (cf. Basso 1996). Moreover, there is a kind of mutual feedback between topogenies as mnemonic devices and the "mnemonic pegs" of landscape features (ibid., 62; cf. Rosaldo 1980, 55–56). In southern Manggarai, travelling past such features can lead to the telling of narratives. In turn, narratives can lead to the memory of specific landscape features, as when the story of a female ancestor who planted a banyan tree in Modo to tie her pigs to recalls the still-standing tree in that village.

MAKING JOURNEYS SAFE

These notions of origin, and of the morality of remembering a landscape of historical connections, inform an important set of practices concerned with making less ordinary journeys safe. As we have seen, Wae Rebo-Kombo people spend much of their lives walking between highlands and lowlands, and while this journeying involves the hazards of hunger or meeting with a spirit, in general (and largely because the path itself is full of familiar, named places) it does not involve any significant physical or spiritual dangers. Similarly, a journey by truck to sell coffee in Ruteng is fraught only with economic and practical dilemmas. By contrast, other kinds of journeys—particularly those connected with new marriage paths and with migration for work or study—are considered more hazardous. As such, these journeys need to be made safe by being "rooted" in a place of origin.

"Rooting" is an extremely profound notion in Manggarai. Though it is clearly connected with the kinds of botanical kinship idioms common in eastern Indonesia (Fox 1971), I want to stress both its *specificity* (and not simply its connection with images of branching or tips and trunks) as well as its role in constituting the historical landscape. Rooting rituals, like topogeny, are concerned with origins in place and time. Rooting stresses where you come from, in order that you may travel safely and productively. Rooting can therefore be seen as continuous with other practices, such as the return to origin rooms for "praising" rituals, or the ways in which people claim a number of different dwellings as their "own house." Rooting procedures normally involve the sacrifice of a chicken and a large, communal meal. Such events may be held in a person's natal home, but often involve travelling back to the village or house of a family's origin source of brides, or "mother-father." Thus, before Teres left Wae Rebo to attend university, a rooting ritual was held in her mother's natal village of Kakor. It was felt that Teres' journey away from Manggarai in search of education should start in the place that was the source of her mother, and therefore of herself. Similarly, Amé Gaba's sister's son made a point of visiting Amé Gaba, who had also partly funded his education, to informally "root" his final journey to Kupang for graduation.

Failing to properly "root" an important journey in this way jeopardizes its chances of success. Whether or not a person succeeds in education or gains a job can be influenced by rooting; for instance, one elderly woman stressed to me that all those Wae Rebo people who had high-status jobs outside Flores had been "rooted by a white chicken." Failure to hold a correct "rooting" event also makes people susceptible to a deadly sickness known as *itang* (which can also be caused by reversing marriage connections or breaking taboos). For example, the death of one new bride was thought to be due to a failure to "root" her marriage journey with her groom's family's original "mother-father." It is the retelling and remembering of such connections that make marital and other journeys safe, and I was continually told that for a person to "just go" on an important journey would be extremely unsatisfactory. Even for shorter journeys, some form of formal leave-taking—a shared meal, a short speech—is required, as seen in Tanta Tin's description of how she is only happy about the travels of her nephew Maka if he first "takes his leave from me."

The acknowledgment of origins and of historical links between specific places is also seen in a common practice when passing through or entering other Manggarai villages. As a village is approached, a member of a travelling party will always take care to stop and "offer a betel quid" to the ancestors of that place, placing it on a rock and saying: "Oh aunt, don't call out in surprise! Don't stroke us! Just look at us." This reflects widespread understandings that, when a person enters an ancestral domain, certain ancestors (an aunt in this case) may be delighted to see their living relatives and may stroke and caress them. However, as the ancestors are "people on the other side," their salutations and caresses can make the living, particularly children, unwell. The gift of a betel quid acknowledges both the ancestors' connection with a place and their desire to show affection to descendants, but is in essence a request for distance from the living. Like a "rooting" ritual, giving betel to ancestors encountered in this manner in the course of a journey materially constitutes the landscape as one of historical connections, but also, like other ritual actions, acknowledges the landscape's hidden interlocutors.

These examples all show the analytical problem in assuming, as do anthropologists who follow Deleuze and Guattari (1987), that an interest in "roots" reflects merely the genealogical or hierarchical obsessions of Western thought. Wae Rebo-Kombo people are themselves interested in roots and worried by the consequences of failing to acknowledge, for example, the significance of "source" villages. However, the Manggarai concern with rooting only makes sense in the context of a landscape of *movement*. Rooting is what makes travel possible and, more important, safe. It is worth recalling that the phrase used to describe such events is *wu'at wa'i,* or "rooting the feet." Such a root is therefore always the beginning of a line of movement. It is rooting that makes growth away from origins possible, ensuring that a person may both *travel* freely and *return* safely.

In addition to "rooting" procedures, a parent or elder may try to ensure the spiritual protection of both travelling people and goods through a range of measures, including prayers, spells, special medicines, and charms. One prayer, spoken to a younger person to secure safe travel, follows ritual speech in its use of paired phrases. These list the dangers the speaker hopes the traveller will circumvent—practical dangers that also symbolize spiritual hazards:

> Oh child, walk carefully.
> Don't be embraced by clouds.
> Don't be met by the sun.
> Don't have a slippery path.
> Don't let any wood fall.
> I'll meet you when you return again, child.

A similar prayer may be said before a *padong,* the accompanied journey made by a newly married couple. Moreover, both bride and groom may be given a range of protective medicines to ensure their safe passage through marriage rituals and journeys.

In general, people can be rather nervous about visits to affinal villages. Away from the protective land and ancestors of home, they fear that they and their possessions will be vulnerable to jealous witchcraft attacks. For example, before I travelled with Nina to a church wedding in Rotok, a village to the east, she insisted that I visit her father, Amé Tranus, for protective medicine. He gave me a piece of dried coconut, as well as protecting my camera against a possible witchcraft attack. Before setting out with Nina, I followed her example by chewing some of this coconut, spitting out the juice into my palms, then touching a little of it on my chest, the base of my throat, and the back of my neck. Although not a baptized Catholic, Amé Tranus said that this had a similar effect to making the sign of the cross. Indeed, protective measures for journeys employ kinds of syncretic language and practices that are not seen in other areas of life: one man told me that "rooting" rituals were held "so that God's thoughts walk together with us." Amé Tranus also blew a prayer into a handkerchief, which I was told to carry with me at all times, particularly when sleeping.

Mary Helms has shown how for a wide range of societies geographical distance is frequently thought to correspond with "supernatural" distance, such that as one moves away geographically from a social center, one moves towards places and people that are increasingly "different," and therefore regarded as increasingly mythical and powerful (1988, 4).[9] One of the main reasons why Helms considers contact with a geographically distant "unknown" comparable to contact with distant spirit levels is because of the "ritual procedures and protection" that may be adopted by "travellers or resource seekers" (1988, 30). Certainly, in southern Manggarai, the kinds of procedures often undergone before a journey away from regular places and pathways are extremely similar to the "medicine" given to pregnant women who might encounter ancestral spirits, or others considered to be in danger of spiritual attack. Moreover, rooting a person in an origin place shares certain similarities with rituals to "collect up the soul" of a person who has been unwell, emphasizing the connection with his/her household room. Nevertheless, despite attempts to make journeys safe, throughout my fieldwork I was aware of rumors and stories that revolved around the unknown dangers of travel, such as a 2001 rumor that a certain "medicine" had been buried next to the path leading down to Kombo and would negatively influence the fate of anyone who touched or went near it. In addition, travel is sometimes thought to be dangerous for rather different reasons, as, for example, when those whom people leave behind may think about or miss them too much, causing them to become unwell. This explains why those travelling faraway are advised to "think only about your journey," and why those left behind take great pains to know the exact date of a traveller's scheduled arrival (after which it is safer to think of them).

Because for most people journeying is full of spiritual dangers, those men with the ability to travel freely in other villages are often thought to be powerful "people with magic." When I first knew him, Fabianus was an imposing man in his forties, the father of six children, an important healer, and a very successful coffee farmer. However, a gap of ten years between his second and third oldest children indicated his rather unusual life history. Between 1980 and 1990, Fabianus left Wae Rebo and his family to travel throughout Manggarai. In our conversations, Fabianus was intriguingly vague about how he had spent these years of travel, stating philosophically that he went to "search for the best way of making a living" and to "gain experience." Moreover, he indicated that this travel was motivated by some kind of command from a guardian spirit or angel, and that he was also looking for healing spells and medicine. It was when he found this, or rather when it was "just given," that he returned to his family in Wae Rebo. This secretive "prayer just of my very own" is now the central element in Fabianus' healing, which is acknowledged by all in the village as highly efficacious, the product of his powerful ability to travel safely through the lands of strangers.

Fabianus' story of his travels through the Manggarai landscape can be read as an individual claim to power and knowledge that obscures as much as it reveals. When I asked him why he never came back to Wae Rebo during his travels, he simply said, "I just didn't." When I asked him if he forgot his family, he said, "My schedule wasn't finished." Fabianus' vague account of his travels is well known in the village, and he himself asserts that his healing powers protect him from harm, because "God doesn't agree with me dying." He stresses that his house, up high in the steep fields above Wae Rebo, is associated with his magic and his protective "angel":

> This place here, that's why I made a house here, never mind if there's a steep ravine above, if I'm here then rocks will not fall. [*He describes how in the past a rock fell from the mountainside and should "really" have hit him.*] But no, never mind, I'm still on this earth, God forbade the rock to fall here, it was a rock this big! It just stopped here on this hill. So, if I travel, I'm not scared, I don't have fear.

Fabianus' travels seem to confirm the second part of Mary Helms' thesis that (since the foreign is equated with a powerful "supernatural" realm) those who travel to geographically distant places "may be accorded an aura of prestige and awe approaching the same order, if not always the same magnitude, as that accorded political-religious specialists or elites in general" (1988, 4). However, recent patterns of migration by young people away from Manggarai introduce more complexity to this picture. As I shall now describe, those who go to university or school, or to work on distant building sites, acquire, not spiritual prowess, but access to new experiences, money, prestige, and other forms of identity.

MIGRATION STORIES

Since Indonesia's economic and political crises of the late 1990s, which led to a rapid fall in value of the rupiah, an increasing number of Indonesians—many of them undocumented—have migrated to work in other countries, particularly Malaysia (Hugo 2008, 60–68). Towards the end of my first period of fieldwork, in 1999, people were increasingly talking about and dealing with the migration of young men from Manggarai to Malaysia. When I next returned to the region in 2001, I heard more stories of migration and met with several men who had returned, either temporarily or permanently, from such travels. One was Stefan, the husband of a Wae Rebo woman living in a village to the west.

Stefan left for Malaysia in the year 2000, shortly after the birth of his son. He worked as a legal migrant on a tea plantation and regularly sent money back to his family in Manggarai. In a letter to his father-in-law in Wae Rebo, he asked him not to be angry about his travels, but stressed that he wanted to earn enough to build a house and pay for his children's future education. Stefan also sent me a letter from Malaysia that was full of precise details about his journey, including the date he had left, his time of arrival at key ports, and the number of nights he had spent in various places along the way. This letter was particularly intriguing to me, as I myself was always being asked to provide such details about my own journeys to and from Flores. Stefan's wife had had a difficult time during the early years of her marriage, falling out with her mother-in-law, becoming ill, and losing her first daughter when the child was only eight months' old. At first she seemed cynical about Stefan's migration, viewing it as another hardship she had to endure. However, Stefan was true to his word. He spent only two years in Malaysia, saved up considerable sums of money, and on his return built a large house for his family. Stefan harbors no desire to return to Malaysia, and now his wife seems less fatalistic and more contented.

If Stefan's story is a success, other migration tales reveal a more ambivalent attitude towards Malaysia, characterized by those left behind as "the outside place where there is apparently lots of money." Many Manggarai men do not realize until they get to Malaysia that they do not have complete papers and thus must work illegally, living in camps subject to sudden police raids. They may work on dangerous building sites and often encounter problems both in receiving wages and in sending remittances home. One afternoon in Kombo in 2001, there was great excitement as a truck stopped in the village to set down Mius, an unmarried man who had been working in Malaysia for a year. As he sat in the house of his married sister, people arrived to welcome him back, and a crowd of young boys gathered near him, admiring the material signs (watch, baseball cap, shoes) of his foreign adventures. Mius described working on building sites in Malaysia while living in a camp "in the forest." He said that he had never slept well in this camp, partly because of fear of police raids, and partly because conditions were crowded and noisy. He described frequent fights between men from Flores and those from Madura and Java. Indeed, such conflicts seem to be a key factor that militated against the cultivation of a pan-"Indonesian" identity during such migrations. To the head shaking of other villagers, Mius described how he had seen men killed by falling from buildings, and how the corpse of a man who was murdered by another was just left in the forest and not given any mortuary rites.

Johan Lindquist has recently described how becoming a migrant in Indonesia "appears to offer a route from the village into the economy of development and particular forms of modernity" (2009, 11). Yet, in his study of Batam, Lindquist notes how, upon arrival, many migrants experience the shock of finding that their places of work and housing are not the middle-class, "advanced" scenarios they had expected. Instead, migrants find themselves in "wild" (*liar*) places associated with a kind of "wild" sociality (ibid., 12–13). This "shock" is similar to that recounted to me by several Manggarai men who have worked as undocumented migrants. Though they may manage to save up large sums of money, in their daily lives as migrants they are forced to live an uncertain, precarious existence "in the forest." When they return, their stories feed into rumors that circulate regarding the dangers of working in Malaysia. One woman told me that one boss offered to pay men five million rupiah each if they lived in a particular house. However, she said, inside the house was a hungry python; the boss would lock the men inside the house, and in the morning only their shoes and clothes would be left. These kinds of rumors of exploitation and predation produce much anxiety among the families of men who have gone to work in other countries or on other Indonesian islands and have not been heard from for many years. These fears also reinforce people's conviction that those who travel to "outside" lands need to be protected spiritually, both through being "rooted" in places of origin and through charms and other protective measures.

Most migration to work outside Flores is undertaken by men, following a common Southeast Asian pattern of male travel to outside realms (Rosaldo 1980, 192; van Reenen 1996, 116; Tsing 1993, 127–128). However, a handful of young women have also migrated to work elsewhere in Manggarai or Indonesia. Some join weaving cooperatives, some go to study and work as teachers, but most look after the children of relatives or work in shops. For example, Eta once worked in a Chinese-Indonesian family's shop in the coastal town of Labuanbajo. She became friends with the owner's daughter and followed her to Surabaya when the daughter went there to study. In Surabaya, she worked in a pharmacy, though she said she spent much of her income on renting a room. When she heard that her father was ill in Kombo she returned to Manggarai and shortly afterwards married her cross-cousin, retaining no further desire to travel beyond the local area. Eta, Stefan, and Mius all demonstrate a pattern of "temporary travel" to seek work beyond Flores. This can be compared with other studies noting that a smaller proportion of the population of East Nusa Tenggara migrates permanently relative to other Indonesian provinces (Williams 2007, 17).

Although it is not always considered "migration" in the literature, children in this context also undertake many journeys to attend school or to live with other relatives. If a person works elsewhere in Flores as a teacher or state official, it is normal for their kin in Wae Rebo-Kombo to send at least one of their children to live with them. These children make a house more "lively" and help out with domestic tasks while enjoying the perceived advantages of a middle-class lifestyle. I know of several children who, at the age of seven, went to start school and live with such relatives. Because of the cost and practicalities of return visits, these children often do not come back to Wae Rebo, or even see their parents, for many years. Their departure is particularly poignant, and it is usually their fathers who go to visit them, taking special foodstuffs such as sun-dried bananas, sweet potatoes, or oranges. One boy, Aben, moved when he was seven to live with his father's brother, a teacher in the west, and did not return to Wae Rebo for nine years. Though an absent member of the Wae Rebo-Kombo community, he is also considered to have taken on some of the identity of the place where he lives, as he now speaks a slightly different Manggarai dialect.

Another form of child migration are the journeys undertaken by older children to attend middle and high school. Though there are two primary schools in the lowlands, the nearest middle schools are several hours' truck drive away from Kombo, in Todo or Iteng. Children who are able to continue with their education beyond primary school must live either with relatives in towns or larger villages, or stay in one of the many boardinghouses (*asrama*). Such children's return journeys to school are dominated by the need to prepare enough rice to last until their next visit home. Parents may also take rice to their children themselves and continually worry about what kind of vegetables these schoolchildren are eating, so far from their family's fields. At times of school holidays, Kombo and Wae Rebo become particularly lively, as these children return to their villages, bringing with them sweets for younger siblings, stories for parents, and, inevitably, small objects of town life (a rucksack, a lipstick, a poster) for themselves.

The phenomenal differences between village places (associated with the forest) and school places (associated with the town) that are established during childhood remain salient for Manggarai adults and are reflected in the lyrics of a popular song. In these, a village girl yearns for her friends who have gone to high school "up in town" where their sandals "flip on their feet." She imagines she hears the noise of a "rolling truck" and of a "clock striking," but these sounds are in fact the movement of a boulder and the noise of a monkey, "west inside the forest." This song reminds us that different kinds of movement (and their attendant sounds) are associated with different kinds of power and status. Noises of boulders rolling, or monkeys moving through the forest, bring home to this girl the fact that she has remained behind in the village, away from the trucks, clocks, and flipping sandals of her friends at school in town.

LANDSCAPES OF MOVEMENT

This chapter has described some of the travelling practices and stories that constitute the Manggarai landscape as a dynamic network of places and pathways. Focusing on ancestral, personal, and everyday mobility allows us to see that pathways and journeys are as significant to bodies and selves as place. Moreover, as we saw with regard to the movements in and out of a house, trails and travel are a fundamental aspect of place making. Despite the local state's focus on the preserved "authenticity" of the highland village of Wae Rebo, the Manggarai landscape is not static. It shifts and changes with time, even as it did in the times of the ancestors. Of course, part of this shifting and changing is caused, not by the journeys of humans, but by the weather—winds that come from particular directions and blow through the permeable house, storms that cause houses to collapse, and the rain that changes the texture and safety of mountain paths. It is no surprise that anti-rain magic is, as we saw in Chapter 4, included in the gamut of Manggarai agricultural practices.

Partial resettlement has led to new forms of productive travel, as people exploit different economic strategies in highlands and lowlands. However, beyond the daily movements of a travelling village, people have a range of perspectives on the desirability of travel, whatever rewards it may bring, and on the spiritual dangers that travel involves. Many young men I know have very little interest in travelling far and are happy to confine their movements to the path between Wae Rebo and Kombo or the local marriage paths of friends and relatives. Nevertheless, migration by men to Malaysia, or by schoolchildren to other places in Flores, does highlight the ways in which paths of travel are differentiated by age and gender. The young travel more than the old, and men tend to travel more than women. Indeed, mothers who remain behind when their sons set off on marriage journeys to their bride's village are often described as the "roots" of those who travel. Thus, outsider women who create or follow paths of connection become, as they age, more associated with and attached to place (particularly to the fires of the hearth), allowing their children to follow their own paths.

Although much of the recent anthropological emphasis on travel and mobility has come from research on migration, displacement, and transnational communities, this study shows how travel can be an essential part of everyday life even in a remote Indonesian village where people are preoccupied with links to the land and "rooting" in place. For Wae Rebo-Kombo people, being a two-placed village means being a village on the move. Indeed, the very greetings of everyday life, and the direction terms they involve, emphasize the importance of acknowledging the movements of others. However, as noted, these movements cannot be separated from or opposed to the concern with creating links between places and people. Indeed, the named land continues to be imagined as an important agent in ensuring the health and productivity of people's lives. Contrary to the predictions of Gupta and Ferguson, in this case, the expanding mobility of people has led neither to a "profound sense of loss of territorial roots" nor to an "erosion of the cultural distinctiveness of places" (1992, 9).

Rather than assuming that travel and movement create a problem for the making of place and culture, perhaps in this context it makes more sense to take mobility in its many forms as a *given*. The issue then becomes one of how to create moments of stillness in the midst of flow. Throughout this book, we have seen how ritual plays an important role in creating such moments, through the (temporary) creation of centers, and through the retracing of paths and connections *back* to a place of origin. Perhaps the most striking image of stillness or shelter in the midst of flow is the umbrella held over a new bride during both her *padong* journey and the "accompanying" rituals. The sense of creating place and relationships out of movement is also seen in ritual phrases spoken at marriage, which evoke an image of house doors moving across the landscape. In considering both family and village growth, we saw how "praising" rituals reconstruct the temporary unity of those originating in a room, following a necessary process of dispersal. Similarly, communal sacrifices at the new-year ritual of *penti* are followed by movements away from the drum house, reconstructing moves to other houses. Such rituals reconstitute not only *place* but also groups with a shared origin. This dynamic of centering and dispersing is also seen in house hospitality that emphasizes the role of the house as a *center*, despite the permeability and mobility of personnel that define it. Significantly, when movements threaten to cause harm, the solution may often be to ritually "stop" or "impede" (*kepet*) such mobility. This was seen in a ritual for a disgraced ancestor held *outside* a house, as well as in agricultural rituals that attempt to temporarily block the pathways of spirits through fields.

A landscape of movement is not simply one where migrants travel to towns or to faraway cities. It is one where rivers carry the fertility of highland ancestors, where a father follows his daughter's marriage path to mourn his deceased grandchild, and where ancestral journeys continue to have implications for relations between villages. Journeys and paths are always connected with place. Thus, at the *end* of a bride's *padong* journey, she is incorporated into a new room. Similarly, before the *start* of a significant journey to seek work or education, a person must be rooted in a place of origin. Such journeys and paths may be commonplace—a walk back to the lowlands in time for school on Monday morning, a trip to the highlands to help with coffee harvesting, a journey by truck to take rice to absent children. Yet journeys and paths may also evoke tears and strong emotions—a bride crying as she leaves on her *padong*, a daughter weeping as she arrives for the final death ritual of her deceased father, a group of relatives listening to the sound of wailing as they bring the soul of a deceased man back to the drum house.

Conclusion

In 1998, in the dying days of Indonesia's New Order regime, the inhabitants of Wae Rebo began the long process of rebuilding their communal drum house with a ritual in which a line of elders faced a chain saw placed at the base of a central house-post. The chain saw belonged to a man employed by the rebuilding project's official coordinators to cut some of the major timbers for the new building. The purpose of the ritual, pragmatically named "sharpening the machete and the axe," was ostensibly to request permission to fell timbers in the forest from its spirits, or "those who are the owners of the trees." In addition, as a chain saw had never been used in the forests of this area before, it was imperative that the machine should be properly introduced to forest and the ancestral spirits, lest they should take fright or offence at its noise and appearance. After the ritual sacrifice, a large crowd of men set out immediately for the forests southwest of the village. Upon arrival at a specific clearing, the ritual speaker insisted that he and the other elders, cradling chickens to be sacrificed, should face in the direction of the village, and that the path be kept clear for any travelling spirits. In his speech, he asked the spirits to "give a little extra energy to those of us working here," and described the chain saw as a "new machete."

Over the following months, through wind and rain, the timber for the new house was gradually felled, and preparations could finally be made for one of the central events of the rebuilding: the carrying into Wae Rebo of the key house-posts and central ridgepole. On the day of this event, most of the village men set off early for the forest, where the timbers were temporarily stored. In the rectangular drum house, which had yet to be dismantled, several old men gathered to chew betel together before helping to prepare the village center for the arrival of the posts. Two old men, dressed smartly in dark sarongs, went out onto the stone *liké* platform immediately in front of the drum house. Here, one of them banged a gong, while the other played a *tambor* drum with sticks, looking up and out towards the surrounding hill-sides, hoping to awaken ancestral spirits. As five women finished their preparations, dressing in ritual costume, one of the older men came into the drum house: "Hurry up a little," he said, "they are nearly here." The women processed out across the village yard, followed by a young man, Sil, rhythmically banging a gong. Others, staying behind in the drum house, quickly began to beat the hand-drums (*tembong*), just as they do when people go to greet a new bride arriving in the village. Afterwards, a number of people remarked, "It really was like a normal bride-greeting."

The procession of women took a path leading down the hill towards a stream. As they arrived, younger men were frantically clearing undergrowth and obstacles from the paths. Then, suddenly, we saw the men coming up the hill, carrying the ridgepole and other posts, supporting poles across their shoulders, and sweating with the exertion. Leading the way were several older men singing out phrases that other men answered. After the ridgepole and main house-post had crossed the stream, one of the women, Iné Kata, went forward and formally greeted the men. Placing her hands on the end of the

FIGURE C.1   Carrying in the ridgepole of the new drum house

ridgepole, she called out "*Roho, roho,*" a phrase that means to make the wood light and easy to carry, as well as an action reminiscent of the way people sometimes show their affection by holding a person's chin. "Should we offer betel now?" asked Iné Kata, uncertain of the correct procedure. Several of the men decided that no, it was about to rain, and the wood was very heavy. Betel quids could be offered later.

Led by the gong-banging Sil, the women then processed back up to the village yard, those carrying the ridgepole and posts following behind. As the drumming still sounded out from the drum house, the two large posts were put down, their "heads" towards the *liké* stone platform. More men burst into song, starting up a circular, stamping dance, which they finished with the trilling sound said to call the land, drums, and spirits. Following these lively songs, men and women all crowded excitedly into the still-standing rectangular drum house. Here, they drank glasses of sweet coffee, prepared by younger women using coffee and sugar collected from all the community's households. Later, when more posts had been brought from the forest, another ritual was held for their arrival. Amé Bertolo, the ritual speaker, held an egg in a basket of special *ngelong* leaves identical to those prepared to welcome a new (human) bride. As he called out the name of each major post or beam, he smeared a little of the cracked egg onto each of them. Throughout this and other procedures, the drum house was not referred to by its real name but simply described as a humble shelter (*sondong*). From this moment on until the completion of the building work, women in the village center were forbidden to weave, and both young children and pregnant women were kept well away from the drum-house site.

After the completion of this ritual, I was called into a large kitchen attached to the back of a rectangular house, where I joined a crowd of women and boys ravenously spooning rice and vegetables from shared plates amidst much excited discussion about the previously witnessed events. One older woman, Iné Aga, remarked that the posts were met just like a young bride. However, a few young women who had been watching the arrival of the timber had a rather different reaction. One of them, Lusi, told me, "Oh...we all had tears in our eyes, we were all crying as we watched the ridgepole being carried in." Lusi confessed that she and others found this sad because the wood looked just like a dead person and was being carried just like a corpse. Besides, she added, the old drum house would be taken down soon, and everyone was thinking of all the "lively" occasions that had been held there. Hearing this, Iné Aga became agitated and whispered to Lusi, "Don't, don't," adding that it was forbidden to talk in this way. Nonetheless, such talk continued in the days that followed, as the old drum house was dismantled. Three young women asked me to take their photograph in front of the rapidly disappearing house. "Oh Auntie," one of them sighed, "we really feel pity for this old house."

These events, and the reactions they provoked, bring together many of the themes of this book: place making through everyday movements and the practices of hospitality; the creation of presence, and of centers, in ritual; the value and implications of the "liveliness" generated by communal gatherings; the significance of marriage as an accompanied journey at the end of which the bride is welcomed to a new place; the necessity of acknowledging the unseen powers of the land; the multiple and sometimes mysterious connections among place, bodies, memories, and fate; and the complex potency of landscapes as lived-in environments.

While some aspects of Manggarai landscapes—whether large boulders, hot springs, or mushrooms that materialize the land's "energy"—are thought by local inhabitants to be simply given, most places and pathways must be *made*. One of the key arguments of this book has been that such place making involves both conscious activity (including speech) and practices that are less conscious, less explicitly concerned with "place creation." In Manggarai, a house is built with the labor and skill of men who fell timbers, tie beams with lengths of rattan, or gather grass to make thatch, but it is also made with the labor of women who boil water for coffee and cook hearty meals to sustain the male builders. When, following the welcoming of the *ngando*, Wae Rebo villagers crowded into the old drum house to drink coffee, they were contributing to the ongoing value of a clan house as a place for such communal effervescence. When, later in the day, women and boys heartily ate together in a back kitchen, they contributed to the ongoing value of that kitchen as a hospitable center. Like houses, villages such as Wae Rebo are also made through continuing explicit and implicit acts of creation. They are created through building or rebuilding a drum house, such that this construction process is described as "making a village." Yet, villages are also made by movements of people along paths to and from fields or other villages, and by movements of words tracing the lines of ancestral or personal narratives.

As we saw in Chapter 5, though it aroused the passions and interests of villagers, the drum-house rebuilding project was not instigated by them. Nor, unlike many other communal rituals, was it held in response to "signs" of the land's needs. Instead, this extremely time-consuming project was developed and funded by the office of the Bupati, the head of the Manggarai district, after his earlier visit. The project was a conscious, top-down attempt to *remake* Wae Rebo's village center as a fully authentic place. Indeed, at the chain-saw ritual, Amé Bertolo dwelt (for the sake of the ancestors) on the pronouncements of the Bupati who, in his words, had "replaced the *raja*" of the ancestors' time. Yet, like many conscious attempts by "outsiders" to remake place (such as church efforts to "inculturate" chapel buildings), the Bupati's project did not go uncontested. Not all villagers accepted the local state's vision of what a drum house or a village should be, or how it should be constructed. Indeed, a persistent doubt in the minds of many villagers was that the procedures for rebuilding the drum house had been as efficacious as they might have been. This was partly because they were rushed, partly because they involved financial payments, and partly because the organizers spoke too much Indonesian. Some months after the chain-saw ritual, one elderly man reported a dream in which two spirits asked him what the strange noise was that they were hearing in the forest. Was this evidence that the forest ritual had not been successful? Should it be repeated? For the Bupati's team, who were eager to keep to their timetable and had a more ceremonial understanding of ritual, such considerations were an irrelevant distraction.

In the course of Manggarai life, people may often express uncertainties about correct ritual procedure. When should they set out for a particular performance? When or where should betel quids be offered? However, despite such uncertainties, it is clear that rituals are not only activities central to the making of places or pathways but also performances that create specific kinds of *presences*. House rituals in which ancestral food is placed on "plates" hanging from the central rafters temporarily (re-)create a house as a center for various spirits as well as for living and deceased humans. Moreover, such house rituals also create a kind of temporary stillness, an inward focus, in the midst of the movements that otherwise define Manggarai social life. Similarly, agricultural rituals—through speech, offerings, and the construction of various kinds of platforms—materially constitute the ritual centers of fields. In part, the temporary presence that is acknowledged and created in rituals is that of specific *agents,* whether ancestors woken by drumming or rooms addressed in ritual speech. Not only do rituals enable such agency to be utilized by humans, they also ensure its continued, hopefully beneficial, presence. For, when it comes to place, no assumptions can be made in our analyses regarding *continuity*. Indeed, this is why my original concern with uncovering the everyday, phenomenological significance of landscape has necessarily been tempered by an appreciation of the creation of presence and place agency that ritual makes possible.

Nevertheless, though "ritual" and "everyday" actions involve different foci and efforts and address different kinds of interlocutors, it would be wrong to see them as opposed kinds of activity. One noteworthy aspect of sacrificial rituals in Manggarai is the fact that they are often given extremely practical names, such as "blood on feet," "accompanying," "sharpening the machete and axe." Indeed, in order to be efficacious, ritual activity sometimes requires a kind of self-conscious projection of a place, object, or activity as everyday or banal, as when a chain saw is described as a "machete," or the drum house is referred to as a humble "shelter." Ritual events, in addition to ritual speech, also utilize the more everyday ways in which places are made— namely, through the offering of greetings, the gift of betel quids, and the presentation of *tuak* and food. Whether these hospitality practices are performed for house-posts, spirits, water sources, or human beings, they all follow the same basic format. In addition, they all aim to increase the "liveliness" that is such a fundamental aspect of valued places. In Manggarai, places enlivened by human bodies and talk assume a kind of protective power; similarly, places enlivened by nonhuman interlocutors also have power, both protective and fertile. Indeed, one of what Keane (1997) would call the "risks" of ritual in this context is that it will fail to produce the requisite human and nonhuman "liveliness." There is a kind of mutual feedback taking place, as a protective place is one where "lively" activities can safely be held but protective rituals are also a key means by which places are enlivened. Thus, large-scale ritual events, such as those conducted for a new drum house or for new communal fields, are partly about satisfying the land's appetite, and ensuring its ongoing involvement with human health, by making *the land itself* "lively."

In treating the central ridgepole of the drum house as a kidnapped mountain bride, the ritual process demonstrates, not only the centrality of marriage journeys to local conceptions of productive life, but also the importance of considering "the house" in connection with the wider landscape. In addition, it acknowledges and re-creates the presence of various unseen interlocutors. Songs are sung to forest-based spirit affines, pregnant women and children are kept away from places that might be full of ancestral spirits, and dreams are interpreted as signs of communication from "the other side." As we have seen throughout this book, the body does not always constitute the boundaries of the self, and people (and their blood) can be entangled with places in often mysterious or not fully understood ways. Thus, thinking too much about a person absent on a journey can make that person unwell, while other forms of illness can be addressed by calling back someone's soul to their natal room. Some days after the ritual to welcome the ridgepole, one man told me that there had been lots of wild pigs around in the forest at the time of carrying in the timbers. However, he said, people had been forbidden to hunt them for fear that they might be the temporary manifestation of "human souls."

Throughout this book, we have seen how memories of and connections with place follow certain common cultural logics but can also be highly individual. Indeed, by moving out in concentric circles from household rooms to houses, stone platforms, and fields, we have explored different scales of entanglement with personal, historical, and ancestral landscapes. Such entanglements can be both beneficial and dangerous. Ritual actions may retell the movements that constitute village histories, or may attempt to re-create communal connections with the land or drums, but people also have their own, subjective experiences and memories of place. This is why—though it has attempted to reveal the sedimentation of meaning within one particular landscape—I nevertheless entitled this book *Potent Landscapes*. As a realm full of kinship memories, where a stone reminds a grandmother of a buried placenta, or a stream induces fear in the father of a drowned child, the landscape of southern Manggarai has multiple significances. For Lusi and her friends, the carrying-in of the ridgepole evoked the image and memory of human corpses being carried out of houses. For others, the dismantling of the old drum house stirred up memories of its many "lively" events, and they felt "pity" for the building as its roof was taken off and its walls dismantled. Landscapes in this context are "potent," not only because places have agency, but because networks of marriage paths, ancestral journeys, fields, houses, and garden-huts have the power to evoke human emotions and to shape future desires and dreams.

Nevertheless, despite the individual and subjective connections between people and places or pathways, this book has also demonstrated the powerful links that exist between the land and its inhabitants. It has explored the ways in which one community has responded to state-sponsored resettlement, and how this community continues to try to negotiate and assert the link between the land and various discourses and practices. Although Indonesian state officials may have the power to order villages to relocate their houses, to open up and manage new fields, or to rebuild drum houses, in local eyes, this power is limited, and sometimes even curtailed, by the power of the land. The ridgepole that is carried into the village as a mountain bride is later transformed into a protective spirit, residing at the heart of the drum house and instructed to "bite angry people." Such a bite was perhaps what killed the overzealous engineer who argued for complete relocation from Wae Rebo. Certainly, what is clear is that, in this context, talk of the "energy of the land" is a powerful discourse not only about the agency of the material environment but about morality, religious change, and outside interference.

In Wae Rebo-Kombo, many people say that ritual practices are "the law of what the land wants" (*ruku ngoéng de tana*) and that, if they are abandoned, both the health of human beings and the fertility of the land will decline. The fate of a community and the fate of the land are inextricably entwined. Moreover, as the Manggarai term *ruku* (which means both "law" and "character, personality") is closely connected with the pan-Indonesian notion of *adat* (custom, tradition), this also points to local perceptions of the close connection between the land and the *adat* of those who inhabit it. Understandings of *adat* in this Indonesian context are not entirely dictated by state officials or urban elites, but remain influenced by local ideas about the agency of the land. Cultural politics are also the politics of landscape. Therefore, when Manggarai people humorously and apologetically say to a visitor, "This is the shape of our land here," they are also declaring, rather less apologetically, "This is our character" and "This is the way we do things."

NOTES

INTRODUCTION

1   This tradition has informed much of the work on Austronesian societies, in which the connection between land and people has been highlighted (see, e.g., Reuter 2006) but in which little attention has been paid to the difference this makes to ordinary people throughout their lives.

2   Despite this strategy informing her first long period of fieldwork, Hoskins' second ethnographic text—*Biographical Objects* (1998)—gives equal weight to the stories of men and women, and to formal and informal speech, in uncovering the nuances of individual biographies and their connections with various objects.

3   Makassarese influence on Manggarai was mainly linguistic, though it is also evident in Manggarai's supplementary-weft *lipa songké* cloth, which is markedly different from the red and brown *ikat* textiles of other Florenese groups (Hamilton 1994). The Bimanese appear to have had the greatest political and economic influence over the region, exerting power through their control of coastal products (Gordon 1975, 56) and instituting the *dalu* system of region divisions in order to facilitate tax collection and administration (Erb 1999, 79, 87).

4   In 2002, the province of NTT had the lowest ranking out of all thirty Indonesian provinces for per capita income, and the third lowest Human Development Index rank (UNDP 2004).

5   Manggarai is classified as a Bima-Sumba language within the Central Malayo-Polynesian language group and has been estimated to have approximately forty-three subdialects (Verheijen and Grimes 1995, 585). Wae Rebo-Kombo villagers generally follow a dialect known as the "s/h shift" (Verheijen 1967, xv–xvi; 1987, 1189–1191), which employs a very different intonation (known locally as "dry speech") from central and western dialects, as well as a partially different vocabulary, and substitutes *h* for *s*, and *s* for *c*. Thus, "dog" is *acu* in central regions, but *asu* in the s/h shift dialect; while *masang* (yesterday) becomes *mahang*. The s/h shift dialect also employs the pronominal system of West Manggarai (Verheijen and Grimes 1995, 588). In this book, I largely follow the system of notation used by Verheijen (1967) in his Manggarai-Indonesian dictionary, though I differ from him in following contemporary Indonesian orthography, using *c* instead of *tj*, *j* instead of *dj*, and *y* instead of *j*.

CHAPTER 1: ROOMS

1 Blackwood (1999) has described similar "negotiations" regarding the transition of Minangkabau rooms and houses from generation to generation. However, in the matrilineal context of Minangkabau, it is the relationship between mother and daughter that is crucial.

2 As in Malaysia (Laderman 1983, 165–166), Manggarai women are strongly discouraged from crying or screaming during childbirth.

3 *Jéngok* is a long, thin, extremely hot root that is highly valued for medicine.

4 *Nana* is used by women as a term of address for men or boys of the same generation or younger. Men use the term only for those much younger than themselves. The equivalent female term is *enu*.

5 A number of rather vague and unspecific healing ideas concern the *lampék* blade, such as "treating" it with burnt coconut should the baby's belly button become infected and burning it in the case of other illnesses or even disagreements. Such an association of the umbilical cord, the blade used to cut it, and the baby's health is common in southeast Asia, where dried and ground umbilical cord may be used to make a medicine to bathe a baby's eyes (Laderman 1983, 158) or added to siblings' coffee by their mother in the case of arguments (Cannell 1999, 55).

6 Similarly, Barraud notes that Tanebar-Evav call childbirth "to be-house" (1990, 220), and describes the house for a newborn baby as "a kind of intermediary womb between heaven and society" (1990, 222).

7 In contrast with areas of Southeast Asia where the placenta is explicitly seen as a kind of "sibling" to the baby (Laderman 1983, 158; Barraud 1990, 229; Carsten 1997, 83–84), I was told that the placenta should be buried near to the room so that "the blood is not far away."

8 The reverse of this example is a situation where the *tungku* link is rather tenuous but is emphasized because of the close relations between two families.

9 When two female "siblings" marry two male "siblings," this necessary separation is performed in a ritual called "crossed gifts." The women are each presented with a water carrier "so they can each fetch water," a plate "so they can each eat separately," and a sarong "so they can each cradle their children." The ritual ensures that each couple will have many healthy children despite the "overlapping bones" of their parents.

10 The importance of separation in extraordinary circumstances is also seen in ideas about cross-sex twins. I was told that when a female twin marries, her twin brother cannot receive any part of the bride-price that is paid for her. Similarly, if the brother marries, his twin sister will not be asked to contribute what is known as *sida* money towards the price of his bride. If either of these things were to occur, it would be like "incest" (*jurak*), as if the female twin had become the

wife of her brother. On the potency of cross-sex twins elsewhere on Flores, see Erb (1987, 527–531) and Howell (1991, 228); and on Bali, see Boon (1990, 224).

11 Anthropologists of other areas of Indonesia have connected such practices with the *semangat* or "soul-stuff" that such body parts as hair or fingernails may contain (Errington 1989, 122; cf. Tsintjilonis 2004, 447), but I did not find such notions to be elaborated in Manggarai.

12 There are a number of different kinds of ritual held to "stem" or "stop" (*kepet*) particular spirits or energies, and they always involve the sacrifice of a gray chicken. See also Gibson (1986, 197) on occasions when Buid ancestors are offered a sacrifice in order to stay away from those inside a house.

13 In other Southeast Asian contexts that stress the placenta's sibling-like nature, the placenta seems to share some of the characteristics of Manggarai "body siblings." For example, McKinley describes how Malays see the placenta as an elder spirit sibling of a newborn baby, with whom it has a "joking relationship" (1983, 372).

14 In the very different context of northern Togo, Blier has argued that the Tamberma see miniature earth mounds outside each house door as sheltering the souls of house occupants (1983, 378).

15 Similarly, in his work on art and agency (and while avoiding the language of fetishism), Alfred Gell (1998) defines agency as intentionality and therefore argues that objects exercise agency only insofar as they act as "extensions" or indexes of *human* agency. By contrast, Actor Network Theory (ANT) proposes a more radical (or "symmetrical") approach to humans and nonhumans, criticizing the priority given to *social* relations in accounts of the material world and breaking down the boundaries between subjects and objects. While Gell defines agency as intentionality, Bruno Latour sees agency as simply the ability to act. Thus, an "actant" for Latour implies "*no* special motivation of *human individual* actors, nor of humans in general" (1996a, 373).

CHAPTER 2: THE PERMEABLE HOUSE

1 Waterson's encyclopedic examination of Southeast Asian houses contains colonial-era photographs of these older house forms (1990, 37–39). People in Wae Rebo-Kombo who remembered elongated oval houses called them *mbaru beruga*.

2 All translations from the original Dutch are by Harold Herrewegh.

3 Gordon, in his thesis on central Manggarai, describes the measurements of these "meter houses" as "four by six meters with a minimum elevation of one and three-fourths meters" (1975, 65).

4 *Niang* houses are constructed from five layers: the floor (*lanté*); the main loft area (*lobo méhé*); a further loft called the *léntar;* the *lémpa-raé;* and finally, a top story called the *hékang kodé* or "monkey-hut." Though other parts of the house

are named, it is only the names of these stories that are known by everyone. One man told me that the five levels of the house were linked with the five levels of Indonesian government, from the president down to village head. This echoes the interpretations of Anakalangese villagers who saw the five levels of the house as paralleling the five-point state ideology of *pancasila* (Keane 1995, 104).

5   Ellen has rightly criticized spatial analyses that aim to uncover an overall order, disputing the notion of the house as a "microcosm" and arguing that connections between different symbolic domains are "partial and variable," dependent on context (1986, 23).

6   The literal meaning of *sumang* is "to meet" or "meeting," and it is the medicine given to those who may have become ill because of an inadvertent meeting with an invisible spirit.

7   Rodman describes how the "impermanence and portability" of housing materials in Longana, Vanuatu, "allows a freedom of movement" in which residence patterns are "part of the interweaving of place and people that creates Longana kinship" (1985, 69). During my first fieldwork in Manggarai, I did not think that houses *themselves* were portable. However, following the Bupati's project to rebuild the Wae Rebo drum house, a large rectangular house was dismantled. When I returned for fieldwork in 2001, I found it had been reassembled near to the path out of the village.

8   This tracing of interconnections is also seen in conversations when people compare alliance or kin relations to show that they are "really" siblings, or that a person is "really" a potential spouse. This language of contrasts between appearance and a more profound or ideal reality was sometimes used as a social critique. For example, one out-married woman, Fita, was said to have a very "hard" mother-in-law. A friend told me that Fita's baby looked thin and unwell (and hence was living temporarily with Fita's parents), even though "really" the child should have been fat and healthy.

9   The use of wage labor (known as working "daily," *harian*) for certain agricultural tasks is becoming more common, particularly by households with only a small labor pool. However, some households still work for one another according to reciprocal work arrangements known as *dodo*.

10 For example, one girl wrote this description of a *pesta kélas* (final death ritual event): "There is an old man speaking with a chicken. There are old mothers cooking. There are also people dancing, and people drunk on *tuak*. There is someone burning a chicken, a person killing a chicken. There are people eating." Another girl wrote of a *ramé kémpu* (bridewealth negotiation): "There is an old man speaking with a chicken. There are young men just sitting. There are people dancing, boys and girls, and there are old mothers cooking in the kitchen, and there is someone burning a chicken in the kitchen. There are young women lifting plates, and there are people lifting glasses of water in the house, and people eating."

11 Although I would not wish to push the analogy too far, it is worth noting the

similarity between my description of ordinary Manggarai houses and the literature on the traditional Southeast Asian polity as a profoundly *centered* but boundary-less realm. Heine-Geldern argued that the structural and spatial organization of Indic states was a microcosmic mirroring of the macrocosmos, in which the capital stood as the "magical center of the empire" (1956 [1942], 3). Later, Tambiah utilized the notion of mandala, a composition of two elements, core and container, to describe such a "galactic polity," a sociospatial configuration visible in temples such as Borobudur on Java (1976, 102). Similarly, Geertz argues that the nineteenth-century Balinese state was a "theatre state," in which the king and court stood as the "exemplary center" (1980, 11–18). Drawing on this literature, Errington characterizes the "houses" of island Southeast Asia as "profoundly centered entities, consisting of a center and a serving group," where the center is a stable object such as a temple or a set of regalia, and the serving group consists of humans who recruit members "through a variety of means" (1989, 239). By contrast, I am arguing that it is hearth-based practices of hospitality that *temporarily* create the ordinary Manggarai house as a center, while other practices of mobility emphasize permeability.

12 Unlike the Nagé (Forth 1991b, 141), Manggarai people have no rules regarding the orientation of corpses *within* the grave.

13 In 2008, these sums were: Rp5,000 and 3 kg rice at the time of the death, and another Rp5,000 and 6 kg rice at the time of the final *kélas* ritual. One man is responsible for maintaining a book in which names of household heads and lists of amounts given are carefully noted.

14 Like another Austronesian people, the Vezo of Madagascar, Manggarai people seek out the fertility that flows from the ancestors, but also attempt to create barriers protecting them from what the Vezo describe as the "longing" that the dead feel for the living (Astuti 1995, 123).

CHAPTER 3: PATHS OF MARRIAGE

1 In the same volume, McWilliam (1997) analyzes paths as a "relationship idiom" among the Meto of West Timor. Significantly, the notion of marriage paths or "roads" also appears to be widespread in Melanesia (see Bonnemaison 1985, 46; 1994, 304; Parmentier 1987, 109; O'Hanlon and Frankland 2003, 168).

2 In central and northern areas of Manggarai, a woman's natal kin are called *anak rona* or "children of men," while the family into which a woman marries, and her descendants, are *anak wina* or "children of women" (Erb 1993, 15). In Wae Rebo-Kombo, these terms were known but were found too impolite to use, since *rona* and *wina* are also rather sexually loaded terms for "husband" and "wife."

3 Other ethnographers of Indonesian societies have also discussed the suitability of these conventional glosses. Sherman argues that it is "impossible to explain how a

married woman could see herself as either 'wife-taker' or 'wife-receiver' in relation to her parents and brothers" (1987, 868) but nevertheless retains the gloss "wife-receiver" as "most suitable" for Toba-Batak practices and values, as the notion of wife-*taking* distorts local understandings of indebtedness and respect between alliance groups. In an interesting parallel with Manggarai terminology, Rodgers notes that the most exact translation of the Batak term *anakboru* (conventionally glossed as "wife-takers" or "wife-receivers") is "daughter-people" (1990, 324).

4 In the case of both *tinu-lalo* and *lili* (when a man married his deceased brother's widow), the new spouse simply substituted for their deceased sibling, and it was unnecessary to pay any extra bride-price or to repeat rituals held for the first marriage. However, under church influence, these forms of marriage have declined in significance. For more on marriage in central and eastern Manggarai, see Gordon (1980) and Erb (1991b). See also Needham (1980) and Hicks (1984) for a somewhat hypothetical and esoteric debate on the theoretical existence and "evolution" of a prescriptive alliance system in Manggarai.

5 Kunst noted a different kind of competitive singing in his colonial-era survey of music on Flores, describing how the inhabitants of opposite mountain slopes in Manggarai "have the habit of holding a kind of singing-duel on quiet evenings, taking their turns at singing 'at' each other from the distance" (1942, 92).

6 For more on bridal makeup, and in particular on the bride as an icon of modern beauty in Manggarai, see Allerton 2007a.

7 The use of umbrellas in these rituals is considered extremely important, perhaps because they are mobile shelters, thus neatly combining the dual characteristics of protective place and dynamic movement.

8 Manggarai marriage events frequently employ what is called *gara-gara*, that is, "mock" speech. For example, when arriving for a marriage ritual, the groom's kin may be told that the girl cannot be found and must have run away. After they present a sum of money, the bride will be miraculously "found" and the ritual can proceed. Similarly, at a "collecting" ritual, each "path" of alliance will be asked to give money to "dress the young man." When asked for this money, the convention is to reply, "If he can't yet dress himself, maybe he shouldn't be getting married." People take great delight in these "jokes" and view them as an important element of alliance relationships.

9 This ritual parallel can be compared with Himalayan India, where the annual pilgrimage of a goddess represents a stylized version of a woman's postmarital journey (Sax 1991, 14).

10 Rodgers (1990, 321) notes that the Batak explicitly contrast the flighty behavior of adolescent girls with the restraint of new brides, while Barnes opposes the bride and groom's "acute embarrassment" to the "exuberant celebrating" of friends in Lamalera (1996, 89).

11 Lembor is a region of West Manggarai well known for its grassy plains where livestock are grazed.

12 To be "eaten" by someone is also a euphemism for sexual intercourse.

13 Similarly, among the Endenese of central Flores, a groom contracting a formal marriage walks along "the neat road, the clean path," while a groom initiating an elopement "slashes the grass to make way" (Nakagawa 1988, 228–229).

CHAPTER 4: EARTH, STONE, WATER

1 The most striking example of the attribution of agency to the landscape came during a small earthquake. As the ground shook beneath them, some women called out, "Hey, there are people here!"

2 Historically, there have been limited employment opportunities outside the agriculture sector throughout the province of Nusa Tenggara Timur (Barlow et al. 1991, 47). This ongoing dependency on agriculture may well have spared many in NTT from the most severe effects of the 1997–1998 Indonesian monetary crisis (Mathews 1998, 75, 84; Forrester 1999, 122; cf. McWilliam 2002, 9).

3 In particular, people said that the *kokak* bird (a kind of honeyeater, *Philemon buceroides neglectus*) was the "watch" of the old people in the past. The bird is said to make its first sound at about 3 p.m. Once you have heard its cry three times, you know it is time to return home. For a comparative account of the significance of chicken calls (as well as buffalo) see Hoskins' work on the structuring of "social and biographical time" in Kodi, Sumba (1993, 67).

4 The sense of domestic categories all having a "wild" or "monkey" counterpart is also found in botanical terminology. For example, just as "monkey-huts" are a "wilder" version of village houses, so a form of wild betel leaf is known as "monkey-betel" (*kala-kodé*), while other wild plants are called "monkey-ginger" (*lia-kodé*) and "monkey-bananas" (*muku-kodé*).

5 If a person has a serious request to make of another, they may hand that other person a small sum of money as they speak, stressing the weight and significance of their words by intoning, "scared you will think it is just my mouth" (*rantang le mu'u*).

6 These "tripods" are called *hanggar* and consist of small sticks split into three at the top, with a piece of bark thrust in the center as a "plate." Their shape echoes that of the three hearthstones used for balancing pots on in the house.

7 *Empo-déhong* (literally, "deceiving/tricking ancestor") seems to correspond with a spirit known in some other parts of Manggarai as *gorak* (Erb 1991a, 121). Erb notes that *gorak* are thought to seek out children's heads for use in concrete construction, and that European missionaries were often the targets of *gorak* rumors (ibid., 118). Erb links these beliefs to the long history of foreign domination and slave raiding in Manggarai, an analysis that is persuasive for southern Manggarai, where in myths and stories slave raiders are called *gorak*.

8 For accounts of myths involving *darat*, see Allerton (2001, 170–171, 269–270).

9   The Manggarai word *muing* is rather difficult to translate into English, as it carries a range of meanings including "correct, true, indeed, fitting, really, just, actually." The term is often used to stress a real or underlying personality, color, character, or flavor. Hence, I have translated the phrase *tana muing* as the rather awkward English "really/actually the land," since the tone people use when uttering this phrase is similar to the tone English speakers use when they wish to emphasize that, actually, something is not quite as it initially appears.

10   Gregory Forth (personal communication) suggests that eels may be "doubly spiritual" in this context, as they not only look like snakes (associated, throughout Flores, with spirits) but also are connected with spiritually potent water sources. In Kédang, to the east of Flores, a snake seen near the spring in an origin village may not be killed, as it may be the guardian spirit/proprietor of the spring (Barnes 1974, 62).

11   As in many areas of Southeast Asia, Manggarai people associate the health of both people and land with coolness and dampness, while "heat" is associated with uncomfortable living, anger, and bad luck (cf. Carsten 1997, 123; Telle 2009, 294). Images of cool, lush, fertile places often appear in Manggarai marriage rituals. For example, when the groom's kin arrive for the bridewealth negotiations, they might state that they have seen the "coolness on the ground" and have discovered that it begins in the village of the bride's kin. Similarly, when presenting a "sarong to shelter," the bride's family might say that it is to ensure "a floor of moistness below, a cover of shade above."

12   Verheijen suggested that these platforms may have contained the graves of influential elders (1967, 713). The *sompang,* which in some villages has a banyan tree growing out of it, can be compared both with the sacrificial posts found in other Florenese societies (Forth 1998, 7; Smedal 1994, 15) and with the stone "boats" of the Tanimbar Islands (McKinnon 1991, 64–83).

13   In southern Manggarai, the association of Christianity with "the outside" is not only a result of the particular conditions of its establishment but also connects with the continued use of Indonesian for prayer meetings and church services. As Kuipers has described for Sumba, even when the local language is used in church, it is ordinary speech that is adopted, not ritual speech (1998, 40). Thus, the sacrificial rituals of the village retain a medium of speech closely associated with the interior realm of the ancestors.

14   Manggarai responses to enculturation appear to be highly localized. By comparison with Wae Rebo-Kombo, Moeliono reports that *penti* in Rura, north Manggarai, has been transformed into a "Catholic ceremony of giving thanks and asking for blessing" (2000, 104). Similarly, Erb describes a *penti* ritual in the hamlet of Tukeq in which spirits were invited to "pray to God" together with the whole village community (2007, 8).

15   Manggarai has many more wet-rice fields (*sawah*) than other areas of Flores. By the late 1980s, following the development of *sawah,* approximately 40% of

the rice production of Nusa Tenggara Timur was grown in Manggarai (Corner 1989, 187). In line with these developments, the area of land used for shifting cultivation in Manggarai declined to 48% in 1983, as against an average Flores proportion of 62% (Barlow et al. 1991, 154).

CHAPTER 5: DRUM HOUSES AND VILLAGE RESETTLEMENT

1 Similar "dual" or "parallel" structures have been noted throughout eastern Indonesia in both traditional offices, conceptions of authority, and patterns of ritual speech (van Wouden 1968, 29; Barnes 1974, 89; Fox 1988).

2 Throughout Indonesia, state policies have sought to promote small, usually single-family dwellings based on an ideal (and often unrealistic) model of nuclear families headed by the husband/father (van Reenen 1996, 4; Blackwood 1999, 49–50; Schrauwers 2000, 99).

3 Despite such labelling, the resettlement of Manggarai villagers is rather different from Indonesian policies of "transmigration" that have involved giving land to settlers in such "outlying" areas as Kalimantan and West Papua (Irian Jaya), often leading to serious interethnic conflict (see Hoey 2003).

4 Other areas of Manggarai do contain communities that have not entirely abandoned their highland sites. Modo, in Lembor, is a small highland site where a few families still live despite the village's relocation to the larger, lowland site of Kakor. Farther east from Kombo is the large village of Narang, composed of several resettled hamlets. One of these, Rotok, retains a connection with an origin village called Pulang. However, in both these cases, the majority of the population has moved to the resettled village.

5 There were rumors of other heirlooms stored in the loft of the drum house, including an old Javanese dagger (keris). However, I never saw any such objects. In Todo, the village of the onetime raja of Manggarai, a small drum is rumored to have been made with the skin of a young female victim of sacrifice (Erb 1999, 81). For an account of the significance of heirlooms to an Indonesian "house society," see Errington 1989.

6 The procedures surrounding the carrying-in of the Wae Rebo drum house-posts have a number of parallels with practices elsewhere in Southeast Asia. Waterson describes how Minangkabau house timbers are carried in to the sound of gongs and drums, Sa'dan Toraja house-posts are "personified and dressed up," and the main house-post in Roti is treated as a "king" (1990, 118).

7 The village of Kéndé, visible from Kombo, has two drum houses. The first of these houses only one clan, while the second unites five clans who arrived in Kéndé at different times in the past. In his thesis, Gordon reports that most Manggarai villages have between six and ten clans (1975, 171). For an account of a multi-clan village with two drum houses, see Moeliono 2000.

8 *Sasi*—called *caci* in central Manggarai—can be compared with other ritual combats in Indonesia (Hoskins 1993, 156–157). Increasingly, these duels are being appropriated by government officials and others as "performance genres" for tourists or special events (Erb 2001; cf. Graham 1994, 126).

9 Writing on the Peruvian Andes, Penelope Harvey argues that "The animate landscape provides an alternative source of power to that of the urban-based state apparatus. However, the relationship is not one of direct opposition, and the historicity of the landscape also entails an entanglement with the agency of the state that dates back to Inka times" (2001, 199). This comment is very pertinent to the situation in Wae Rebo-Kombo, where the agency of "the land" sometimes clashes with that of the state, but where understandings of the land's agency are in part shaped by the implications of state-sponsored resettlement.

10 The value of the rupiah rose from Rp9,000 to US$1 in mid-1998, to Rp13,000 by the end of the year. The project therefore cost well over US$2,000, a huge amount of money by local rural standards.

11 The language of preservation dominated press reports on the Bupati's visit. One headline read: "Authentic Manggarai settlement: Wae Rebo, a site which needs to be preserved" (*Pos Kupang,* 2.1.98).

12 It is noteworthy that by far the largest number of visitors to the drum house since its construction have not been foreign tourists (whose numbers are in fact very low, usually single figures for each year) but students from the tourism high school in Ruteng, who come to the village on "practice" field trips.

13 Similarly, some Todo people referred to their rebuilt *niang* house as an *Inpres,* a "Presidential" development project (Erb 1998, 186).

14 Wae Rebo villagers themselves are perfectly capable of adopting this discourse on authenticity and are increasingly speaking of their dialect as the "original" Manggarai language that other villages, most notably Todo, have lost or forgotten. Statements about the greater authenticity of the s/h shift are also an explicit rejection of central Manggarai views of this dialect as rather "backward" and humorous.

CHAPTER 6: ROOTS AND MOBILITY

1 As Nils Bubandt notes, "surprise and confusion…in coming to terms with an Austronesian spatial system has not gone unreported in the anthropological literature" (1997, 136; cf. Barnes 1974, 84; Forth 1991b, 139; Wassman and Dasen 1998, 690).

2 Direction terms may undergo various shifts of meaning in response to wider influences. Forth argues that in the Nagé region of Flores, direction terms are coming to be used "more and more as simple equivalents of…Bahasa Indonesia words" (1991b, 143). Although in Manggarai, people would sometimes translate *lé* as the Indonesian *utara* (north) and *lau* as *selatan* (south), I was not aware

of the Manggarai terms being used as cardinal directions. Bubandt argues that Christianity has entailed a transfer of "symbolic significance" from the Buli "downward" direction, traditionally the place of the dead, towards the "upward" direction to which dead Christians should ascend (1997, 150–151). In southern Manggarai, "heaven" (*surga*) has not proven a particularly catchy idea, and the dead continue to be described as "towards the mountains" (*lé*).

3 Wassman and Dasen (1998, 693–694) give an interesting overview of accounts of the confusion and disorientation felt by Balinese people when they similarly lose their bearings. Their own study, employing both ethnographic and psychological methods, argues for "moderate linguistic relativity," showing how Balinese language (and culture)—which lacks the "egocentric encoding" assumed by developmental psychology—does (moderately) constrain conceptualization of space.

4 In central Manggarai, the expression "the drums inside, the fields outside" (*gendangn oné, lingkon pé'ang*) is used to refer to the symbolic unity of a drum community and its land. Both Erb (2001, 2007) and Moeliono (2000) emphasize the significance of this notion to Manggarai understandings of place, as well as the disruption of the link between *gendang* and *lingko* in the modern era, in which land is increasingly conceived as private property. In Wae Rebo-Kombo, other contrasting pairs tend to be used to express the unity of land and people, particularly "hill where we sit, land where we live" (*golo lonto, tana ka'éng*).

5 An intriguing comparison is found in Bubandt's description of how a young Buli boy once asked him, "Is your town close to Japan or is it still farther up?" (1997, 148). In the Buli orientation system, the "upward" direction seems to have many of the connotations of both the Manggarai "seaward" and "outside."

6 Visits to other villages also involve transporting goods such as tobacco or coffee, because people stress that, when journeying farther afield in Manggarai to the villages of kin or affines, it is important always to take along something as "fruit of the hands" (*wua de limé*).

7 Despite the expectation of safe walking, massages are freely given to friends and kin on the understanding that throughout the course of a normal life all people have "little falls" that produce "cooked blood" in knots in their feet, hands, and knees. Falls, particularly while carrying a heavy basket, are also used as the explanation for backache, because the "cooked blood" is thought to travel away from the sprained limb up to the neck and shoulders.

8 The claim that Manggarai people originated in Minangkabau seems to be one of some longevity; see Keers 1948, 49; Kunst 1942, 1; and Erb 1999, 85–86.

9 Similar notions have been discovered by ethnographers of other Indonesian societies. For example, Jane Atkinson has described how the Wana conceptualize "knowledge, power and wealth" as originating in distant lands (1989, 315), while Danilyn Rutherford (2003) has investigated the multiple allures and domestications of "the foreign" on Biak.

REFERENCES

Acciaioli, Greg. 1985. "Culture as art: From practice to spectacle in Indonesia." *Canberra Anthropology* 8, nos. 1 and 2:148–172.

Adams, Kathleen. 1984. "Come to Tana Toraja, 'Land of the heavenly kings': Travel agents as brokers in ethnicity." *Annals of Tourism Research* 2:469–485.

Allerton, Catherine. 2001. "Places, paths and persons: The landscape of kinship and history in southern Manggarai, Flores, Indonesia." Ph.D. diss., University of London.

———. 2003. "Authentic housing, authentic culture? Transforming a village into a 'tourist site' in Manggarai, eastern Indonesia." *Indonesia and the Malay World* 31 (Issue 89): 119–128.

———. 2007a. "Lipsticked brides and powdered children: Cosmetics and the allure of modernity in an eastern Indonesian village." In *Body arts and modernity,* ed. Michael O'Hanlon and Elizabeth Ewart, pp. 108–125. Wantage, UK: Sean Kingston Publishing.

———. 2007b. "The secret life of sarongs: Manggarai textiles as super-skins." *Journal of Material Culture* 12, no.1:22–46.

———. 2007c. "What does it mean to be alone?" In *Questions of anthropology,* ed. Rita Astuti, Jonathan Parry, and Charles Stafford, pp. 1–27. Oxford: Berg.

———. 2009. "Introduction: Spiritual Landscapes of Southeast Asia." *Anthropological Forum* 19, no. 3:235–251. Special Edition on Spiritual Landscapes of Southeast Asia.

———. 2012. "Making guests, making 'liveliness': The transformative substances and sounds of Manggarai hospitality." *Journal of the Royal Anthropological Institute* (n.s.) 18:S49–S62.

Anderson, Benedict R. O'G. 1990 [1972]. "The idea of power in Javanese culture." In *Language and power: Exploring political cultures in Indonesia,* pp. 17–77. Ithaca, N.Y.: Cornell University Press.

Anderson, David G. 2000. *Identity and ecology in Arctic Siberia: The number one reindeer brigade.* Oxford: Oxford University Press.

Anderson, Robert T. 2003. "Constraint and freedom in Icelandic conversions." In *The anthropology of religious conversion,* ed. A. Buckser and S. D. Glazier, pp. 123–145. Oxford: Rowman and Littlefield.

Appadurai, Arjun, ed. 1986. *The social life of things: Commodities in cultural perspective.* Cambridge: Cambridge University Press.

———. 1996. *Modernity at large: Cultural dimensions of globalization.* Minneapolis: University of Minnesota Press.

Astuti, Rita. 1995. *People of the sea: Identity and descent among the Vezo of Madagascar.* Cambridge: Cambridge University Press.

Atkinson, Jane Monnig. 1989. *The art and politics of Wana shamanship.* Berkeley: University of California Press.

Bachelard, Gaston. 1994 [1964]. *The poetics of space.* Boston: Beacon Press.

Bahloul, Joëlle. 1996. *The architecture of memory: A Jewish-Muslim household in colonial Algeria, 1937–1962.* Cambridge: Cambridge University Press.

Barlow, C., A. Bellis, and K. Andrews, eds. 1991. *Nusa Tenggara Timur: The challenges of development.* Canberra: The Australian National University.

Barlow, Colin, and Joan Hardjono. 1996. *Indonesia Assessment 1995: Development in Eastern Indonesia.* Singapore: Institute of Southeast Asian Studies.

Barnes, R. H. 1974. *Kédang: A study of the collective thought of an eastern Indonesia people.* Oxford: Clarendon Press.

———. 1980. "Concordance, structure and variation: Considerations of alliance in Kédang." In *The flow of life: Essays on eastern Indonesia,* ed. James J. Fox, pp. 68–97. Cambridge, Mass.: Harvard University Press.

———. 1992. A Catholic mission and the purification of culture: Experiences in an Indonesian community. *Journal of the Anthropological Society of Oxford* (hereafter *JASO*) 23:169–180.

———. 1996. *Sea hunters of Indonesia: Fishers and weavers of Lamalera.* Oxford: Clarendon Press.

———. 1999. "Marriage by capture." *Journal of the Royal Anthropological Institute* (n.s.) 5:57–73.

Barraud, Cécile. 1990. "Wife-givers as ancestors and ultimate values in the Kei islands." *Bijdragen tot de Taal-, Land- en Volkenkunde* 146:193–225.

Basso, Keith. 1996. *Wisdom sits in places: Landscape and language among the Western Apache.* Albuquerque: University of New Mexico Press.

Beatty, Andrew. 1990. Asymmetric alliance in Nias, Indonesia. *Man* (n.s.) 25:454–471.

Bender, Barbara. 2001. "Introduction." In *Contested landscapes: Movement, exile and place,* ed. B. Bender and M. Winer, pp. 1–18. Oxford: Berg.

Beusch, Andreas, P. Hartmann, R. C. Petts, and P. Winkelmann. 1997. *Low cost road construction in Indonesia: Labour-based road projects in Manggarai district.* Bern: Intercooperation.

Bird-David, Nurit. 1999. "'Animism' revisited: Personhood, environment and relational epistemology." *Current Anthropology* 40 (Supplement): S67–S91.

Blackwood, Evelyn. 1999. "Big houses and small houses: Doing matriliny in West Sumatra." *Ethnos* 64, no. 1:32–56.

Blier, Suzanne Preston. 1983. "Houses are human: Architectural self-images of Africa's Tamberma." *The Journal of the Society of Architectural Historians.* 42, no. 4:371–382.

Bloch, Maurice. 1978. "Marriage amongst equals: An analysis of the marriage ceremony of the Merina of Madagascar." *Man* (n.s.) 13, no. 1:21–33.

———. 1991. "Language, anthropology and cognitive science." *Man* (n.s.) 26, no. 2:183–198.

———. 1995a. "The resurrection of the house amongst the Zafiminary of Madagascar." In *About the house: Lévi-Strauss and beyond,* ed. J. Carsten and S. Hugh-Jones, pp. 69–83. Cambridge: Cambridge University Press.

———. 1995b. "People into places: Zafimaniry concepts of clarity." In *The anthropology of landscape: Perspectives on place and space,* ed. E. Hirsch and M. O'Hanlon, pp. 63–77. Oxford: Clarendon Press.

———. 1998 [1992]. "What goes without saying: The conceptualization of Zafimaniry society." In *How we think they think: Anthropological approaches to cognition, memory and literacy,* pp. 22–38. Boulder, Colo., and Oxford: Westview Press.

Bonnemaison, Joel. 1985. "The tree and the canoe; roots and mobility in Vanuatu society." *Pacific Viewpoint,* 26:30–62. Special Issue on mobility and identity in the island Pacific.

———. 1994. *The tree and the canoe: History and ethnogeography of Tanna.* Honolulu: University of Hawai'i Press.

Boon, James A. 1990. "Balinese twins times two: Gender, birth order and 'households' in Indonesia/Indo-Europe." In *Power and difference: Gender in island southeast Asia,* ed. J. M. Atkinson and S. Errington, pp. 209–234. Stanford, Calif.: Stanford University Press.

Bourdieu, Pierre. 1973 [1971]. "The Berber house." In *Rules and meanings: The anthropology of everyday knowledge,* ed. Mary Douglas, pp. 98–110. Harmondsworth, UK: Penguin.

Bovensiepen, Judith. 2009. "Spiritual landscapes of life and death in the central highlands of East Timor." *Anthropological Forum* 19, no. 3:323–338. Special edition on Spiritual Landscapes of Southeast Asia.

Bowen, J. 2003. *Muslims through discourse: Religion and ritual in Gayo society.* Princeton, N.J.: Princeton University Press.

Brenner, Suzanne. 1998. *The domestication of desire: Women, wealth, and modernity in Java.* Princeton, N.J.: Princeton University Press.

Bubandt, Nils. 1997. "Speaking of places: Spatial poesis and localized identity in Buli." In *The poetic power of place: Comparative perspectives on Austronesian ideas of locality,* ed. J. J. Fox, pp. 132–162. Canberra: The Australian National University.

Cannell, Fenella. 1999. *Power and intimacy in the Christian Philippines.* Cambridge: Cambridge University Press.

———. 2006. "Introduction: The anthropology of Christianity." In *The anthropology of Christianity,* ed. F. Cannell, pp. 1–50. Durham, N.C.: Duke University Press.

Carsten, Janet, and Stephen Hugh-Jones. 1995. "Introduction: About the house—Lévi-Strauss and beyond." In *About the house: Lévi-Strauss and beyond,* ed.

J. Carsten and S. Hugh-Jones, pp. 1–46. Cambridge: Cambridge University Press.

Carsten, Janet. 1995. "The substance of kinship and the heat of the hearth: Feeding, personhood and relatedness among Malays of Pulau Langkawi." *American Ethnologist* 22, no. 2:223–241.

———. 1997. *The heat of the hearth: The process of kinship in a Malay fishing community*. Oxford: Clarendon Press.

———. 2004. *After kinship*. Cambridge: Cambridge University Press.

Casey, Edward S. 1996. "How to get from space to place in a fairly short stretch of time. Phenomenological prolegomena." In *Senses of place*, ed. Steven Feld and Keith H. Basso, pp. 13–52. Santa Fe, N. Mex.: School of American Research Press.

Clifford, James. 1997. *Routes: Travel and translation in the late twentieth century*. Cambridge, Mass., and London: Harvard University Press.

Cole, Stroma. 2007. *Tourism, culture and development: Hopes, dreams and realities from Eastern Indonesia*. Clevedon, UK: Channel View Publications.

Colombijn, F. 2002. Introduction to "On the road: The social impact of new roads in Southeast Asia" (Special Issue). *Bijdragen tot de Taal-, Land- en Volkenkunde* 158, no. 4:595–617.

Condominas, George. 1994 [1957]. *We have eaten the forest. The story of a Montagnard village in the central highlands of Vietnam*. Translated by Adrienne Foulke, introduction by Richard Critchfield. New York: Kodansha International.

Corner, L. 1989. "East and West Nusa Tenggara: Isolation and poverty." In *Unity and diversity: Regional economic development in Indonesia since 1970*, ed. H. Hill. Singapore: Oxford University Press.

Cosgrove, Denis, and Stephen Daniels. 1988. *The iconography of landscape*. Cambridge: Cambridge University Press.

Cunningham, Clark E. 1964. "Order in the Atoni house." *Bijdragen tot de Taal-, Land- en Volkenkunde* 120:34–68.

Deleuze, Gilles, and Félix Guattari. 1987. *A thousand plateaus: Capitalism and schizophrenia*. Translated by Brian Massumi. London and New York: Continuum.

Dietrich, Stefan. 1983. "Flores in the nineteenth century: Aspects of Dutch colonialism on a non-profitable island." *Indonesia Circle* 31:39–58.

———. 1992. "Mission, local culture and the 'Catholic ethnology' of Pater Schmidt." *JASO* 23, no. 2:111–125.

Dix Grimes, Barbara. 1997. "Knowing your place: Representing relations of precedence and origin on the Buru landscape." In *The poetic power of place: Comparative perspectives on Austronesian ideas of locality*, ed. J. J. Fox, pp. 116–131. Canberra: The Australian National University.

———. 2006. "Mapping Buru: The politics of territory and settlement on an Eastern Indonesian island." In *Sharing the earth, dividing the land: Land and territory in the Austronesian world*, ed. Thomas Reuter, pp. 135–155. Canberra: The Australian National University.

Duncan, Christopher R. 2002. Resettlement and natural resources in Halmahera, Indonesia. In *Conservation and mobile indigenous peoples: Displacement, forced settlement and sustainable development,* ed. Dawn Chatty and Marcus Colchester, pp. 347–361. Oxford: Berghahn.

Durkheim, Emile, and Marcel Mauss. 1963 [1903]. *Primitive classification,* ed. Rodney Needham. Chicago: University of Chicago Press.

Ellen, Roy F. 1986. Microcosm, macrocosm and the Nuaulu house: Concerning the reductionist fallacy as applied to metaphoric levels. *Bijdragen tot de Taal-, Land- en Volkenkunde* 142:1–30.

Erb, Maribeth. 1987. "When rocks were young and the earth was soft: Ritual and mythology in northeastern Manggarai." Ph.D. diss., State University of New York.

———. 1991a "Construction sacrifice, rumors and kidnapping scares in Manggarai: Further comparative notes from Flores." *Oceania* 62:114–126.

———. 1991b. "Stealing women and living in sin; adaptation and conflict in morals and customary law in Rembong, northeastern Manggarai." *Anthropos* 86:59–73.

———. 1993. "Becoming complete among the Rembong: This life and the next." *Southeast Asian Journal of Social Science* 21:10–36.

———. 1996. "Talking and eating: Sacrificial ritual among the Rembong." In *For the sake of our future: Sacrificing in eastern Indonesia,* ed. S. Howell, pp. 27–42. Leiden: Research School CNWS.

———. 1998. "Tourism space in Manggarai, western Flores, Indonesia: The house as a contested place." *Singapore Journal of Tropical Geography* 19, no. 2:177–192.

———. 1999. *The Manggaraians: A guide to traditional lifestyles.* Singapore: Times Editions.

———. 2001. "Conceptualising culture in a global age: Playing caci in Manggarai." Department of Sociology, National University of Singapore. Working paper no. 160.

———. 2006. "Between empowerment and power: The rise of the self-supporting church in western Flores, eastern Indonesia." *Sojourn* 21, no. 2:204–229.

———. 2007. "Adat revivalism in western Flores: Culture, religion and land." In *The revival of tradition in Indonesian politics: The deployment of adat from colonialism to indigenism,* ed. Jamie S. Davidson and David Henley, pp. 247–274. New York: Routledge.

Errington, Shelly. 1989. *Meaning and power in a southeast Asian realm.* Princeton, N.J.: Princeton University Press.

———. 1990. "Recasting sex, gender and power: A theoretical and regional overview." In *Power and difference: Gender in island Southeast Asia,* ed. J. M. Atkinson and S. Errington, pp. 1–58. Stanford, Calif.: Stanford University Press.

Fairhead, James. 1992. "Paths of authority: Roads, the state and the market in Eastern Zaire." *European Journal of Development Research* 4, no. 2:17–35.

Feeley-Harnik, Gillian. 1980. "The Sakalava house (Madagascar)." *Anthropos* 75:559–585.

Feld, Steven, and Keith H. Basso, eds. 1996. *Senses of Place.* Santa Fe, N. Mex.: School of American Research Press.

Feuchtwang, Stephan. 2004. "Theorising place." In *Making place: State projects, globalisation and local responses in China,* ed. S. Feuchtwang, pp. 3–30. London: UCL Press.

Forrester, Geoff, ed. 1999. *Post-Soeharto Indonesia: Renewal or chaos?* Leiden: KITLV Press.

Fortes, Meyer, and E. E. Evans-Pritchard, eds. 1940. *African political systems.* Oxford: Oxford University Press.

Forth, Gregory. 1991a. *Space and place in eastern Indonesia.* Canterbury: University of Kent, Centre of Southeast Asian Studies.

———. 1991b. "Nagé directions: An eastern Indonesian system of spatial orientation." In *Social space: Human spatial behaviour in dwellings and settlements. Proceedings of an interdisciplinary conference,* ed. O. Gron et al., pp. 138–148. Odense: Odense University Press.

———. 1998. *Beneath the volcano: Religion, cosmology and spirit classification among the Nage of eastern Indonesia.* Leiden: KITLV Press.

———. 2001. *Dualism and hierarchy; processes of binary combination in Keo society.* Oxford: Oxford University Press.

Fox, James J. 1971. "Sister's child as plant—metaphors in an idiom of consanguinity." In *Rethinking kinship and marriage,* ed. R. Needham, pp. 219–262. London: Tavistock.

———, ed. 1980. *The flow of life: Essays on eastern Indonesia.* Cambridge, Mass.: Harvard University Press.

———. 1987. "The house as a type of social organization on the island of Roti." In *De la hutte au palais: Sociétés 'à maison' en Asie du sud-est insulaire,* ed. C. Macdonald, pp. 171–178. Paris: Éditions du CNRS.

———, ed. 1988. *To speak in pairs: Essays on the ritual languages of eastern Indonesia.* Cambridge: Cambridge University Press.

———. 1993. "Memories of ridge-poles and cross-beams: The categorical foundations of a Rotinese cultural design." In *Inside Austronesian houses: Perspectives on domestic designs for living,* ed. J. J. Fox, pp. 140–177. Canberra: The Australian National University.

———. 1996. "Introduction." In *Origins, ancestry and alliance: Explorations in Austronesian ethnography,* ed. J. J. Fox and C. Sather, pp. 1–17. Canberra: The Australian National University.

———. 1997a. "Place and landscape in comparative Austronesian perspective." In *The poetic power of place: Comparative perspectives on Austronesian ideas of locality,* ed. J. J. Fox, pp. 1–21. Canberra: The Australian National University.

———. 1997b. "Genealogy and topogeny: Towards an ethnography of Rotinese ritual place names." In *The poetic power of place: Comparative perspectives on Austronesian ideas of locality,* ed. J.J.Fox, pp. 91–102. Canberra: The Australian National University.

Freeman, Derek. 1970 [1955]. *Report on the Iban.* London: Athlone Press.

Geertz, Clifford. 1980. *Negara: The theatre state in nineteenth-century Bali.* Princeton, N.J.: Princeton University Press.

Gell, Alfred. 1998. *Art and agency: An anthropological theory.* Oxford: Clarendon Press.

Gennep, A.van. 1977 [1908]. *The rites of passage.* Translated by M.B.Vizedom and G.L.Caffee. London: Routledge and Kegan Paul.

Gibson, Thomas. 1986. *Sacrifice and sharing in the Philippine highlands: Religion and society among the Buid of Mindoro.* London: Athlone Press.

Gordon, John L. 1975. "The Manggarai: Economic and social transformation in an eastern Indonesian society." Ph.D. diss., Harvard University.

———. 1980. "The marriage nexus among the Manggarai of West Flores." In *The flow of life: Essays on eastern Indonesia,* ed. J.J.Fox, pp. 48–67. Cambridge, Mass.: Harvard University Press.

Graham, Penelope. 1994. "Rhetorics of consensus, politics of diversity: Church, state and local identity in eastern Indonesia." *Social Analysis* 35:122–143.

Gullestad, Marianne. 1991. "The transformation of the Norwegian notion of everyday life." *American Ethnologist* 18, no. 3:480–499.

Gupta, Akhil, and James Ferguson. 1992. "Beyond 'culture': Space, identity and the politics of difference." *Cultural Anthropology* 7, no. 1:6–23.

Hamilton, Roy, ed. 1994. *Gift of the cotton maiden: Textiles of Flores and the Solor islands.* Los Angeles, Calif.: Fowler Museum of Cultural History.

Harrison, Robert. 1979. "Where have all the rituals gone? Ritual presence among the Ranau Dusun of Sabah, Malaysia." In *The imagination of reality: Essays in Southeast Asian coherence systems,* ed. A.L.Becker and A.A.Yengoyan, pp. 55–83. Norwood, N.J.: Ablex Publishing Corporation.

Harvey, Penelope. 2001. "Landscape and commerce: Creating contexts for the exercise of power." In *Contested landscapes: Movement, exile and place,* ed. B.Bender and M.Winer, pp. 197–210. Oxford: Berg.

———. 2005. "The materiality of state-effects: An ethnography of a road in the Peruvian Andes." In *State formation: Anthropological perspectives,* ed. Christian Krohn-Hansen and Knut G. Nustad, pp. 123–141. London and Ann Arbor, Mich.: Pluto Press.

Headley, Stephen C. 1987. "The idiom of siblingship: One definition of 'House' societies in southeast Asia." In *De la hutte au palais: Sociétés 'à maison' en Asie du sud-est insulaire,* ed. C.Macdonald, pp. 209–218. Paris: Éditions du CNRS.

Heine-Geldern, R. 1956 [1942]. *Conceptions of state and kingship in Southeast Asia.* Data paper number 18. Southeast Asia Program, Department of Asian Studies, Cornell University.

Helliwell, Christine. 1993. "Good walls make bad neighbours: The Dayak long-house as a community of voices." In *Inside Austronesian houses: Perspectives on domestic designs for living,* ed. J. J. Fox, pp. 44–62. Canberra: The Australian National University.

Helms, Mary W. 1988. *Ulysses' sail: An ethnographic odyssey of power, knowledge and geographical distance.* Princeton, N.J.: Princeton University Press.

Henley, David, and Jamie S. Davidson. 2007. "Introduction. Radical conservatism—the protean politics of adat." In *The revival of tradition in Indonesian politics: The deployment of adat from colonialism to indigenism,* ed. Jamie S. Davidson and David Henley, pp. 1–49. New York: Routledge.

Hicks, David. 1976. *Tetum ghosts and kin: Fieldwork in an Indonesian community.* Palo Alto, Calif.: Mayfield Publishing Company.

———. 1984. "A relationship terminology of asymmetric prescriptive alliance among the Manggarai of eastern Indonesia." *Anthropos* 79:517–521.

Hitchcock, M. 1998. "Tourism, *Taman Mini,* and national identity." *Indonesia and the Malay World* 26:124–135.

Hoey, Brian A. 2003. "Nationalism in Indonesia: Building imagined community and intentional communities through transmigration." *Ethnology* 42, no. 2:109–126.

Hoskins, Janet. 1993. *The play of time: Kodi perspectives on calendars, history and exchange.* Berkeley and London: University of California Press.

———. 1998. *Biographical objects: How things tell the stories of people's lives.* New York and London: Routledge.

Howell, Signe. 1991. "Access to the ancestors: Reconstructions of the past in non-literate society." In *The ecology of choice and symbol: Essays in honour of Fredrik Barth,* ed. R. Gronhaus, G. Haaland, and G. Henriksen, pp. 225–243. Bergen: Alma Mater.

———. 1995. "The Lio house: Building, category, idea." In *About the house: Lévi-Strauss and beyond,* ed. J. Carsten and S. Hugh-Jones, pp. 149–169. Cambridge: Cambridge University Press.

———. 2001. "Recontextualizing tradition: 'Religion,' 'state' and 'tradition' as coexisting modes of sociality among the northern Lio of Indonesia." In *Locating cultural creativity,* ed. J. Liep, pp. 144–158. London: Pluto Press.

Huber, Mary Taylor. 1988. *The bishop's progress: A historical ethnography of the Catholic missionary experience on the Sepik frontier.* Washington, D.C., and London: Smithsonian Institution Press.

Hugo, Graeme. 2008. "Migration in Indonesia: Recent trends and implications." In *Horizons of home: Nation, gender and migrancy in island Southeast Asia,* ed. Penelope Graham, pp. 45–70. Clayton, Victoria: Monash Asia Institute Press.

Hutajulu, R. 1995. "Tourism's impact on Toba Batak ceremony." *Bijdragen tot de Taal-, Land- en Volkenkunde* 151, no. 4:639–655.

Ingold, Tim. 2000. *The perception of the environment: Essays in livelihood, dwelling and skill.* London: Routledge.

———. 2006. "Rethinking the animate, re-animating thought." *Ethnos* 71, no.1:9–20.

———. 2007. *Lines: A brief history.* London: Routledge.

Jackson, John Brinckerhoff. 1997 [1960]. *Landscape in sight: Looking at America,* ed. Helen Lefkowitz Horowitz. New Haven, Conn.: Yale University Press.

Janowski, Monica, and Fiona Kerlogue, eds. 2007. *Kinship and food in Southeast Asia.* Copenhagen: NIAS Press.

Kahn, Miriam. 1990. "The stone-faced ancestors: The spatial anchoring of myth in Wamira, Papua New Guinea." *Ethnology* 29:51–66.

———. 1996. "Your place and mine: Sharing emotional landscapes in Wamira, Papua New Guinea." In *Senses of place,* ed. S. Feld and K. H. Basso, pp. 167–196. Santa Fe, N. Mex.: School of American Research Press.

Kammerer, Cornelia Ann, and Nicola Tannenbaum. 2003. "Introduction." In *Founders' cults in Southeast Asia: Ancestors, polity and identity,* ed. N. Tannenbaum and C. A. Kammerer, pp. 1–14. New Haven, Conn.: Yale University Southeast Asia Studies.

Kana, N. L. 1980. "The order and significance of the Savunese house." In *The flow of life: Essays on eastern Indonesia,* ed. J. J. Fox, pp. 221–230. Cambridge, Mass.: Harvard University Press.

Kartomi, Margaret J. 1995. "'Traditional music weeps' and other themes in the discourse on music, dance and theatre of Indonesia, Malaysia and Thailand." *Journal of Southeast Asian Studies* 26:366–400.

Keane, Webb. 1995. "The spoken house: Text, act and object in eastern Indonesia." *American Ethnologist* 22, no. 1:102–124.

———. 1997. *Signs of recognition: Powers and hazards of representation in an Indonesian society.* Berkeley: University of California Press.

———. 2003. "Semiotics and the social analysis of material things." *Language and Communication* 23:409–425. Special issue on "Words and beyond: Linguistic and semiotic studies of sociocultural order," ed. P. Manning.

———. 2004. "Where on earth is Eastern Indonesia? A review essay." *Indonesia* 77:146–155.

———. 2007. *Christian moderns: Freedom and fetish in the mission encounter.* Berkeley: University of California Press.

Keers, W. 1948. *An anthropological survey of the Eastern Little Sunda Islands.* Amsterdam: Iutgave van het Indisch Instituut.

Kipp, Rita Smith. 1993. *Dissociated identities: Ethnicity, religion and class in an Indonesian society.* Ann Arbor: University of Michigan Press.

Kipp, Rita Smith, and Susan Rodgers, eds. 1987. *Indonesian religions in transition.* Tucson: Arizona University Press.

Kopytoff, Igor. 1986. "The cultural biography of things: Commoditization as process." In *The social life of things: Commmodities in cultural perspective,* ed. Arjun Appadurai, pp. 64–91. Cambridge: Cambridge University Press.

Küchler, Susanne. 1993. "Landscape as memory: The mapping of process and its representation in a Melanesian society." In *Landscape: Politics and perspectives,* ed. Barbara Bender, pp. 85–106. Oxford: Berg.

Kuipers, Joel C. 1998. *Language, identity and marginality in Indonesia. The changing nature of ritual speech on the island of Sumba.* Cambridge: Cambridge University Press. Studies in the Social and Cultural Foundations of Language, no. 18.

———. 2003. "Citizens as spectators: Citizenship as communicative practice on the eastern Indonesian island of Sumba." In *Cultural citizenship in island Southeast Asia,* ed. Renato Rosaldo, pp. 162–191. Berkeley: University of California Press.

Kunst, Jaap. 1942. *Music in Flores: A study of the vocal and instrumental music among the tribes living in Flores.* Leiden: E. J. Brill.

Laderman, C. 1983. *Wives and midwives: Childbirth and nutrition in rural Malaysia.* Berkeley: University of California Press.

Latour, Bruno. 1996a. "On actor-network theory." *Soziale Welt* 47, no. 4:369–381.

———. 1996b. "On Interobjectivity." *Mind, Culture and Activity: An International Journal* 3, no. 4:228–245.

Lévi-Strauss, Claude. 1983. *The way of the masks.* Translated by Sylvia Modelski. London: Jonathan Cape.

———. 1987. *Anthropology and myth: Lectures 1951–1982.* Oxford: Blackwell.

Lewis, E. Douglas. 1988. *People of the source: The social and ceremonial order of Tana Wai Brama on Flores.* Dordrecht: Foris Publications.

Lindquist, Johan A. 2008. *The anxieties of mobility: Migration and tourism in the Indonesian borderlands.* Honolulu: University of Hawai'i Press.

Locher, G. W. 1968. "Preface" to F. A. E. van Wouden, *Types of social structure in eastern Indonesia* [1935]. The Hague: Martinus Nijhoff.

Malkki, Liisa H. 1997. "National geographic: The rooting of peoples and the territorialization of national identity among scholars and refugees." In *Culture, power, place: Explorations in critical anthropology,* ed. Akhil Gupta and James Ferguson, pp. 52–74. Durham, N.C.: Duke University Press.

Mathews, Richard. 1998. "The impact of the May crisis in Bali, West Nusa Tenggara, East Nusa Tenggara and East Timor." In *The fall of Soeharto,* ed. G. Forrester and R. J. May, pp. 70–92. Bathurst, N.S.W.: Crawford House Publishing.

McKinley, Robert. 1983. "Cain and Abel on the Malay peninsula." In *Siblingship in Oceania: Studies in the meaning of kin relations,* ed. Mac Marshall, pp. 335–387. ASAO Monograph No. 8.

McKinnon, Susan. 1991. *From a shattered sun: Hierarchy, gender and alliance in the Tanimbar islands.* Madison: University of Wisconsin Press.

McWilliam, Andrew. 1997. "Mapping with memories: Cultural topographies in West Timor." In *The poetic power of place: Comparative perspectives on Austronesian ideas of locality,* ed. J. J. Fox, pp. 103–115. Canberra: The Australian National University.

———. 2002. *Paths of origin, gates of life: A study of place and precedence in southwest Timor.* Leiden: KITLV Press.

Metzner, J. K. 1982. *Agriculture and population pressure in Sikka, Isle of Flores: A contribution to the study of the stability of agriculture systems in the wet and dry tropics.* Canberra: Development Studies Centre, The Australian National University.

Miller, Daniel, ed. 2001. *Car cultures.* Oxford: Berg.

Mitchell, Jon P. 2006. "Performance." In *Handbook of material culture,* ed. Christopher Tilley et al., pp. 384–401. London: Sage.

Moeliono, Moira M. M. 2000. "The drums of Rura: Land tenure and the making of place in Manggarai, West Flores, Indonesia." Ph.D. diss., University of Hawai'i.

Molnar, Andrea K. 1997. "Christianity and traditional religion among the Hoga Sara of West-Central Flores." *Anthropos* 92:393–408.

Munn, Nancy D. 1970. "The transformation of subjects into objects in Walbiri and Pitjantjatjara myth." In *Australian Aboriginal anthropology: Modern studies in the social anthropology of the Australian Aborigines,* ed. Ronald M. Berndt, pp. 141–163. Perth: University of Western Australia Press.

———. 1986. *The fame of Gawa: A symbolic study of value transformation in a Massim (Papua New Guinea) society.* Durham, N.C., and London: Duke University Press.

———. 1996. "Excluded spaces: The figure in the Australian Aboriginal landscape." *Critical Inquiry* 22, no. 3:446–465.

Nadasdy, Paul. 2007. "The gift in the animal: The ontology of hunting and human-animal sociality." *American Ethnologist* 34, no. 1:25–43.

Nakagawa, Satoshi. 1988. "The journey of the bridegroom: Idioms of marriage among the Endenese." In *To speak in pairs: Essays on the ritual languages of eastern Indonesia,* ed. J. J. Fox, pp. 228–245. Cambridge: Cambridge University Press.

Needham, Rodney. 1958. "A structural analysis of Purum society." *American Anthropologist* 60:75–101.

———. 1966. "Terminology and alliance, I: Garo, Manggarai." *Sociologus* 16:141–157.

———. 1980. "Principles and variations in the structure of Sumbanese society." In *The flow of life: Essays on eastern Indonesia,* ed. J. J. Fox, pp. 21–47. Cambridge, Mass.: Harvard University Press.

Nooteboom, C. 1939. "Versieringen van Manggaraische huizen" (Decorations of Manggaraian houses). *Tijdschrift voor Indische Taal-, Land- en Volkenkunde* 79:221–238.

O'Hanlon, Michael, and Linda Frankland. 2003. "Co-present landscapes: Routes and rootedness as sources of identity in Highland New Guinea." In *Landscape, memory and history: Anthropological perspectives,* ed. Pamela J. Stewart and Andrew J. Strathern, pp. 166–188. London: Pluto Press.

Orta, Andrew. 2004. *Catechizing culture: Missionaries, Aymara and the "new evangelization."* New York: Columbia University Press.

————. 2006. "Dusty signs and roots of faith: The limits of Christian meaning in highland Bolivia." In *The limits of meaning: Case studies in the anthropology of Christianity,* ed. M. Engelke and M. Tomlinson, pp. 165–188. Oxford: Berghahn.

Palmer, Andie Diane. 2005. *Maps of experience: The anchoring of land to story in Secwepemc discourse.* Toronto: University of Toronto Press.

Pannell, Sandra. 2007. "Of gods and monsters: Indigenous sea cosmologies, promiscuous geographies and the depths of local sovereignty." In *A world of water: Rain, rivers, and seas in Southeast Asian histories,* ed. P. Boomgaard, pp. 71–102. Leiden: KITLV Press.

Parkin, David. 2007. "Wafting on the wind: Smell and the cycle of spirit and matter." *Journal of the Royal Anthropological Institute.* Special issue, *Wind, life, health: Anthropological and historical perspectives,* S39–S53.

Parmentier, Richard J. 1987. *The sacred remains: Myth, history and polity in Belau.* Chicago and London: University of Chicago Press.

Pedersen, Morten A. 2003. "Networking the nomadic landscape: Place, power and decision making in Northern Mongolia." In *Imagining nature: Practices of cosmology and identity,* ed. A. Roepstorff, N. Bubandt, and K. Kull, pp. 238–259. Aarhus: Aarhus University Press.

Pemberton, John. 1994. *On the subject of "Java."* Ithaca, N.Y.: Cornell University Press.

Picard, M. 1997. "Cultural tourism, nation-building and regional culture: The making of a Balinese identity." In *Tourism, ethnicity and the state in Asian and Pacific societies,* ed. M. Picard and R. E. Wood, pp. 181–214. Honolulu: University of Hawai'i Press.

Pietz, William. 1985. "The problem of the fetish, I." RES: *Journal of Anthropology and Aesthetics* 9:5–17.

Povinelli, Elizabeth. 1995. "Do rocks listen? The cultural politics of apprehending Australian Aboriginal labor." *American Anthropologist* 97, no. 3:505–518.

Prior, John M. 1988. *Church and marriage in an Indonesian village: A study of customary and church marriage among the Ata Lio of central Flores, Indonesia, as a paradigm of the ecclesiastical interrelationship between village and institutional Catholicism.* Studies in the Intercultural History of Christianity, no. 55. Frankfurt: Peter Lang.

Rafael, Vicente L. 1993. *Contracting colonialism: Translation and Christian conversion in Tagalog society under early Spanish rule.* Durham, N.C.: Duke University Press.

Reenen, Joke van. 1996. *Central pillars of the house: Sisters, wives and mothers in a rural community in Minangkabau, West Sumatra.* Leiden: Research School CNWS.

Reid, Anthony. 1988. *Southeast Asia in the age of commerce, 1450–1680. Vol. 1: The lands below the winds.* London: Yale University Press.

Reuter, Thomas. 1992. "Precedence in Sumatra: An analysis of the construction of status in affinal relations and origin groups." *Bijdragen tot de Taal-, Land- en Volkenkunde* 148 (3–4): 489–520.

———, ed. 2006. *Sharing the earth, dividing the land: Land and territory in the Austronesian world.* Canberra: The Australian National University Press.

Rodgers, Susan. 1990. "The symbolic representation of women in a changing Batak culture." In *Power and difference: Gender in island southeast Asia,* ed. J. M. Atkinson and S. Errington, pp. 307–344. Stanford, Calif.: Stanford University Press.

Rodman, Margaret C. 1992. "Empowering place: Multilocality and multivocality." *American Ethnologist* 94, no. 3:640–656.

———. 1985. "Moving houses: Residential mobility and the mobility of residences in Longana, Vanuatu." *American Anthropologist* 87:56–72.

Rosaldo, Renato. 1980. *Ilongot headhunting 1883–1974. A study in society and history.* Stanford, Calif.: Stanford University Press.

Rubin, Gayle. 1975. "The traffic in women: Notes on the 'political economy' of sex." In *Toward an anthropology of women,* ed. R. R. Reiter, pp. 157–210. New York and London: Monthly Review Press.

Rutherford, Danilyn. 1997. *Raiding the land of the foreigners: The limits of the nation on an Indonesian frontier.* Princeton, N.J.: Princeton University Press.

Sakai, Minako. 1997. "Ancestors and place in the Gumai society of south Sumatra." In *The poetic power of place: Comparative perspectives on Austronesian ideas of locality,* ed. J. J. Fox, pp. 42–62. Canberra: The Australian National University.

Sather, Clifford. 1993. "Posts, hearths and thresholds: The Iban longhouse as a ritual structure." In *Inside Austronesian houses: Perspectives on domestic designs for living,* ed. J. J. Fox, pp. 64–115. Canberra: The Australian National University.

Sax, William. 1991. *Mountain goddess: Gender and politics in a Himalayan pilgrimage.* New York and Oxford: Oxford University Press.

Schieffelin, Edward L. 1998. "Problematizing performance." In *Ritual, performance, media,* ed. Felicia Hughes-Freeland, pp. 194–207. ASA Monographs No. 35. London and New York: Routledge.

Schrauwers, Albert. 2000. *Colonial 'reformation' in the highlands of Central Sulawesi, Indonesia, 1892–1995.* Toronto: University of Toronto Press.

Schulte Nordholt, Henk G. 1971. *The political system of the Atoni of Timor.* The Hague: Martinus Nijhoff.

———. 1980. "The symbolic classification of the Atoni of Timor." In *The flow of life: Essays on eastern Indonesia,* ed. J. J. Fox, pp. 231–247. Cambridge, Mass.: Harvard University Press.

Scott, James C. 1998. *Seeing like a state: How certain schemes to improve the human condition have failed.* New Haven, Conn.: Yale University Press.

Scott, Michael W. 2007. *The severed snake: Matrilineages, making place and a Mela-*

nesian Christianity in Southeast Solomon Islands. Durham, N.C.: Carolina Academic Press.

Sherman, D. George. 1987. "Men who are called 'women' in Toba-Batak: Marriage, fundamental sex-role differences and the suitability of the gloss 'wife-receivers.'" *American Anthropologist* 89, no. 4:867–878.

Smedal, Olaf. 1994. "Making place: Houses, lands and relationships among Ngadha, central Flores." Ph.D. diss., University of Oslo.

Spyer, Patricia. 2000. *The memory of trade: Modernity's entanglements on an Eastern Indonesian island.* Durham, N.C.: Duke University Press.

Steenbrink, K. 2007. *Catholics in Indonesia, 1808–1942: A documented history. Volume 2: The spectacular growth of a self-confident minority, 1903–1942.* Leiden: KITLV Press.

Stewart, Charles, and Rosalind Shaw, eds. 1994. *Syncretism/Anti-Syncretism: The politics of religious synthesis.* London: Routledge.

Strathern, Marilyn. 1972. *Women in between; Female roles in a male world: Mount Hagen, New Guinea.* London and New York: Seminar Press.

Sugishima, T. 1994. "Double descent, alliance and botanical metaphors among the Lionese of central Flores." *Bijdragen tot de Taal-, Land- en Volkenkunde* 150:146–170.

Tambiah, Stanley. 1976. *World conqueror and world renouncer: A study of Buddhism and polity in Thailand against a historical background.* Cambridge: Cambridge University Press.

Telle, Kari. 2007. "Entangled biographies: Rebuilding a Sasak house." *Ethnos* 72, no. 2:195–218.

———. 2009. "Spirited places and ritual dynamics among Sasak Muslims on Lombok." *Anthropological Forum* 19, no. 3:289–306. Special edition on "Spiritual Landscapes of Southeast Asia."

Thomas, Philip. 1997. "The water that blesses, the river that flows: Place and the ritual imagination among the Temanambondro of southeast Madagascar." In *The poetic power of place: Comparative perspectives on Austronesian ideas of locality,* ed. J. J. Fox, pp. 22–41. Canberra: The Australian National University.

———. 1998. "Conspicuous construction: Houses, consumption and 'relocalization' in Manambondro, southern Madagascar." *Journal of the Royal Anthropological Institute* 4, no. 3:425–446.

Tilley, Christopher. 1994. *A phenomenology of landscape: Places, paths and monuments.* Oxford: Berg.

———. 2004. *The materiality of stone: Explorations in landscape phenomenology.* Oxford: Berg.

Traube, Elizabeth. 1986. *Cosmology and social life: Ritual exchange among the Mambai of East Timor.* Chicago and London: Chicago University Press.

Trawick, Margaret. 1992. *Notes on love in a Tamil family.* Berkeley: University of California Press.

Tsing, Anna Lowenhaupt. 1993. *In the realm of the diamond queen: Marginality in an out-of-the-way place.* Princeton, N.J.: Princeton University Press.

Tsintjilonis, Dimitri. 2004. "The flow of life in Buntao': Southeast Asian animism reconsidered." *Bijdragen tot de Taal-, Land- en Volkenkunde* 160, no. 4:425–455.

Tuan, Yi-Fu. 1974. *Topophilia: A study of environmental perception, attitudes and values.* Englewood Cliffs, N. J.: Prentice-Hall.

Turner, Victor. 1973. "The center out there: Pilgrim's goal." *History of religions* 12:191–230.

UNDP. 2004. "The Economics of Democracy: Financing Human Development in Indonesia." http://www.undp.or.id/pubs/ihdr2004/ihdr2004_full.pdf (accessed Sept. 1, 2011).

Urry, J. 1990. *The tourist gaze: Leisure and travel in contemporary societies.* London: Sage.

Vel, Jacqueline A. C. 2001. "Tribal battle in a remote island: Crisis and violence in Sumba (Eastern Indonesia)." *Indonesia* 72:141–158.

Verheijen, J. A. J. 1951. *Het hoogste wezen bij de Manggaraiers* (The supreme being among the Manggarai). Wien-Mödling: Drukkerij van het Missiehuis St. Gabriël.

———. 1967. *Kamus Manggarai I. Manggarai—Indonesia.* The Hague: Martinus Nijhoff.

———. 1987. "Dialek-dialek dan kelompok-kelompok Bahasa Manggarai." In *Manggarai texts XII: 'Manggarai barat,'* pp. 1189–1191. Ruteng: Regio SVD.

Verheijen, J. A. J., and Charles E. Grimes. 1995. "Manggarai." In *Comparative Austronesian dictionary: An introduction to Austronesian studies, Part 1: Fascicle 1,* ed. Darrell T. Tryon, pp. 585–592. Berlin and New York: Mouton de Gruyter.

Wassman, Jurg, and Pierre R. Dasen. 1998. "Balinese spatial orientation: Some empirical evidence of moderate linguistic relativity." *Journal of the Royal Anthropological Institute* 4:689–711.

Waterson, Roxanna. 1990. *The living house: An anthropology of architecture in southeast Asia.* Singapore: Oxford University Press.

Weiner, James F. 2001. *Tree leaf talk: A Heideggerian anthropology.* Oxford: Berg.

Williams, Catharina Purwani. 2007. *Maiden voyages: Eastern Indonesian women on the move.* Singapore: Institute of Southeast Asian Studies.

Wilson, Fiona. 2004. "Towards a political economy of roads: Experiences from Peru." *Development and Change* 35, no. 3:525–546.

Wood, R. E. 1992. "Tourism, culture and the sociology of development." In *Tourism in southeast Asia,* ed. M. Hitchcock, V. T. King, and M. J. G. Parnwell, pp. 48–70. London: Routledge.

Wouden, F. A. E. van. 1968 [1935]. *Types of social structure in eastern Indonesia.* Translated by R. Needham. The Hague: Martinus Nijhoff.

INDEX

adat (custom): conceptions of, 11, 117, 118, 119, 127, 144, 145, 146, 148, 185; connection with land, 98; discourses on "authenticity," 142, 144, 145, 147, 157, 196n14; and houses, 60, 143–147; relationship with Catholicism, 11, 77, 103–104, 116–120, 125, 194n13. *See also* Manggarai: idea of pan-Manggarai culture; ritual leader (*tu'a adat*)

adoption, 35–36

affinity. *See* marriage alliance

agency: created in performance, 42–43, 182; of drums and gongs, 131–132; of houses, 41–43, 64–65; of land, 98, 109, 111–112, 118, 122–123, 126, 139, 141, 146, 184–185, 193n1, 196n9; of place, 19, 21, 27–28, 38, 40, 42, 64–65, 96, 97–98, 112, 114–115, 135, 182. *See also* landscape: as animate; signs (communicated by the land)

agriculture, 12, 98–103. *See also* fields; ritual: agricultural rituals

ahé-ka'é. *See* siblingship

ancestors: ancestors of the land, 106–107, 110, 122, 123–124, 125–126; conceptions of, 8, 103, 109–110, 112, 123–124, 139, 166, 182; and drums, 131, 132, 135, 182; as harmful, 38, 72, 168, 191n14; and houses, 71, 106, 189n12; and the land, 106–107, 112, 113–114, 118, 123–124, 139, 140, 141, 168, 178–179; relationship with descendants, 21, 32–33, 134–135, 138, 146, 168, 191n14; and rooms, 21, 32–33, 37, 41, 43, 72, 134–135; of Wae Rebo, 112, 113, 114, 130, 134, 139, 140, 141, 165–166. *See also* food and eating: food for ancestors; mobility: of ancestors; ritual: praising rituals; ritual: to "stop up/impede"Anderson, Benedict, 3–4

animism: agricultural animism, 123–124; phenomenological approaches to, 4, 121–122, 123

anti-syncretism, 117–118, 120, 124. *See also* syncretism

Bird-David, Nurit, 121, 123

Bloch, Maurice, 8, 86, 115

blood: "body-blood" as destiny, 37, 38; "cooked" blood, 197n7; "green/unripe" blood, 37–38, 41, 43, 66–67; lack of, 55; and ritual, 20–21, 27, 121. *See also* marriage: "blood on feet" ritual

Bonnemaison, Joel, 115

Bowen, John, 124

bridewealth: contributions towards, 34, 77, 188n10; negotiations, 79, 81, 90, 190n10, 194n11

Bupati's visit. *See* state: visit to Wae Rebo

Carsten, Janet, 35–36, 38

Casey, Edward, 142

Catholicism: charismatic, 71, 103, 124, 145; and death, 69, 124; identity as Catholic, 11, 13; inculturation, 104, 116–117, 118; and landscape, 98, 115–119, 123; priests, 103–104, 116, 119, 120, 143; and protection, 120, 169; relationship with *adat* (custom), 11, 77, 103–104, 116–120, 125, 194n13; religious teachers (*guru agama*), 68, 103, 117. *See also* grotto; ritual: Catholic Church's views on; SVD

childbirth, 24–27, 36, 37–38, 188n7. *See also* names: naming ritual

children: being taught about kinship, 34; moving between houses, 53, 56, 61; and place, 20, 25–26, 28–30, 35, 36, 50, 52–53, 56, 164; and ritual, 63–64,

lowlands, 127, 156–161; and history,
151–152; between houses or huts, 53,
56–59; idea of "swinging," 57–58; limits
to, 70; and marriage paths, 75–76,
80–81, 82–83, 88, 89–90, 90–91,
92–94, 177; spirit paths, 97, 109, 122,
160, 177, 178; talk about, 129, 155–156,
157, 172; theoretical approaches to, 152,
157, 176–177; as transformative, 88,
90; traveling practices, 120, 158–159,
163–165, 168. *See also* children: traveling to school; direction terms; kinship:
and travel; landscape: of mobility; marriage: journey; marriage: paths; ritual:
and travel; roads

money: "dirty money," 34; given at death,
67–68, 191n13; "money to accom-
pany," 81; *sida*, 69, 91, 188n10. *See also*
bridewealth

monkey-huts. *See* garden-huts

mother-in-law and daughter-in-law relationship, 23–24, 89

names: of fields, 99, 108; naming ritual, 27,
28, 39; old names of months, 100; of
places, 118, 128, 137, 138, 148, 154, 158,
165–167

New Order, 45, 128–129, 130, 143, 178

origins: concern with among Austronesian
societies, 32, 78, 113; importance of
remembering, 32, 165, 167; origin village, 93, 136–137, 195n4; place of origin,
33, 41, 56, 70, 112, 135, 137, 149, 152, 167,
168, 176, 177; roots and, 93, 94, 96, 152,
153, 169, 170

phenomenological approaches: to animism, 4, 121–122, 123; to landscape, 5,
105–106, 121; limitations of, 105–106,
148, 182

place: and agency, 19, 21, 27–28, 38, 40, 42,
64–65, 96, 97–98, 112, 114–115, 135, 182;
creation of value of, 50, 71, 75, 142, 148,
149, 181; and culture, 148–149; as dangerous, 37–39, 122–123; entanglement

with people, 18, 25, 36–37, 40, 55, 148,
174, 176, 183–184; life cycle of, 19–20,
29–30, 40–41, 149; made through
travel, 158–161, 166, 176–177; as person,
21–22, 41–42; as protective, 26, 27, 38,
39, 55, 65, 67, 71–72, 183, 192n7; sensory
approach to, 7, 50, 70, 106. *See also*
ancestors; gender: and place; grotto;
houses; language: place-specific ways of
talking; memory: and place; names: of
places; origins: place of origin; ritual:
and place; spirits: spirit-places; stones
and stone platforms; villages; Wae
Rebo-Kombo

political leader, 33, 127, 129, 165. *See also*
ritual leader

precedence, 33, 35, 114

priests. *See* Catholicism

ritual: to "accompany," 79, 81; agricultural
rituals, 103–107, 111–112, 182; Catholic
Church's views on, 103–104, 116–117,
118; to "collect up souls," 39–40, 43,
112, 149, 170; contrasted with everyday
activities, 9, 64, 65, 182–183; hearth-
based activities during, 52, 62–64;
"moving in to the house" ritual,
64–65, 139; new year ritual (*penti*),
112–113, 114, 120, **132**, 134–135, 194n14;
offerings, 32, 104, 105, 106–107, 114,
122, 123; as performance that creates
presence, 16, 32–33, 42–43, 65, 98,
112, 181, 182, 183; and place, 9, 32–33,
42–43, 71–72, 98, 105, 148–150, 182;
praising rituals (*mora*), 32–33, 35, 42,
135–136, 137, 149, 167; to "stop up/
impede," 38, 122, 177, 189n12; and
travel, 176–177; variation in ritual
practice, 103–104, 116–120, 121, 145;
for water sources, 111–113, 119, 120, 123,
124–125. *See also* death; drum house:
construction rituals; fields; houses;
marriage: "blood on feet" ritual; state:
perspectives on ritual

ritual leader (*tu'a adat*), 117, 118, 119, 127, 131.
See also political leader

ABOUT THE AUTHOR

Catherine Allerton is a lecturer in anthropology at the London School of Economics, where she has taught since 2003. She studied social and political sciences at the University of Cambridge and social anthropology at the London School of Economics. In addition to her research on places, paths, and landscapes, Dr. Allerton has published articles and book chapters on loneliness and unmarried women, sarongs, tourism, cosmetics, and ideas of beauty. In 2009 she guest-edited a special edition of *Anthropological Forum* entitled "Spiritual Landscapes of Southeast Asia: Changing Geographies of Religion and Potency," which explored the consequences for the varied spiritual landscapes of the region of new religious forms, migration, and varied political and military projects.

OTHER VOLUMES IN THE SERIES

HARD BARGAINING IN SUMATRA:
Western Travelers and Toba Bataks in the Marketplace of Souvenirs
Andrew Causey

PRINT AND POWER:
Confucianism, Communism, and Buddhism in the Making of Modern Vietnam
Shawn Frederick McHale

INVESTING IN MIRACLES:
El Shaddai and the Transformation of Popular Catholicism in the Philippines
Katherine L. Wiegele

TOMS AND DEES:
Transgender Identity and Female Same-Sex Relationships in Thailand
Megan J. Sinnott

IN THE NAME OF CIVIL SOCIETY:
From Free Election Movements to People Power in the Philippines
Eva-Lotta E. Hedman

THE TÂY SƠN UPRISING:
Society and Rebellion in Eighteenth-Century Vietnam
George Dutton

SPREADING THE DHAMMA:
Writing, Orality, and Textual Transmission in Buddhist Northern Thailand
Daniel M. Veidlinger

ART AS POLITICS:
Re-Crafting Identities, Tourism, and Power in Tana Toraja, Indonesia
Kathleen M. Adams

CAMBODGE:
The Cultivation of a Nation, 1860–1945
Penny Edwards

HOW TO BEHAVE:
Buddhism and Modernity in Colonial Cambodia, 1860–1931
Anne Ruth Hansen

Production Notes for Allerton / *Potent Landscapes*
Cover design by Mardee Melton
Interior design by Richard Hendel and composition by Wanda China
    with display type in Optima LT and text in Garamond Premier Pro
Printing and binding by Sheridan Books, Inc.
Printed on 55 lb. House White Hi-Bulk D37, 360 ppi.